Landscaping with
Native Plants

of the Southwest

George Oxford Miller

Voyageur Press

First published in 2007 by Voyageur Press, an imprint of MBI Publishing Company, Galtier Plaza, Suite 200, 380 Jackson Street, St. Paul, MN 55101-3885 USA

The information in this book is true and complete to the best of our knowledge. All recommendations are made without any guarantee on the part of the author or Publisher, who also disclaim any liability incurred in connection with the use of this data or specific details.

This publication has been prepared solely by MBI Publishing Company and is not approved or licensed by any other entity. We recognize that some words, model names, and designations mentioned herein are the property of the trademark holder. We use them for identification purposes only. This is not an official publication.

Voyageur Press titles are also available at discounts in bulk quantity for industrial or sales-promotional use. For details write to Special Sales Manager at MBI Publishing Company, Galtier Plaza, Suite 200, 380 Jackson Street, St. Paul, MN 55101-3885 USA.

Editor: Josh Leventhal
Designer: LeAnn Kuhlmann
Printed in China

Library of Congress Cataloging-in-Publication Data
Miller, George Oxford, 1943-
  Landscaping with native plants of the Southwest / by George Oxford Miller.
     p. cm.
  Includes bibliographical references and index.
  ISBN-13: 978-0-7603-2968-9 (softbound)
  ISBN-10: 0-7603-2968-0 (softbound)
 1. Native plants for cultivation—Southwestern States. 2. Native plant gardening—Southwestern States.
3. Landscape gardening—Southwestern States. 4. Drought-tolerant plants—Varieties—Southwestern States.
5. Xeriscaping—Southwestern States. I. Title.
SB439.24.S69M55 2007
635.9'5179—dc22
                              2006027180

On the front cover: Organ pipe cactus (*Stenocereus thurberi*) and brittlebush (*Encelia farinosa*) at Organ Pipe National Monument, Arizona. Photo © Ron Niebrugge/wildnatureimages.com

On the back cover: (top) Landscape of agave species. *(bottom)* Field of sunflowers (*Helianthus annuus*), Arizona.

On the title page: Goodding's verbena (*Glandularia gooddingii*) and palo verde (*Parkinsonia florida*).

Contents

O Friend!

In the garden of thy heart plant naught but the rose of love.

— Bahá'u'lláh, founder of the Baha'i Faith

Acknowledgments

A book such as this, necessarily, is a composite of many people's knowledge, research, opinions, and experience. Professors, landscapers, gardeners, horticulturists, nursery owners, and native-plant enthusiasts all influenced this book to a great extent. There have been too many people through the years to name individually here, but I do appreciate the cumulative help and encouragement I received.

A special thanks to Martha Latta, past president of the National Xeriscape Council, Inc., and former owner of Garden Villa in San Marcos, Texas, who provided valuable editorial comments and the landscape drawings that illustrate the chapter "The ABCs of Native Plant Landscaping."

Desert Botanical Gardens, Phoenix

An Introduction to

Landscaping with

Native Plants
of the Southwest

Ocotillo (*Fouquieria splendens*) in bloom

This book assumes four premises. First, landscaping increases property values and aesthetic appeal and can decrease monthly utility expenses. Second, indigenous plants are superior to most imported species for landscaping because natives are naturally adapted to the region's climate and soil. Third, and to me most important, landscaping with plants from your area helps repair the environment. Human development can be expected to alter the countryside from its natural state, but it doesn't have to eradicate the biological heritage of our native plants and animals. We can all do our part by replacing some of the plants removed to build our houses, streets, and businesses. Lastly, by drawing on the rich native plant life of the Southwest, we can create stunning garden designs that appeal to all the senses and offer a peaceful retreat in our own backyards.

The botanical diversity of the Southwest encompasses mile-high mesas, foothills, mountains with snow-capped peaks, conifer forests, alpine meadows, canyonlands, and all four North American deserts. That a plant is native to Arizona or New Mexico, however, does not imply that it can be planted anywhere within the region. Each of the fifteen (or more) major vegetative provinces recognized by botanists has a unique community of plants adapted to its specific soil and climatic conditions. For the purposes of landscape applications, this book divides the Southwest into seven landscape zones, depending on the temperature variations, frost-free days, moisture, and altitude gradients. This book will help you to analyze your yard and decide which plants best match your specific habitat.

Many of the thousands of native plants growing in our region have characteristics that will enhance your landscape with attractive foliage, flowers, fruit, or bark throughout the year. This book describes about 280 species of trees, shrubs, vines, wildflowers, groundcovers, and cacti with exceptional landscape merit. I have favored plants with a wide landscape range over those with very specific or demanding habitat requirements, though some exceptional specialties are included. The "Native Plant Profiles" describe each species and variety in detail, including each plant's range; specific soil, moisture, and shade requirements; temperature tolerance; size, shape, and suitable landscaping uses; and flower, foliage, and fruit characteristics. Photographs of the selected species will further help homeowners, nursery workers, and landscapers decide which plants can best suit their needs.

Before going out and buying new plants, however, every gardener must first come to understand his or her own landscape and the requirements of establishing a garden using native plants. The maps and listing of Southwest landscape zones in the book will help you identify the rainfall and temperature variation within your area. The individual chapters address the issues of landscape maintenance, landscaping to attract wildlife, and landscaping for energy and water conservation, including xeriscaping with drought-tolerant species, with listings of appropriate plants for each situation. The appendices at the back of the book offer suggestions of plants for specific landscape needs. Separate listings itemize evergreen plants and tell you how to colorscape for year-round beauty with flowering trees and shrubs. When used together, this book's chapters, plant descriptions, and appendices answer the majority of questions that a homeowner will have about landscaping with native plants.

A Note on Nomenclature

Through the decades and centuries, the native plants that cover our landscape have been known by dozens of common names. The same plants have many names, and different plants have the same name. To avoid confusion, botanists apply Latin plant names according to the strict protocol of the classification system developed in the eighteenth century by botanist Carl Linneaus. Yet, as research expands, some plant species are lumped together, and others are split and given new names. Then someone redoes the work with a different methodology (such as DNA analysis), and everything is rearranged again. For a standard for plant names, I used the latest accepted nomenclature for each plant according to the Integrated Taxonomic Information System, referenced at www.itis.usda.gov. Discontinued scientific names and names still used by some state agencies are listed in parentheses.

In the hierarchy of taxonomic classification, botanists group plants that share a wide range of similar physical characteristics into families. Families are divided into smaller groups called genera, which are further subdivided into species. A species may be split into subspecies and varieties. Taxonomists group plants primarily by flower type, since, unlike foliage and growth habit, the flower characteristics of a species are not altered by climatic differences. Species with similar flower types are grouped together as a genus. For example, the genus *Lupinus* contains the 27 species of lupines in Arizona and New Mexico. The many similar genera around the world are grouped with *Lupinus* into the legume family, Fabaceae, a huge family that includes peas, beans, acacias, and mesquites.

Within a species, the basic structure of the flower remains constant, though slight genetic variations can cause differences in flower or foliage color. If a difference is widespread through a population of the same species, it may be classified as a variety or even a subspecies. Horticulturists search for varieties with particular ornamental value and often crossbreed them, and then clone them, to produce cultivars (cultivated varieties). The new plants may vary from the type species in foliage or flower color, fruit size, growth habit, or tolerance to cold or drought, to name a few variations.

Blooming evening primrose and cholla

7

The botanical diversity of the Southwest offers a treasure-trove of options for color, form, and function, as illustrated by this yucca plant amidst a field of blooming firewheel plants.

Why Use
Native Plants?

Nearly 4,000 species and subspecies of flowering plants grow within the borders of Arizona and New Mexico. Approximately 1,000 of these are trees and shrubs, about half of which could be used as ornamental plants. Our rich botanical heritage is a treasure chest for landscapers. But beyond the diversity of plants available, other compelling reasons exist why we should landscape our homes, businesses, and public properties predominantly with native plants.

Interest in landscaping with native plants has mushroomed since the early 1990s. From state agriculture departments to local garden clubs, native plants have become top-agenda topics. Water-conscious cities, such as Phoenix, Tucson, and Albuquerque, have initiated xeriscape programs to encourage planting drought-tolerant species, and county extension agents carry the message to local groups and organizations.

Environmental Repair

Most of us are uninformed about, and isolated from, our natural environment. Instead of placing an inherent value on nature—the source of all life and the root of human material and technological success—modern society relates to fast food and high-tech toys. Even the plants in our neighborhoods reflect our loss of identity with our natural environment. The trees, hedges, and shrubs planted around our houses typically come from some distant country via the Home Depot or Kmart garden center.

Today, as agriculture, ranching, and urban sprawl eliminate many natural plant communities, a growing number of people are concerned about preserving what remains of our natural environment. Community colleges, nature centers, and universities offer classes on ecology and conservation issues. Many people visit state and city parks and greenbelts looking for natural areas representative of the native flora and fauna. In most metropolitan areas, the natural associations of indigenous plants remain only in parklands and preserved sanctuaries.

Why can't our neighborhoods represent the natural plant diversity that occurs in nature or that existed before our houses were built? Plants are a part of our great natural heritage. The plants that have sunk their roots in Southwest soil since the last Ice Age can help us understand that our psyches and society are equally rooted to the earth. A stroll down our own streets could be a lesson in native plant ecology. Our children could grow up familiar with the same plants that provided food and fiber for the Native Americans who have lived in the Southwest for thousands of years. We could live among the same plants that mystified the botanists who accompanied the first European explorers.

Wildlife species also benefit from the native plants in our yards. Few of the plants that provide forage and shelter for wildlife are left in the wake of urban and agricultural development. As subdivision developers destroy native plants and replant with mass-produced imported species, our songbirds are replaced by starlings and English sparrows, themselves immigrants from Europe. We can encourage the return of our native birds and other wildlife by landscaping with plants that provide food and shelter. As the plants mature and begin to flower and fruit, we will once again be rewarded by the sight of butterflies dancing from flower to flower and by the melodies of birds singing in our trees.

Low Maintenance

Why choose native species over the readily available, inexpensive foreign species? Because they are low maintenance—and that means dollars saved. By selecting plants native to your area, you create a landscape that is naturally adapted to whatever weather extremes may occur. After tens of thousands of years of climatic vicissitudes, only those species that were able to adapt have survived. As a result, these plants will be able to cope with whatever Mother Nature throws at them in a landscape setting.

When a landscape plant is firmly established, it will require little supplemental water, even in the driest years. Unusually frigid winters may nip tender twigs, but the plant will survive and fully recover with the next spring growth. Fewer plants will die and require costly replacement. Other than normal landscape maintenance, such as pruning, a native plant requires little attention.

While the low-maintenance feature of our native plants is attractive for homeowners, it is an essential consideration for commercial landscapers. Large businesses allocate sizable budgets for landscaping office buildings and commercial developments. States and municipalities are concerned with plantings for buildings, parks, greenbelts, and thousands of miles of streets and highways. State governments spend millions of dollars on landscaping. Plants that minimize water use and labor costs mean sizable savings to you as a homeowner, a businessperson, and a taxpayer.

Variety

Southwest native plants come in all sizes, shapes, and colors. Why not use a variety of plants that provides visual interest throughout the year? You can plant a mixed assortment of natives for spring, summer, and fall flowers and colorful fruit. You can choose evergreen species with green, gray, or whitish foliage, or deciduous plants with spectacular autumn colors.

The plants native to Southwest soil offer so much variety that you can use them in an almost endless combination of landscape designs. And native plants provide a unique and regionally distinct beauty to our neighborhoods, parks, and commercial districts. Residents of Arizona and New Mexico pride themselves on the natural beauty of the Southwest. Many of the plants that are indigenous to the Southwest grow nowhere else on earth. Why not landscape our homes, resorts, and businesses with indigenous plants so that our cities and neighborhoods look like the Southwest and not a clone of New Orleans, Atlanta, or Miami? As Lady Bird Johnson, former First Lady and founder of the Lady Bird Johnson Wildflower Center, said, "I want places to look like where they are. I want Alabama to look like Alabama, and Texas to look like Texas."

Sparrow on blooming saguaro (*Carnegica gigantean*)

Pioneers in Native Plant Landscaping

The availability of native plants has evolved greatly over the last two decades. In the 1980s, many people lauded the virtues of landscaping with native plants, but homeowners faced one major obstacle: Where could they buy those wonderful plants? Not at the local garden center. Wholesale nurseries didn't grow natives because there wasn't enough demand.

Nurturing native landscaping from a niche movement into a major horticultural industry required decades of individual passion, public education, experimentation by university agricultural departments and agencies, private nurseries willing to take a risk, and city, state, and industry designers demanding water-wise, budget-saving plants. Each plant or variety discovered by an agricultural extension agent, propagated by a grower, and placed on the market by a local nursery added to the synergy between supply and demand.

Growing Both Markets and Plants

When Plants of the Southwest Nursery started in 1978, native plants still grew beneath the radar of most nurseries. Beyond ornamental classics such as Texas ranger, blue spruce, yuccas, and cacti, about the only place to buy natives was at the periodic sales held by nature centers and the scattered Native Plant Society chapters in Arizona and New Mexico.

Gail Haggard and David Deardorff began hand collecting seeds and sowing them in Gail's backyard in Santa Fe to sell at the annual plant sale of the New Mexico Native Plant Society. After a few years of trial-and-error propagation, they opened Plants of the Southwest, one of the first nurseries dedicated exclusively to regional native plants.

Through the years, the nursery thrived as the familiarity and popularity of native plants increased. The Plants of the Southwest catalog became an educational tool that introduced the public to the ornamental wonders of our local plant heritage. It provides plant descriptions, planting guidelines, and tips for care and propagation. The nursery sells retail and wholesale quantities of plants indigenous to New Mexico, Arizona, Texas, and the Oklahoma panhandle.

"We have a four-acre nursery near Socorro [New Mexico] where we have greenhouses and grow one- and five-gallon field stock," said Susan Westbrook, director of the Santa Fe nursery. "We use no insecticides and a minimum of fertilizers. We also buy a lot from small, backyard growers, especially cacti and herbs. Supporting the local economy is part of our philosophy."

Native plant horticulture has been a part of Susan's life for 30 years. She still collects seeds from her favorite

Plant display at Boyce Thompson Arboretum in Superior, Arizona

plants, such as blackfoot daisy, chocolate flower, Jacob's ladder, and chamisa. "You become intimate with plants when you follow their cycle all the way around from seeds to flowering," she said. "Native plants help people see the beauty of where we live, wherever it is."

Plants of the Southwest Nursery continues to grow and expand the market. It has one of the best native plant Web sites on the Internet (www.plantsofthesouthwest.com) and plans to open a slow-food restaurant at the Santa Fe nursery that specializes in cooking with native foods fresh from the fields.

With Plants of the Southwest and many other owner-operated nurseries, native plants are as much a lifestyle as a business. Such nurseries in every major city in the

Southwest continue to play a pivotal role in raising the public awareness of native plants and stimulating both sides of the supply and demand equation.

During the 1980s and 1990s, native plant landscaping grew from a concept to an industry embraced by home-owners, municipalities, developers, and landscapers. Many commercial businesses realize that native plants help create a link with the unique ambiance of a locality. Hotels, art galleries, and resorts throughout Arizona and New Mexico thrive on the Southwest image.

Creating a Sense of Place: Resort Trends

The hospitality industry and retail merchants in the Southwest have always recognized the marketing value of the surrounding mountains, canyons, and deserts. Now, more and more are realizing that indigenous planting is a major feature that contributes to the scenic landscape that makes the Southwest so special.

Tucson Desert Oasis

Resorts know that first impressions count. They lavishly landscape their entrance drives, porticos, and courtyards with colorful and luxuriant plants. In most cases the plants are exotic ornamentals, which does not bedazzle the native plant enthusiast. From sun-baked Phoenix to tropical Key West, gardens of petunias and poolside palms greet the guests. The only sense of place that many properties want to impart is the sense of their own place.

But not the Westward Look Resort in Tucson. Sitting at 2,450 feet altitude in the foothills of the Santa Catalina Mountains, the resort embraces its desert surroundings. Instead of trying to turn the water-thirsty desert into the lush Caribbean-style landscape typical of many Sun Belt resorts, Westward Look glories in the natural beauty of its Sonoran Desert setting.

The resort sits on 80 acres of prime Sonoran Desert real estate, originally a family homestead established in 1912. Surrounded by encroaching housing developments,

Westward Look Resort, Tucson

the resort set aside twenty-three acres as a pristine Sonoran Desert preserve with walking and equestrian trails. The undisturbed native vegetation grows right up to the paved hiking/jogging trail that circles the developed portion of the property. Immaculately landscaped gardens surround the buildings, border the walkways and entrance drive, and decorate the courtyards. But instead of imported species from distant climes, a majority of the landscape plants are native to the surrounding hillsides.

"Our focus is to create a sense of place," said Sandra Esparza, the regional director of Gemstone Resorts and general manager of Westward Look. "We want the visitors to discover the beauty and tranquility of the desert. If they can experience the soul of the desert, they can leave with something they didn't have before."

Landscape mix at Westward Look Resort

Esparza began the process of converting the landscape to exclusively native plants—a $100,000 project—in the spring of 2005. "We want people to know firsthand what the Sonoran Desert is by seeing the diversity of plant life," she said.

The master architect and creative genius of Westward Look's remarkable scenery is landscape manager Reymundo Ocampo. Ocampo, a Zapotecan Indian from Oaxaca, Mexico, began his career as a government accountant, but soon found the confinement of four walls too stifling. He quit and returned to his first love: native plants. He's been working his magic on resort landscapes since 1986.

Ocampo combines a mixture of formal and informal designs on the property. Around the rooms, he shears the hedges, but not hedges of yew or boxwood; he uses Texas ranger, jojoba, and desert hackberry. With a stroke of artistic flair, he blended woolly butterflybush and Texas ranger. Both have fuzzy, gray leaves, but radically different flowers. The gumball-like orange flowers of the butterfly-bush lace through the ashen foliage with a splash of unexpected color. The blue Texas ranger flowers add a striking contrast to the combination.

"I've never seen butterflies come to the butterflybush, but the hummingbirds love it," Ocampo said.

To attract more hummingbirds to the grounds, the resort consulted with the Arizona Sonoran Desert Museum about installing a hummingbird garden. Ocampo planted salvias, ocotillo, chuparosa, and justicias, then added a little stream of flowing water. Now the hummers zip through the garden like trucks on the interstate.

Blue and foothills palo verde trees and huisache shade the room balconies while adding brilliant spring color. "I like the 'Desert Museum' palo verde," Ocampo says. "It's a cross between the blue and foothills palo verdes and Texas palo verde. It has larger flowers, a longer bloom period, and no thorns."

No space escapes Ocampo's creative touch. Desert bird of paradise, desert willow, fairy duster, Texas ebony, desert ironwood, and dozens of species of agave, yucca, prickly pear, cholla, and other cacti accent the border and courtyard gardens. Gregg's dalea, lantanas, and verbenas cover slope plantings and drape over walls.

Besides designing the gardens and directing the work, Ocampo shares his passion for native plants with visitors on morning nature walks along the one-mile loop trail around the perimeter of the property. "When you learn about one native plant, you get hooked and want to learn more and more," he said.

Ocampo explains the traditional edible and medicinal uses of the plants. He shows how agave fibers can be woven into sisal rope and points out the oil-rich nuts of jojoba, a popular additive to cosmetics and bath products. He also describes the landscape uses of the plants and which ones are particularly beneficial for wildlife.

"When choosing a landscape plant, it's location, location, location," he said. "Understand the microclimate of your yard. Because of a few hundred feet difference in elevation, we can grow flowers that don't survive in hotter downtown Tucson. A flower planted by a boulder can absorb enough heat to bloom several weeks earlier and survive a colder winter."

Admittedly, Ocampo departs from the purest native plant philosophy by using plants from beyond his desert valley. Because the resort must present a beautiful landscape all year round, his landscape palette includes plants from the deserts of northern Mexico, Texas, and California. Along walkways, he plants Mexican agaves without catclaw spines, as a safety precaution. He uses Texas ebony and Texas mountain laurel, two premier trees from the Chihuahuan Desert, which extends into southeastern Arizona. He plants species of justicias and desert bird of paradise from nearby Mexico. But all come from similar habitats and are similar to local natives.

In the cool of the morning, I sit on my balcony and drink coffee and watch the verdins and house finches feed among the buttery blossoms of the huisache. A cactus wren is building a nest in a cholla beside the walkway, and a phainopepla flycatcher swoops after insects from its tree-limb perch. The birds don't seem to know where the desert stops and the resort starts, which is as it should be.

Santa Fe Escape

When Noble House Hotels, owners of a dozen properties from Seattle to Key West, acquired the Inn at Loretto in Santa Fe, they asked their in-house landscape architect, John Farrar, to upgrade the exterior. Farrar consulted with local landscape architect Bill Hutchinson of Green Edge, Inc., and they put together a plan to beautify the Pueblo-Revival-style complex.

"I want each hotel in our collection to look like it belongs to its particular region," Farrar said. "If we have enough property, it's important to create a habitat, to take an area and make it work together, instead of just placing a plant here and there."

Farrar and Hutchinson installed pinyon pines and aspens around the entrance and New Mexican privet, chimisa, native grasses, perennial flowers, and sculptures around the entrance drive and along the wall separating the hotel from the neighboring Loretto Chapel, built in 1878.

"The front of the inn was a parking lot. When possible, I'm removing parking lots that were installed in the 1950s when people didn't care about nature," Farrar said.

Inn at Loretto, Santa Fe

"Now, we use valet parking and add more green around the hotels. I believe in using native plants to give back something to the natural environment."

Instead of a harsh asphalt entrance, a vibrant and dynamic landscape greets the visitor. The aspens and pinyons highlighted against the adobe-colored walls create the unmistakable feel of the Southwest. The landscape visually connects the hotel with the Loretto Chapel. The quaking leaves of the aspen, the scent of the pinyon, and the colorful beds of perennials on the hotel property mirrors the peacefulness of the historic gothic cathedral.

Landscape Zones

With elevations ranging from 100 feet above sea level at Yuma to 12,600 feet on the San Francisco Peaks near Flagstaff and 13,161 feet atop Wheeler Peak in New Mexico, the Southwest encompasses an incredibly wide diversity of plant communities. Climate factors vary from blazing deserts that never freeze and receive less than 8 inches of rain annually to alpine tundra with more than 44 inches of precipitation and plants you'll find in Alaska.

According to the classical Merriam Vertical Life Zone concept—that every 1,000-foot gain in elevation is equivalent to a 600-mile change in latitude to the north—the Southwest contains every life zone found in North America. More exact studies expanded Merriam's six life zones into more detailed bioclimatic vegetative communities and then subdivided those into more specific plant associations. This wide divergence of environmental conditions gives the Southwest one of the highest biodiversity ratings north of the tropics. Arizona alone has 3,666 species of native and naturalized plants, including 74 species of cacti and nearly 100 species of ferns.

When choosing plants for your garden, whether natives or imported species, the first essential step is understanding the particular conditions of the site. Many factors can influence a plant's ability to survive and thrive, and growing conditions can vary within a region and even within your property.

As a starting point for determining which plants are candidates for landscaping in your particular area, this book divides the Southwest into seven landscape zones based on the 14 or so major vegetative biomes described for Arizona and New Mexico.

The four low-desert biomes for the Mohave and Sonoran deserts are combined into Landscape Zone 1. The Chihuahuan Desert Scrub and Chihuahuan Desert Grasslands are Landscape Zone 2. The Interior Chaparral belt is Zone 3, and the Pinyon-Juniper woodlands Zone 4. The High Plains Grasslands of New Mexico comprise Zone 5, and the Desert Scrub and Plains Grassland of the Great Basin are combined for Zone 6. The Ponderosa-Oak Forest becomes the highest elevation Landscape Zone 7. The Spruce-Alpine forest biome and the Alpine-Tundra biomes—higher than most people live—are not included.

The U.S. Department of Agriculture's Plant Hardiness Map, which considers only temperature, is broadly accurate, but as a planting guideline for the Southwest, it ignores several critical factors. This book bases the Landscape Zone divisions on the four most important factors affecting plant survival: elevation, moisture, air and soil temperature variation, and natural plant communities within each area. With this classification scheme, you can determine which plants are candidates for landscaping in your particular area.

Selecting plants for your yard involves more than simply determining your Landscape Zone, however. A plant has specific habitat requirements and rarely has a continuous geographical distribution throughout its range. Plants have adapted to certain environmental factors—moisture, exposure, soil chemistry, drainage, humidity, temperature, and number of frost-free days, to name a few. A plant thrives in habitats where it finds these parameters in the optimum combinations and grows in limited numbers in more marginal areas.

Depending on the microhabitat of your yard, a plant may not be suitable for your landscape even though it is listed as belonging to your zone. Conversely, a plant native to an adjacent zone may thrive in your yard if it finds the right niche. Each species entry describes in detail what the plant requires to thrive and be healthy and attractive. By choosing those plants most suitable for the environmental conditions of your yard, you can have a beautiful landscape for years, even generations, with relatively little maintenance.

Landscape Zone Versus Native Range

You can be sure that the plants growing in the wild around your home are the ones best adapted to survive in your yard. They not only are adapted to the local habitat

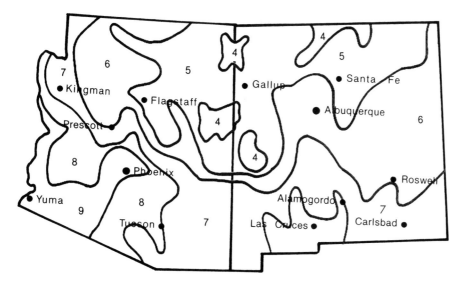

Map of Hardiness Zones

Approximate Ranges of Average
Annual Minimum Temperatures
for Each Zone

4.	-30° to -20° F.
5.	-20° to -10° F.
6.	-10° to 0° F.
7.	0° to +10° F.
8.	+10° to +20° F.
9.	+20° to +30° F.
10.	+30° to +40° F.

Based on the USDA Plant Hardiness Zones Map

conditions, but they also have formed symbiotic relationships with the soil fungi and bacteria that link and enhance the survival of all members of the particular plant association. Choosing members of the local plant community will minimize your worries. In some cases, this book recommends landscape zones that extend beyond a plant's natural range, mainly for plants that have become well established in the nursery trade. Since many plants native to specific habitats within the Southwest are sold throughout the Southwest, you should know which ones will thrive in your yard and which ones you should avoid.

The landscape zones listed for each species include regions with similar soil types, moisture, and temperatures as the native range, especially for popular plants with widespread use. For instance, if you live in Phoenix or Tucson, you probably have sandy or rocky, fast-draining soil. Many of the trees and shrubs from the Sonoran and Chihuahuan deserts, and even from northern Mexico and Baja California, will grow well in your yard (although the occasional freeze may damage the more southern United States or northern Mexican desert species). If you live in the higher elevations of the Great Basin Desert, many of the plants from the Pinyon-Juniper Woodlands or Mountain Conifer Forests will be suitable. As a general rule of thumb, look for plants that are similar species to the local plant community so that they can share the symbiotic relationships with the soil organisms.

Expanding the latitude of the Landscape Zone of a plant beyond its natural range may seem contrary to the basic principle of landscaping with natives, but once a plant proves its worth, growers will push it to its geographical and ecological limits. A plant such as Texas ranger (*Leucophyllum frutescens*) is native to the Chihuahuan Desert in New Mexico and Texas, but it thrives equally well in landscape settings across much of desert Arizona.

When selecting a plant, you should always remember that plants don't recognize arbitrary lines drawn on maps. A plant's range naturally expands and contracts over the decades and centuries, and often includes discontinuous

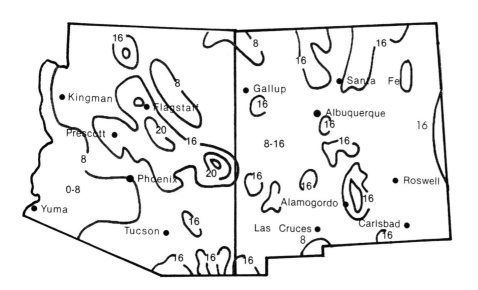

Mean Annual
Precipitation in Inches

Based on *The National Atlas of the United States of America*, compiled by the U.S. Geological Survey, Washington, D.C.

populations. Your yard may naturally match its requirements. The goal of this book is to help you understand a plant's growth needs, as well as its versatility, so that you won't plant it in a soil type, exposure, or temperature zone that's too marginal to foster years of enjoyment.

A plant species always has the same basic habitat needs regardless of the landscape setting, but we can control or eliminate other limiting factors, such as competition and predation. In the wild, a plant competes with other plants for light, moisture, and soil nutrients. By choosing the proper exposure and soil and by isolating the plant from competitors, we give the plant an ecological advantage that it might never have in the wild. Besides competition, we try to eliminate herbivores and insect predation on our landscape plants. Trimming dead limbs helps prevent insect and fungal enemies from entering the plant. Watering and fertilizing the plant until it is established improve its chances of success far beyond those of plants in the wild.

In some areas, the difference in plant communities between bordering landscape zones is dramatic. As U.S. Interstate 17 heads north from Phoenix, gaining elevation, it passes through hills of saguaros and brittlebush until just north of Black Canyon City. Then it winds through a pass and emerges into grasslands dotted with juniper, mesquite, and prickly pear cactus. Conversely, in many places, the transition from one vegetation type to another is gradual and hardly recognizable. The Pinyon-Juniper belt in northern New Mexico often merges with the Ponderosa-Oak belt, with broad ranges of both associations mixed together.

In determining plants suitable for your landscape zone, carefully analyze the specific conditions of your yard. In addition to the overall climatic factors, look at features that determine your yard's specific habitat, or microhabitat—such as the soil, slope, sun exposure, and the drying or chilling effects of wind.

Landscape Zones of the Southwest

Zone 1, Sonoran Desert Scrub

This low- and mid-altitude region (500 to 4,000 feet) receives 12 inches or less of rain annually. Summer highs exceed 100°F and winter lows occasionally dip into the 20s. The growing season extends from mid-February through November. Xeriscape landscaping is a must. Plant cool-season annuals, perennials, and trees and shrubs from September through November to allow the root systems to become established before summer. Cities in this zone include Phoenix, Yuma, Wickenburg, and Tucson. Select landscape plants adapted to sandy soil, extreme heat, low humidity, light frosts, and extended drought. Characteristic desert shrub associations include creosote bush, mesquite, cholla, prickly pear, brittlebush. Desert foothill plant associations include palo verde, ocotillo, saguaro.

Zone 2, Chihuahuan High Desert Scrub

This arid region consists of washes, basins, dunes, grasslands, and undulating plains and mesas with few permanent rivers. It encompasses the northern extremity of the Chihuahuan Desert and includes southeastern Arizona, southern New Mexico, and the Rio Grande Valley north to Albuquerque. Elevation ranges from 3,000 to 5,000 feet. Winter temperatures regularly drop below freezing, hitting lows of 10 to 20°F. The growing season averages 200 to 220 frost-free days from mid-March through November and precipitation varies from 8 to 16 inches annually. Cities in this Zone include Albuquerque, Alamogordo, Las Cruces, Carlsbad, Wilcox, and Sierra Vista. Select landscape plants adapted to sandy, alkaline soil, extreme heat, low humidity, occasional freezes, and extended drought. Characteristic plant associations include honey mesquite, yuccas, agaves, prickly pears, sotols, beargrass, creosote bush, lechugilla, acacia shrubs. Cottonwoods occur along streams and junipers, pinyon pine, and oaks at higher elevations.

Zone 3, Interior Chaparral

This zone encompasses the hilly to mountainous area (3,000 to 8,000 feet) south of the Mogollon Rim in central Arizona from near Seligman to Stafford. The discontinuous band of evergreen shrubs and trees extends from the desert grasslands to the Pinyon-Juniper woodlands. Emory, gray, and Arizona oaks, alligator juniper, pinyon pine, Arizona cypress commonly occur. Shrub associations include mariola, manzanitas, desert ceaonothus, silktassel, and sugar sumac. Rainfall averages 12 to 16 inches annually with last frost between March 15 and April 15; temperature lows reach 10 to 20°F. Cities in this Zone include Prescott, Stafford, and Globe.

Zone 4, Pinyon-Juniper-Oak Woodlands

Influenced by Rocky Mountain flora, the Pinion-Juniper/mixed conifer woodlands dominate the northern half of Arizona and New Mexico. Common shrubs include Standbury cliff rose, chamisa, mountain mahogany, ephedras, and Apache plume. A slightly different tree-shrub association influenced by the Sierra Madres in Mexico dominates the southern mountains in New Mexico. Silverleaf, Arizona, and Mexican blue oaks, Mexican pinyon, and Arizona madrone occur there. Annual precipitation varies from 12 to 24 inches. The growing season extends from early May through September and winters see extended freezes and snow (low temperatures of 0 to 10°F). Elevations range from 4,500 to 7,500 feet. Cities in this Zone include Santa Fe, Sedona, and Payson.

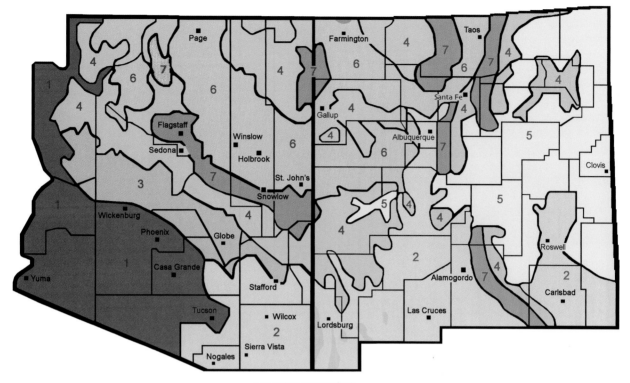

LANDSCAPE ZONES

1. Sonoran Desert Scrub (500-4,000 feet; 20 to 30° F.)
2. Chihuahuan High Desert Scrub (3,000-5,000 feet; 10 to 20° F.)
3. Interior Chaparral (3,000-8,000 feet; 0 to 10° F.)
4. Pinyon-Juniper-Oak Woodlands (4,500-7,500 feet; 0 to 10° F.)
5. High Plains Grassland (5,000-7,000 feet; 0 to -10° F.)
6. Great Basin Desert Scrub and Grasslands (3,000-5,000 feet; 0 to -10° F.)
7. Pine-Oak Forest (6,500-8,000 feet; -10 to -15° F.)

Zone 5, High Plains Grassland

This western extension of the Great Plains Grasslands includes the flat, open expanses of the eastern half of New Mexico and extends into the High Plains of West Texas, with elevations ranging from 3,000 to 7,000 feet. Saline and shallow, stony soils are common with pockets of deep sand. Annual rainfall varies from 20 inches in the east to 12 inches in the west and the growing season extends from April through November. Temperatures can drop to 0 to –10°F in winter. Tall and mid-high grasses and cholla cacti dominated the original prairie vegetation. Landscape plants should be adapted to well-draining, alkaline soil, drought, and extremely hard winters. Clovis and Santa Rosa are in this region.

Zone 6, Great Basin Desert Scrub and Grassland

The cool plateaus (3,000 to 5,000 feet) of the Great Basin Desert and Grasslands experience hard winters with cold, drying winds, snow, and frozen ground. The growing season is early May through September with 150 to 200 frost-free days and low temperatures of 0 to –10°F. Annual precipitation ranges from 10 to 20 inches. Large expanses of open grasslands and unbroken stands of chamisa, big sagebrush, winterfat, and joint fir typify the area. Plants selected for this Zone should be cold hardy, drought tolerant, and adapted to salt-affected soils. Cities in this Zone include Winslow, Holbrook, Farmington, and Gallup.

Zone 7, Pine-Oak Forest

Ponderosa pine and Gambel oak dominate this transition zone between the Pinyon-Juniper woodlands and Rocky Mountain coniferous forests, but species from the bordering biomes mix freely with the Pine-Oak community depending on elevation, slope, and exposure. This unbroken ponderosa forest, at elevations of 6,500 to 8,000 feet, extends for 225 miles in Arizona along the southern rim of the Colorado Plateau. The growing season extends from June through August with extended winters and extended periods of snow cover. Temperatures drop as low as –10 to –15°F. Soils tend to be dry and sandy, and annual precipitation averages 16 to 28 inches. Plants selected for this Zone should be adapted to harsh winters and a short growing season. Flagstaff and the North Rim of the Grand Canyon are in this Zone.

A layered mix of native trees, shrubs, groundcovers, and cacti create a pleasing year-round display.

The ABCs of
Native Plant Landscaping

At least two schools of thought have developed concerning landscaping with indigenous plants. The traditional approach substitutes native plants for the commonly used imported species. Native plants can be used for foundation hedges around buildings, border hedges along walks and drives, and sheared hedges; as accent shrubs planted alone; or as container plants. They can be used in any formal or informal landscape design. At the other end of the spectrum is the attempt to duplicate the natural plant associations found in the wild, whether prairie, desert, or woodland. With this approach, a yard would in effect be a microcosm of nature. In the purest version, there would be no hedges or shaped shrubs, nor species not from the immediate area.

Selecting and grouping species from the plant associations that have evolved together for millennia is at the heart of the native plant concept, whether you want a formal landscape or a wildscape. As with viewing an iceberg, the plant life you see above ground is only a fraction of the ecosystem. Of equal importance to the vascular plants, and perhaps more important to the health of the ecosystem, is the complex of mycorrhizal fungi and bacteria in the soil. Each plant association has its community of soil organisms that interconnect all the roots and allow the member plants to share moisture and nutrients. This underground mycorrhizal infrastructure allows plants to exist in a symbiotic relationship over hundreds and sometimes thousands of acres, and ideally in your yard. If you plant a species that is similar to members of the native community, it is easily incorporated into the water-nutrient sharing network. A species that is not adapted to share the association's mycorrhizal support system struggles while its neighbors thrive through mutual cooperation. The take-home message is to select plants from your area's natural plant association and you'll seldom have to water, fertilize, or even weed once the plant is established.

Many intermediate designs lie between the formal and wild landscape designs. One approach that combines the concepts of maintaining natural plant associations and using plants to visually accent open areas is to create landscape islands. Instead of delineating an area by hedges and a few accent shrubs or trees, use a mass planting, or island, of mixed species from the same plant association. A landscape island can be completely contained in an open area or curve out from a building. It can include one side of a drive or accent a corner. Cacti and xeriscape gardens exemplify the landscape island concept.

Mass plantings combine compatible species to make your landscape visually dramatic. Always choose species with the same habitat requirements within the broader plant association. Plants that complement each as design elements have foliage of a similar color, size, and shape. Or they may contrast each other with varying shades of foliage and leaf patterns. Species with gray foliage provide a dramatic combination with green-leafed species. A tree yucca or palo verde adds a vertical accent for low-growing shrubs such as fairy dusters and brittlebushes.

A group planting can have a different accent for every season. You can provide year-round color, as well as food and shelter for birds and butterflies. Use deciduous plants to provide shades of bright green with new spring leaves and spectacular autumn hues. Use evergreens to add foliage color during the barren winter months. Hedges, borders, and backgrounds do not have to consist of a single evergreen species, but can combine the best nature has to offer. The flexibility of the landscape island concept provides a multitude of design possibilities for an attractive yard throughout each season.

Four Steps for Developing a Master Plan
Step 1: The Dreaming Stage
Landscaping your yard is an investment of money and a commitment to the time a plant takes to mature. You want plants that will be healthy and vigorous and at the same time fulfill your long-term landscaping needs. The first step is to decide what you need and expect from a plant. Do you want a large tree with an expansive canopy, or a small tree to shade an entranceway? Do you want an evergreen or a deciduous tree, a loosely growing shrub, or a dense shrub that can be shaped? If you are just starting to landscape your yard, you want to develop a master plan for the entire lot, taking into account these and other considerations. Don't worry about selecting particular species at this point.

The photographs and landscape drawings in this book will give you many ideas for landscaping your yard. Besides the utilitarian benefits (shade, windbreaks, etc.), plants provide a visual highlight for an area. Plants add beauty to driveways, sidewalks, patios, pools, porches, corners, and courtyards. Use border plantings to enhance walls, fences, and building foundations. A distinctive plant at the corner of the house or entryway adds special visual appeal. Mass plantings of shrubs or vines beautify slopes, medians, open areas.

Decide where you want hedges, border plants, large and small shade trees, vines, and groundcovers. Choose

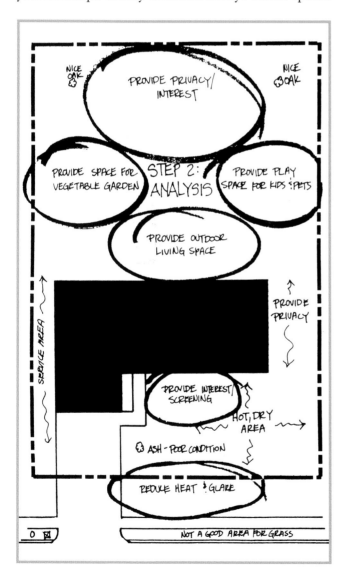

The Dreaming Stage. The first step in developing a master plan for your landscape is making a site plan.

evergreens where you want year-round shade, deciduous species for winter sun, and spring- and fall-flowering species for color throughout the year. Use tall evergreen hedges for visual privacy, and densely branching or thorny species to provide physical barrier hedges. Keep in mind that you don't need to plant everything at once, but you can add the plants year by year as budget and time allow.

Some shrubs will naturally grow into densely branching, thickly foliated, rounded plants; others seem to flail their limbs at random regardless of how much you prune the errant branches. Decide whether you want a formal or informal look for your design. Patios, courtyards, entryways, and foundation hedges often require a more refined-looking shrub or tree, while border hedges along fences and walls, background shrubs in mass plantings, and xeriscape gardens shine with the wildscape look.

Whether you are a home or professional landscaper, minimizing the time and money spent on yard maintenance may be an important consideration. You can save on utility costs throughout the year by planting proper combinations of native deciduous and evergreen trees and shrubs, and by using drought-tolerant species in arid climates. The chapter "Landscaping for Energy and Water Conservation" will guide you through some of these important decisions for your garden plan. The section on xeriscaping tells you how to reduce your summer water bill by as much as 44 percent by using drought-tolerant species.

Planting native groundcovers is another way to reduce yard maintenance, prevent erosion, and add an extra touch of beauty. Many shrubs naturally spread by rhizomes or branch rooting and form thick mats; others form dense thickets in nature. Not every low-growing, thicket-forming plant can serve as a groundcover, however, so look for species with densely foliated branching, multiseason attraction, and a growth profile that matches your height requirements. The chapter "Landscaping with Groundcovers" explains alternative uses for many of the plants described in this book.

The chapter "Landscaping with Vines" describes numerous vines that will enhance any landscape. Vines are fast growing, and most tolerate either sun or shade, making them adaptable to almost any landscape design.

Native plants are also useful for attracting birds and other animals to your yard, further enhancing the beauty and enjoyment of the landscape. Many species offer year-round flowers, fruits, and berries for birds, butterflies, squirrels, and other desirable urban wildlife. The chapter "Landscaping to Attract Wildlife" provides a useful overview and planting suggestions.

Once you have determined your goals and needs for your landscape, you will be able to assess which native plant species are best for you.

Soil Types and Improvement

The first step in analyzing the landscape potential of your yard or site is to determine the characteristics of the soil. The most important factors are the composition of the soil, which determines drainage, and the soil pH, which influences nutrition. Many soils can be improved with a regular composting and mulching program, which helps balance the pH and improves both fertility and drainage. But before you start plowing in the compost, remember that a native plant planted in its preferred soil type doesn't need soil amenities—it's already good to go.

Composition
The ageless physical and biological processes that break down rock into soil produce three basic types of soil: sand, silt, and clay. Loam is a mixture of the three and may be classified as sandy, silty, or clay-like, depending on the relative percentages of each. A well-balanced loam contains about two-fifths sand, two-fifths silt, and one-fifth clay.

Sand
Soils that are composed of 50 percent or more sand contain large grains that drain quickly, retain little moisture, and dry rapidly after watering. The faster a soil drains, the more nutrients are leached away, so soils classified as sandy or sandy loams tend to be infertile. If your site consists of sandy soil, you should either select plants adapted to sandy habitats or develop a program of improving the soil with organic matter and fertilizers and mulching. Be sure to select species that are adapted to fast-draining, infertile conditions. On the plus side, sandy soils are easy to work and easy to improve, and they warm quickly in the spring, allowing early-germinating species to thrive.

Silt
Silt contains small- to medium-sized particles, smaller than sand and larger than clay. Silt and silty loams retain water and nutrients, and they are easy to work. Silky when wet, this soil type may require additional sand to improve drainage. Silt is often deposited by floods or otherwise transported by water.

Clay

Clay is the finest-grained soil type, with particles so small that they bind water molecules very tightly, making absorption by roots difficult or impossible. Soils with more than 40 percent clay retain water, are difficult to work, compact easily, and are slow to warm in the spring. Clay soils should be improved with the addition of organic matter on a yearly basis. Take care when adding sand—too little can turn clay into adobe brick. A good soil mixture will crumble in your hand when dry.

Limestone

The sandy, limestone-derived soils of eastern and southern New Mexico and southern Arizona often contain considerable caliche, or small particles of limestone rock. The soil drains rapidly, is alkaline, and is usually shallow. Limestone can be improved by adding organic matter. Select species adapted to alkaline, fast-draining soils.

Soil Analysis

To determine the type of soil in your yard or site, you can send a sample to a lab for a full-blown chemical analysis, but usually a few backyard tests will tell you what you need to know to make judicious plant selections.

If you enjoy kitchen chemistry, put about one-third of a quart of soil in a quart jar and fill the jar with water. Shake and let it sit for a day, or until all the soil settles to the bottom and the water is clear, with the organic matter floating at the top. You should be able to see the different strata of soil components. Sand, the heaviest, will settle first, followed by silt, and then clay. Measure the thickness of each layer. A layer of sand that equals half or more of the total indicates sandy soil. Similarly, if half is silt, you have silty soil. If the top layer is more than one-quarter of the total, your soil tends toward clay. A well-balanced loam will have nearly equal layers of sand and silt, with less clay.

If you prefer the quick-and-dirty method, squeeze a handful of wet soil through your fingers. Sandy soil is gritty and crumbles, silty soil is firm and silky, and you can make a baseball from clay.

Drainage Test

Soils with either a high clay or sand content may have drainage problems. Conduct a percolation test before you make any soil modifications or plant selections. Dig a round hole in the soil about 6 inches in diameter and 10 inches deep. Fill with water and let it drain completely, then fill it again, and note how long it takes to drain the second time. One hour is an indication of excellent drainage. One to four hours is average to poor, but acceptable. If it takes more than four hours or less than fifteen minutes for the water to drain, you should develop a long-term composting and mulching plan.

Soil pH

Depending on the parent materials, soil varies from acidic to alkaline in its chemical makeup. The pH scale (pH stands for "potential Hydrogen ions") runs from 0 to 14. A rating of 7 is neutral, higher than 7 indicates alkaline soils, and lower than 7 is acidic. Most Southwest plants prefer soil with a pH between 6 and 7.5, though some species require highly acidic or alkaline soil; such preferences are indicated in the Plant Profiles in this book.

If the pH of your soil is too high or too low, some minerals become insoluble and cannot be absorbed by the plant's root system. The most important minerals—nitrogen, phosphorus, and potassium—are available over a wide range of pH, but iron, manganese, and boron become limited if the pH gets much above 7.5. Plants deprived of these minerals develop chlorotic, or yellow, leaves. An iron deficiency causes the newer leaves to become yellow with green veins, while a magnesium deficiency causes older leaves to develop the yellow patches.

To adjust the pH of your soil, add lime to overly acidic soils, those with a pH below 6.5; manure, compost, or in the extreme, sulfur can be added to soils that are too alkaline (pH above 7.5). The amount of additive depends on both the soil composition and the original pH level.

Soil additives can alter the pH by one point or so, but the best option is to select plants that are adapted to your soil. Garden centers sell easy-to-use pH test kits.

Step 2: Site Analysis

One of the most important factors determining a landscape plant's success is its location. In the wild, a plant casts its seeds to the wind, trusting that a few will find an optimum habitat and survive. We can't afford this trial-and-error method in our yards. We want our plants to not just survive, but to grow vigorously and be attractive. Before you turn a spade of soil, carefully analyze the environmental conditions of your yard and choose plants that are naturally adapted to the existing growth conditions. This is the most important step for low-maintenance landscaping.

For optimum performance, the plant must be adapted to four major habitat parameters: the soil, moisture, drainage, and exposure of your yard. Just because a plant grows in your landscape zone and altitude range, or even in your immediate area, does not mean that it will grow well in your yard. Many plants have very exacting requirements. Look at your soil, and not just the fill soil the developer may have spread over your lot. Is the soil in which you intend to plant sandy loam, blackland clay, or rocky soil?

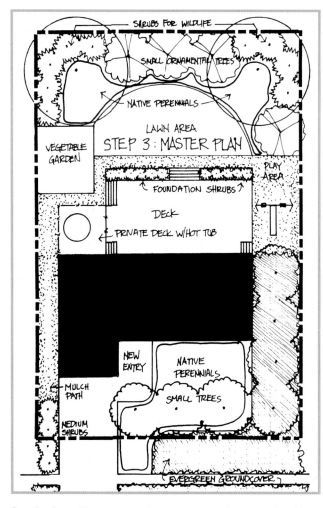

Site Analysis. Determining how you intend to use the different spaces in your landscape requires an understanding of the site's conditions.

How fast does it drain after a heavy rain? If your yard stays soggy for a day or so after a rain, don't plant species that require fast-draining soil.

Even a small yard has subtle differences in exposure, reflected light and heat, and drainage variations that can greatly affect the survivability and healthy appearance of a plant. Plants on the north side of the house receive much less sun and heat than those planted on the south. Shade-tolerant species and those more cold hardy should be used for northern exposures. A southern exposure receives sunlight most of the day, making it hotter and drier in the summer and warmer in the winter. Select sun-loving, drought-tolerant species for southern exposures. Plants along a concrete drive or patio, or in a rock garden, receive an extra dose of radiated heat that may create a low-desert habitat. Shaded entryways, on the other hand, might provide the shade and coolness of a ponderosa forest.

The way you prepare the soil for planting also can create significantly different growth conditions. In general, native plants rely more on the mycorrhizal root network than on the soil amenities and fertilizers that zealous landscapers are wont to apply annually. Mycorrhizal fungi require that the top 6 inches of soil be loose and aerated, and they can easily be damaged by excess phosphate and nitrate fertilizers or by too much moisture. Many drought-tolerant plants are adapted to seasonal rainfall, and regular watering will inhibit their growth or even kill them. A layer of mulch several inches thick will keep a plant's roots from drying out in the dry season, protect against excessive heating, suppress weeds, and foster healthy soil organisms.

The microhabitats in your yard can change as your landscape matures. In nature, plants modify their environment enough to allow a succession of different plant associations through time. This can also occur in your yard. Years of mulching, or years of hot, dry exposure, can change the soil conditions significantly. As saplings develop into large trees, their shade changes the habitat around them. Sun-loving species may die out, and shade-loving ones thrive under these new conditions. When designing your master plan, consider the mature sizes of the species you choose and what they will look like in five or ten years. Choose plants that will remain compatible as your landscape matures. For instance, you might rather plant several small understory trees instead of one large tree that would eventually shade your entire yard.

Step 3: Choosing the Plants

After you have determined the growth characteristics that match your landscape space, exposure, soil, and drainage, you are ready to compile a list of plant species. The plants most adapted to your local growing conditions are those that grew in your area before it was developed. If you're a native-plant purist, stick to plants from your locality. However, many nurseries and landscapers consider the entire Southwest and northern Mexico as the home range for plant selection. Regardless of your philosophy, you will find an abundance of trees and shrubs with striking flowers, fruit, and seeds that make them excellent ornamental landscape plants. After you have selected the trees and shrubs that will be the dominant features in your landscape, you can choose the shorter-lived native wildflowers, groundcovers, vines, and other accent plants to complement your design.

The first step in the plant-selection process is to identify your altitude and zone from the map of landscape zones earlier in this book. The closer that the plants you choose match those two parameters, the better their chances of thriving. Next, refer to the species descriptions of each plant in the "Native Plant Profiles" to determine which are compatible with your particular growing conditions. The species are listed in alphabetical order by scientific name. Additional information about plants for specific purposes or characteristics can be found in the appendices of evergreen plants and flowering trees and shrubs as well as in the chapters on attracting wildlife and on energy and water conservation. Armed with a list of the trees, shrubs, wildflowers, vines, and groundcovers possessing the same habitat requirements as your yard, you are ready to begin shopping for plants.

Step 4: Planting

Most plants should be transplanted in the dormant season (December through February) or before the last frost in the spring. A freshly dug plant can survive the shock of having most of its roots removed in the winter because its leaves are not demanding a constant supply of water. Container plants planted at this time will also have time to grow an expanded root system before the stress of summer.

You can give your plant a head start with proper soil preparation. Preparing the soil correctly helps the plant to begin growing immediately and establish a healthy root system. Dig a hole about twice as wide as the plant's root ball or container. Large trees should have one foot of clearance around the root ball. This allows for loose, well-prepared soil to surround the root system and stimulate growth. Dig the hole deep enough for 6 inches of loose soil on the bottom. Very importantly, the plant should not be planted too deeply. Maintain the original juncture of the base of the plant with the soil.

The most important roots of a plant are the surface feeder roots. These tiny rootlets, located just below the surface of the soil, absorb the moisture and nutrients essential for a plant's growth. Soil compaction will physically impede the growth and spread of the rootlets, which directly limits the development of the entire plant, and waterlogged soil will drown the roots. Before you set your plant, loosen the soil 6 to 12 inches deep for several yards around the hole, depending on the size of the plant. Once a plant is established, you should never disturb the surface roots by tilling the area underneath the plant or by covering it with more than an inch of fill dirt.

After placing the plant and filling the hole, form a slight ridge of soil around the circumference of the hole to create a basin to hold in water. Saturate the soil immediately after planting. Weekly watering, particularly of small plants, may be necessary through the first summer, especially if temperatures are extreme. Mulching around the base of the plant reduces water loss and heat buildup in the soil. It also keeps grass from growing around the plant and competing for water. Grasses can reduce the growth of a plant by as much as 50 percent, so keep the area around the plant clear of grass. Some effective mulch materials include bark or wood chips, leaves, grass clippings, straw or hay, and crushed stone or gravel.

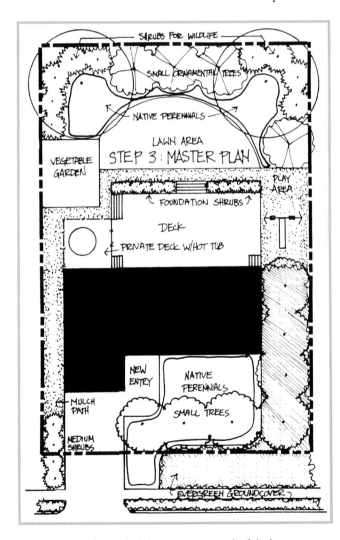

Choosing the Plants. With so many wonderful plants available, identifying those best-suited to your landscape involves careful consideration.

Adding fertilizer granules or time-release fertilizer pellets to the fill around the plant will stimulate plant growth and sometimes double or even triple the growth rate normal in a wild setting. For example, some nurseries use a regular fertilizing and watering schedule to achieve 6 to 8 feet of growth on oak seedlings in their first year. Remember, until a plant grows a network of surface feeder roots, it will need tender loving care and water during dry periods.

For the first year, the plant is vulnerable and should be protected against climatic extremes. Water as frequently as necessary during the first summer. Observe the plant, and water when signs of stress appear. A slight leaf wilt or curl, loss of vibrant green color, and browning around the leaf margins are sure signs of insufficient water. If the surface feeder roots die, recovery is slow and growth inhibited. For plants whose main growing season is spring and summer, watering during the first summer after transplanting is even more important. By the second summer, the plant has gone through two spring growing seasons and should be hardy enough to survive on its own without irrigation, unless the summer is abnormally dry.

By ensuring that lack of water does not inhibit a plant's growth for the first season, you enable the new plant to grow rapidly and become well established. But be careful to avoid overwatering. Most natives dislike wet feet. Overwatering quickly kills species adapted to well-draining soil, a lesson hard learned by those of us accustomed to thirsty plants from wet climates.

So Where Can I Find Those Wonderful Natives?

A trip to the garden center in Lowes, Home Depot, or Kmart reveals the same selection of nonnative ornamentals. A few plants native to the Southwest have made the mix, but most large-volume retailers carry a combination of alpine meadow flowers, tropical patio plants, Asian flowering shrubs, and naturalized tree hybrids and cultivars.

Fortunately, many locally owned nurseries are well stocked with native trees, shrubs, wildflowers, and seeds, and some sell indigenous plants exclusively. Wholesale growers now propagate natives in large quantities to meet the growing demand for home and commercial landscaping. Arboretums, nature centers, parks, and plant societies often sponsor seasonal native plant sales. Get on their mailing lists, or better yet, join one near you and visit regularly.

When selecting plants, container or nursery-conditioned stock is much preferred to transplanting plants straight from the fields, because the former have better developed root systems. In the wild, a shrub or tree's roots spread out over a large area to gather water and nutrients. When transplanted, the plant loses many of its roots and is more susceptible to losing important branches or dying.

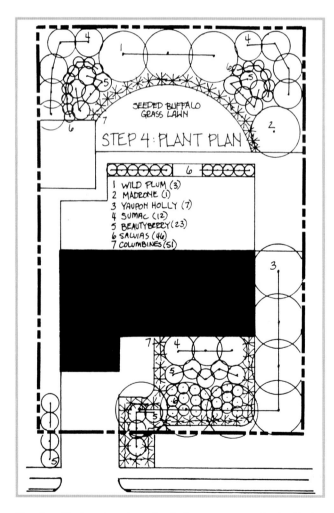

Planting. Placing the plants in their proper spot is the final phase of creating your dream garden.

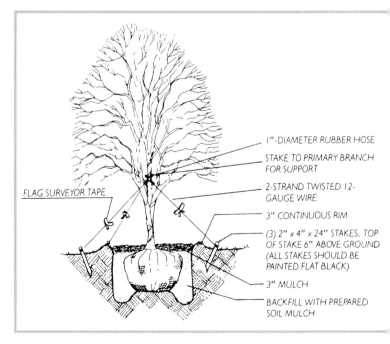

Tree Planting and Staking Detail (not to scale).

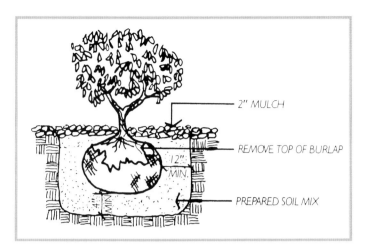

Shrub Planting Detail (not to scale).

After a tree transplanted from its natural habitat has been nursery conditioned (watered, pruned, and fertilized), it has more roots in its ball or container and is more likely to grow rapidly when planted in your yard. Ask the nursery about the history and age of the trees and shrubs before buying them. If you can find a retailer knowledgeable in natives, he or she will probably be willing and eager to advise you on plants suitable for your landscaping situations.

Digging of trees and shrubs from the wild by home landscapers almost always results in the death of the plant, and may be in violation of plant-protection laws. Transplanting is best done by professionals who have the experience, equipment, knowledge, and proper permits. Without the use of expensive mechanized equipment, digging a large root ball is a labor-intensive operation, and no shortcuts make the job easier. Besides the slim chance of success and possible legal prohibitions, digging plants from the wild also impoverishes the countryside. Once a popular plant is deemed economically valuable, it can be removed from nature much faster than it can naturally replenish itself. Over 30 percent of the cacti in the United States are endangered or threatened with extinction because of over-collection from the wild. Northern Mexico, where there are fewer restrictions, suffers even more from plant poaching. Stripping plants from nature contradicts the major philosophy of the native-plant movement: repairing our damaged environment. Demand nursery-propagated plants. It is more ecologically sound and economically wise.

Arizona Plant Collection Laws

Arizona is home to a vast array of rare and unusual plant species, and to protect this natural botanical heritage, the State of Arizona has enacted rigid laws to regulate the collection, removal, and salvage of native plants. Listed plants cannot be removed from any lands, whether privately owned or managed by a government agency, without permission and a permit from the Arizona Department of Agriculture. Theft of protected native plants from private, state, or federal lands may result in a felony charge.

Arizona's Native Plant Law protects all cacti, yuccas, agaves, ocotillo, most trees, and many smaller plants from theft, vandalism, or unnecessary destruction. Protected plants may not be legally possessed or transported from the growing site without a permit. A landowner may destroy, remove, sell, or give away plants on his or her own property, but the landowner is required to notify the state department of agriculture 20 to 60 days prior to the destruction of any protected native plants.

The Arizona Department of Agriculture checks all areas of the state on a regular basis for the use of native plants as landscape material. They closely monitor new

Agave murpheyi is one of many protected Arizona native species.

subdivisions and commercial developments. If a protected plant is found without a tag, it is confiscated.

For the official list of regulations and protected plants, see the Arizona Department of Agriculture's website (www.azda.gov/ESD/nativeplants.htm).

Regular maintenance will keep your native plants lush and vibrant throughout the seasons.

Maintaining Your Landscape

Every landscape design requires some amount of maintenance, and fertilizing, soil conditioning, spraying, pruning, and replacing dead plants to keep the garden healthy and attractive can represent a continual expense. But while no home or commercial landscape is totally maintenance-free, hardy native plants come close to that ideal. Indigenous plants require far less care than many imported exotic species, so a landscape design that incorporates the natural shape and size of natives will require much less periodic attention and seasonal expense than one using exotic species.

For the last decade, the Southwest has been in the midst of a record-breaking drought. In the wild, a plant often reacts to extremes of drought and temperature by leaf loss, twig damage, dieback, or a generally shabby appearance. In our landscape, however, we want to avoid these extreme responses and maintain the optimum—or at least average—growing conditions, regardless of how stressful the weather may be. For example, even though the plants might easily survive periods of drought, we may want to provide supplemental watering if the appearance begins to suffer.

Keep in mind, too, that drought-tolerant species require a certain amount of drought stress to remain healthy, so avoid overwatering. A plant adapted to 12 inches of annual precipitation will die if given the equivalent of 20 inches through irrigation. Likewise, a plant adapted to seasonal rain may react adversely to an abundance of water in its dry season. A firmly established, vigorously growing plant that has adjusted to its exposure and survived several growing seasons needs little attention. If

Brittlebush (*Encelia farinosa*) is more densely foliaged and floriferous with regular pruning.

Your chamisa (*Ericameria nauseosa*) will benefit from light pruning in the dormant season.

properly chosen, it will not outgrow its setting and will survive whatever extremes nature has to offer.

Regardless of which plants you use in your landscape, some basic knowledge and skills in plant husbandry will help you keep your plants healthy and attractive. The following information will help you develop the landscape skills required to keep your yard beautiful.

Fertilizing

Fertilizing with a complete fertilizer in the spring stimulates foliage, flower, and fruit production, the primary characteristics we desire in our landscape plants. Fertilizing helps a plant develop its maximum genetic potential, just as it would in an optimum habitat in nature. Fertilizers are great for turf lawns, fruit orchards, and vegetable gardens, but in general, native plants with an active mycorrhizal root network don't need supplemental fertilizers. Once a plant is well established and adapted to its new location, fertilizing is usually unnecessary and unwanted.

Complete fertilizers supply the three main nutrients required for a plant's growth: nitrogen, phosphorus, and potassium. In general, nitrogen stimulates foliage growth; phosphorous, root growth; and potassium, flower and fruit production. The three-number rating of a fertilizer expresses the percentage of these compounds. A 10-6-4 fertilizer, for example, contains 10 percent nitrogen, 6 percent phosphorus, and 4 percent potash, or potassium.

When required, fertilizer should be applied early in the year—January or February—before the spring growth begins. Fertilizing can be time consuming and expensive, so don't waste money buying unnecessary fertilizers. Before applying fertilizers, have your soil analyzed to determine if nutrients are lacking. Your county agricultural extension agent provides this useful and inexpensive service.

Pruning

Even though you've chosen a plant because its natural growth habit complements your landscape conditions, trees and shrubs often display little regard for our wishes. A shrub may grow scattered branches or a tree produce wayward limbs. Even in the best-designed landscape, some degree of pruning is usually required to direct plant growth and maintain tidiness. Just as water and fertilizer maximize growth, intelligent and timely pruning helps the plant to rapidly develop a full size and attractive shape. Almost every tree and shrub in your landscape will at one time or another require pruning.

Perhaps one reason plant growers and landscapers have ignored native plants for so long is their often-unsightly appearance in nature. A wild shrub may have dead limbs, spreading branches, an irregular profile, and other characteristics undesirable for a landscape setting. The unkempt appearance of wild plants results from lack of care. Pruning can transform many native plants into premier landscape specimens. It can make a plant tall or short, open branching or densely foliated, or even convert a tree into a hedge. Pruning encourages compactness if the shrub is naturally intricately branching. Some species, such as New Mexican privet and little-leaf sumac, make densely foliated shaped or sheared hedges. Others, such as bee brush and false indigo, are open branching and more suitable for informal hedges.

The Cardinal Rules of Pruning

Swear allegiance to the following principles of pruning before grasping your shears or saw.

1. Know the natural growth habit (shape and size) of the plant. Unless you are developing a shaped hedge, pruning should train the plant toward its natural form. Pruning against the natural growth pattern is fighting the plant instead of training it and will require regular maintenance.

2. Make cuts that will heal rapidly. Every tree branch has a collar of growing cells that reinforces the limb and seals it off from the trunk if it dies. If you trim limbs flush with the trunk, you remove this protective collar and expose the conductive tissues to possible invasion by fungi. Branch collars vary greatly among species; some are prominent, while others are less distinct. Look for a bulge or series of ridges in the bark around the base of the limb. Make your cut flush with the branch collar, and it will heal rapidly.

   Remove large limbs in sections, or at least with three cuts. First, cut into the limb on the underside six inches from the collar. Remove the limb with a second cut four inches farther out; and finally, cut the stub, leaving the branch collar bulging from the trunk. This procedure prevents a partially severed limb from falling and peeling a strip of bark down the trunk. Always use sharp tools suited for the size of the job.

3. Avoid topping a tree. Removing the terminal growing section of a tree destroys its natural shape and appearance, stunts its growth, and weakens it. You probably will want to remove limbs that compete with the terminal leader, however.

4. Prune in the right season. Evergreens and most deciduous trees and shrubs should be pruned in the dormant season, December through February.

   Wait to prune until after the first freeze to avoid stimulating new growth, which can occur if pruning is done during the growing season. Plants that bloom in the late spring and fall usually produce flowers on the current season's new growth. Pruning in the dormant season allows them to produce new wood in the spring before blooming.

Species that flower in early spring, such as redbuds, produce blooms on the previous year's new growth. Prune them immediately after flowering, before new growth starts.

There are two important exceptions to these seasonal guidelines. Broken or otherwise damaged limbs should be removed immediately, and foliage should be trimmed back on a transplanted tree. The diminished root system of a transplanted specimen cannot supply water to the full canopy of foliage, and the plant may die unless the foliage is reduced in proportion to the root loss. In this situation, trim back the branch tips, or remove most of the leaves.

5. Prune for a reason. Carefully consider the four primary objectives of pruning: improving appearance, directing growth, encouraging fruit or flowers, and maintaining health. Remove a limb only for a very specific purpose; don't vent your frustration from a stalled lawn mower on a nearby shrub.

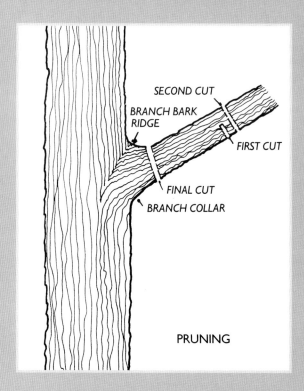

SECOND CUT
BRANCH BARK RIDGE
FIRST CUT
FINAL CUT
BRANCH COLLAR

PRUNING

Cuts made in the right places will help your pruned tree heal quickly.

Mexican elder (*Sambucus nigra* subsp. *canadensis*) can be trained into a handsome tree with some help from the pruning shears.

Know the growth habit of your plant before you assault it with pruning shears. The descriptions in the "Native Plant Profiles" section of this book indicate the growth habits and pruning requirements of most species. Following are some general guidelines for pruning that will help ensure a healthy and attractive plant.

Directing Growth by Thinning

Thinning maintains the symmetrical shape and desired size of a tree or shrub by removing excessive or unsightly branches. Removing wayward limbs channels the plant's growth into the desirable limbs. A developing young tree or shrub, especially if it is rapid growing, produces numerous branches, some of which compete with each other for light. The ones that win the race for the sun will shade the others, which then eventually die. Removing these vulnerable branches from the beginning prevents the tree from wasting nutrients and growth on limbs destined to die.

After a hard freeze or severe pruning, a tree often produces water sprouts—straight, rapid-growing, vertical limbs that branch from the trunk or older interior limbs. These shoots can destroy the tree's natural shape and should be removed. Thinning also keeps the lower limbs from obstructing vision or blocking access at the base of the tree.

When thinning small branches, you should make a smooth cut where the branch connects with the main stem. You can change the direction a branch is growing by pruning it one-fourth to one-half inch beyond a twig that is already growing in the desired direction. The twig will assume the primary growth of the branch. Light pruning of the branch tips of many shrub species stimulates new growth and gives the plant a fuller appearance.

Rejuvenation

As some plants age, such as desert willow and Texas ranger, they develop unproductive wood that produces few leaves or flowers. Cutting back the old limbs, or even cutting back the entire plant nearly to the ground, will stimulate growth of vigorous new branches. You may need to remove the old branches over a two- or three-year interval and thin the new branches as they appear.

Encouraging Flowers and Fruit

Many flowering shrubs benefit from light pruning in the dormant season. Pruning the branch tips of salvias, brittlebush, and chamisa produces denser foliage and more flowers. Thinning the interior limbs of a flowering or fruiting plant allows light to penetrate and stimulate more blooms. Some plants, such as desert bird of paradise, desert willow, and yellow trumpet flower, must be severely pruned every few years to maintain an attractive, full-flowering condition.

Maintaining Health

A plant will not only be more attractive, it will be healthier if damaged, dead, or diseased limbs are removed. Limbs broken by winds, freezes, or careless handling are open doors for invasions of fungi and parasites. Remove them immediately.

Pine Bark Beetle Infestation

The composition and appearance of the forests of the Southwest have changed dramatically since the beginning of the new millennium. A massive die-off of pinyon and ponderosa pines began in 2002. Surveys indicate that tree mortality peaked in 2004, although the impact will be felt for many years. Aerial photos of Arizona and New Mexico show heavy tree loss across 1.3 million acres of ponderosa pine forests and 2.1 million acres of pinyon-juniper woodlands. In the Santa Fe–Taos region, up to 90 percent of the pinyon pines died. The combined stresses of the worst drought in the West in 500 years and abnormally high tree densities due to improper forest management and fire suppression created an unlimited buffet for the tiny pine bark beetles. As the drought worsened and the number of susceptible pines increased, the small numbers of beetles that normally exist in the forests underwent a population explosion.

A healthy pine tree has adequate defenses against the 1/8-inch beetles. When an adult beetle bores a pinhole through the bark, the tree exudes enough sap to expel the pest. Drought-starved trees, however, cannot produce the surplus sap needed to withstand an attack.

When a bark beetle attacks a tree, it emits a scent, or pheromone, that attracts swarms of other beetles. The members of the colony mate and lay eggs between the bark and the wood. When the eggs hatch, the larvae feed on the nutritious inner bark layer, the cambium. The beetles also spread a blue stain fungus that clogs the water- and nutrient-conducting tissues of the cambium, further weakening the tree. When the beetle larvae mature into adults, they leave the infected tree to start the life cycle anew. At the height of an infestation, beetles produce multiple generations between February and October. Adults overwinter inside dead or dying trees.

The U.S. Forest Service advises that no treatment or cure exists for an infected tree, and that prevention is uncertain at best. Removing infected and dead trees has little effect on the spread of the beetles during an infestation. The current beetle population is so overwhelming that removing one tree is like killing one ant on a swarming ant hill. Of course, any time a tree dies in your landscape, remove it immediately for aesthetic and safety reasons.

In areas that are not infested with the beetle, you should be sure to prune any damaged limbs and remove and dispose of dying trees so that the next generation of beetles won't emerge and attack nearby trees. Time your pruning so as not to create fresh wounds during the beetle flight season, February through October. Do not pile unseasoned, freshly cut wood near landscape plants. Firewood that is cut from dying or newly dead trees provides a breeding source for wood-boring beetles. Tightly seal firewood beneath clear plastic in a sunny location for several months to exclude beetles and kill any already in the wood.

Home Remedies

Homeowners can take several precautions to protect high-value pinyon or ponderosa pines in their yards. First, during drought conditions, water specimen trees regularly to maintain their health and natural ability to repel bark beetles. Saturate the feeder roots with water-wise drip irrigation or soaker hoses placed all the way to the drip line of the canopy, the point to which the longest tree branches extend. You should water on a weekly basis during the heat of spring and summer and once a month in the winter. A four-inch layer of mulch around the tree will help to cool the soil and conserve water. Be sure to remove weeds, vines, and other water-hogging vegetation from around the tree.

Chemicals

Insecticides that kill the beetles are effective only if a tree has not yet been attacked. Permethrin (PDF) and carbaryl (PDF) will kill adult beetles that attempt to bore into the bark, but no insecticide will kill the eggs or larvae under the bark. Treatment must kill the adults before they can lay eggs. Systemic insecticides implanted or injected through the bark or applied to soil beneath trees do not control bark beetles. The main trunk must be drenched and the bark of all branches greater than one inch in diameter thoroughly saturated—an awesome task with a mature ponderosa or even a pinyon.

Since pine bark beetles overwinter under the bark of dead or dying trees, insecticides should be applied when the beetles begin to emerge, as early as mid-February in warm areas and April at cooler, higher elevations. Consult with the county agricultural extension agent and exterminator professionals in your area to determine the most effective treatment schedule for the local conditions. Carbaryl reportedly lasts one year when properly applied, and permethrin for about six months, so at least one application per season is required. Since bark beetles produce as many as five generations in a year, a second application may be needed in ensure protection.

Some products for preventing pine bark beetle infestation may not be available to home users, but only to licensed pesticide applicators. High-pressure spray equipment may be required to treat large trees. Be sure to use a product that is labeled for trunk applications and apply it at the proper rate for trunk treatment. Label rates for foliage treatment will not be effective. Whenever you are using insecticides, mix only what is needed. Apply the entire mix according to the label, and never pour leftover insecticide down a drain or allow runoff to seep into waterways.

Thinning

Property owners with wooded acreage can thin their tree cover to maintain the overall health of the plants. By reducing competition for sunlight, nutrients, and moisture, thinning increases the vigor of the remaining trees and makes them more resistant to bark beetle attack. Select the best trees to leave standing, including young specimens for future woodland development. Prune in the winter, when beetles are least active, and remove all slash that might attract beetles. When thinning and pruning, you should protect trees from physical injury. Be especially careful when using edgers around the base of trees and shrubs. Pruning, mowing, and weeding can accidentally injure a tree and induce pitch flow, which weakens a plant and attracts bark beetles and borers. Large properties should be thinned over a period of several years to minimize stress on the remaining trees caused by the altered exposure and runoff patterns. Thinning and removing dead trees also decreases the fire hazard, which is a major concern in forests with considerable dead wood.

Revegetation Considerations

The mortality of millions of pinyons and ponderosa pines across the Southwest landscape has dramatically altered the type and quality of habitat available for plants and animals. Likewise, losing one large pine from your yard will have a major affect on the plants in your landscape. If you do suffer tree loss, take the opportunity to consider the short- and long-term possibilities for creating a native landscape that brings out the best in nature.

In the coming decades, the appearance and species makeup of the Southwest mesas and mountains will change significantly. Native juniper and grass species and understory forest vegetation will increase in severely damaged forests and woodlands. The loss of tree cover also opens new habitat for invasive exotic species, such as Russian olive, Siberian elm, tall morning glory, ragwort, purple loosestrife, tamarix (salt cedar), and introduced range grasses. As homeowners, we have the added responsibility of avoiding nonnative species in our yards that might escape into nature. Other important considerations for revegetation may include landscaping to reduce the risks of fire and for erosion control.

Healthy and vigorously growing plants provide their own best defense against pests and diseases in the landscape. Take care to select plants that are adapted to the

Mexican pinyon pine, *Pinus cembroides*

specific microhabitats of your yard, and treat them with TLC until well established. With this approach, native plants will do what they do best: survive and thrive in the environment that has sustained them for thousands of years.

As a further note, global warming over the last two decades has caused record-breaking warm winters, hot summers, and drought conditions over much of North America. Without severe winters to limit the bark beetle populations, the numbers have increased dramatically and decimated forests from Arizona to Canada and Alaska. On the Kenai Peninsula of Alaska and the south-central region of the state, a decade-long infestation of spruce bark beetles has killed more than 6,000 square miles of trees, an area larger than Connecticut. In British Columbia, the mountain pine bark beetle has turned millions of acres of lodgepole pine into dead-standing forests. As unseasonably warm winters continue, scientists fear additional new infestations across the continent from native bark beetles, as well as alien species of long-horned, sawyer, bark, bud, and shoot beetles from Asia, Europe, and the Mediterranean.

Xeriscape garden in Albuquerque.

Landscaping for
Energy and
Water Conservation,
and Xeriscaping

The Southwest deserts sizzle in the summer, and bone-chilling blizzards sweep across the high plateaus in the winter. Summer temperatures in excess of 90ºF strike in April and linger far into September, and winters are as unpredictable as the north wind. We insulate ourselves from the extremes of nature by adjusting the thermostats in our climate-controlled houses and offices. But we pay the price for this independence from nature. Our creature comforts cost us every 30 days when we receive our utility bills. A judicious choice of landscape plants and a well-thought-out landscape design can reduce your heating and cooling expenses, make your house more comfortable throughout the year, and make your yard a more enjoyable recreational space.

The walls of your house provide a buffer between the outdoors and the interior environment, and landscape plants can be an effective extension of that protection. Trees, shrubs, vines, and groundcovers reduce direct sunlight and reflected heat, provide cooling shade, increase humidity, and block the chilling breezes of winter. Landscaping yields tangible utilitarian benefits, as well as beautifying your home.

With the rising cost of utilities, homeowners cannot afford to pass up the bargain that landscaping represents.

Planting a deciduous tree, such as desert willow (*Chilopsis linearis*), near your home will provide cooling shade in summer yet allow the warming sun to come through in winter.

A beautifully landscaped yard can add thousands of dollars to the value of your house, makes it easier to sell, makes your living space more attractive and enjoyable, and reduces monthly utility expenses. In short, it pays to landscape.

The Deciduous Solution

Nature has its own energy-conservation program: deciduous plants. The purpose of a leaf is to capture solar energy and convert it into food, and this is most efficiently accomplished in the spring and summer. Many plants have adopted the strategy of losing their leaves in the winter. This prevents water loss through the leaves at a time when food production is at a minimum. Thanks to nature's ingenious scheme, we have plants that provide cooling shade in the summer, yet allow the sun's warming rays to penetrate in the winter.

Summertime Shade

In the summer, the southern and western walls of a structure receive direct radiation from the sun from dawn to dusk. Regardless of how well insulated it is, a house absorbs a tremendous heat load that your air-conditioning system must dissipate. Anything that reduces that heat load reduces utility bills. A deciduous tree provides the perfect solution. A tree large enough to shade the roof can reduce the interior temperature of a house by 8 to 10 degrees.

For optimum shading, a deciduous tree should be planted 15 to 20 feet away from a building. Choose a tree that grows tall enough so that the lower limbs do not block air circulation around the house. Ashes, maples, and oaks are traditional favorites and have superior landscaping qualities, though other indigenous trees, such as walnut, ironwood, New Mexico locust, and huisache, will suffice beautifully. Avoid the temptation to plant fast-growing species that are short-lived and prone to wind damage, an especially important consideration for trees with limbs near the roof.

You probably will want to shade the east side of your house without completely blocking the cheerful morning rays of the sun. Low shrubs and trees, such as desert willow, mesquite, and palo verde, let morning light filter in while blocking heat buildup. Xeriscape gardens (other than rock gardens) and groundcovers help by reducing heat reflected from the ground.

Another way to obtain summer shading is by planting vines, either climbing on a trellis or arbor or clinging directly to a masonry wall. The layer of vegetation against the side of your house will block the sun's rays and provide an insulating dead-air space. Note, though, that the hold-fasts of larger vines can penetrate the mortar and eventually cause damage to the structure, and vines on a wooden exterior tend to hasten decomposition and must be removed when your house needs painting. An arbor both shades the side of the house and provides a shady outdoor area for recreation. Arbors especially enhance pools, porches, and patios.

The air-conditioning compressors of many houses are placed without regard to exposure. A unit on the south side of a house is in the sun continually and must labor much harder than one in the shade. You can increase the efficiency and life of the compressor by planting a tree or shrub nearby to provide shade without blocking airflow. For the same amount of energy, the compressor may keep the interior temperature as much as three degrees cooler.

Broad circle drives leading to your front door, paved patios, and rock gardens may be attractive, but they absorb and radiate heat just like a shopping mall parking lot. The air temperature above grass and groundcovers may be as much as 15 degrees cooler than above concrete or rock aggregate. You can reduce the heat radiated onto your house and make your patio or pool more bearable in the summer by planting around walks and drives.

Winter Role Reversals

In the summer, we resent the villainous sun and welcome the gentle breezes, but in the winter the roles reverse, and we praise the warming sun and curse the wind. Deciduous shade trees cooperate by dropping their leaf cover and allowing the sun's heat to warm our houses. Trees and shrubs can also alter the airflow around your house and buffer the chilling winter

A rock garden makes an effective and attractive water-conserving landscape.

breezes. A row of evergreen trees or large shrubs planted on the northwest side of your house will deflect the arctic north winds without blocking the cooling summer southern breezes. An evergreen hedge five feet from the house will reduce the wind velocity striking the structure and create an insulating dead-air space. This decreases the airflow, and resulting heat loss, through the outside walls of the house. Tests have shown that a 30-foot-tall evergreen planting reduces wind velocity by 55 percent, an effect felt as far as 320 feet downwind of the planting.

Xeriscaping

Anyone contemplating landscaping a home or business is concerned with the time and expense of plant maintenance.

One of the primary expenses of maintaining a landscape is water, and expensive summer watering bills can offset some of the savings plants provide in air-conditioning costs. As much as 60 percent of residential water consumption goes to watering yards, but with a careful choice of plants, you can greatly reduce the moisture required to keep your landscape attractive and healthy. Of the thousands of plants native to the Southwest, some are water spendthrifts, and some are as frugal as a Depression-era loan officer.

A plant grows by capturing solar energy and converting raw elements, through the process of photosynthesis, into useful nutrients. Plant roots absorb water and dissolved minerals, which are channeled through the plant's vascular system to the food factories in the leaves. The

Mesquite and various species of cacti in xeriscape design in Tubac, Arizona.

leaves transpire, or lose, a major portion of the water supplied by the roots. Some plants have developed ingenious methods to reduce water loss from the leaves, and many of these species have exceptional landscape value. Plants combat water loss through the leaf surface by producing small leaves or leaves covered with a waxy or woolly coating, as well as by internal cellular and structural adaptations. These xerophytic, or drought-tolerant, plants thrive under conditions that would kill or severely stress plants native to more moist areas.

The term *xeriscape*—derived by combining the Greek word for "dry," *xeri*, with "landscape"—became a buzzword in the 1990s among gardeners, landscapers, and urban planners looking for more cost-efficient approaches to planting. Cities, industries, and farmers all recognize water as their state's most precious resource. Most metropolises in the Southwest must find ways to conserve water, or their reservoirs and wells will run dry in the near future. In response, many cities and counties in the Southwest have initiated xeriscape programs to actively encourage property owners to landscape with plants that have a low water consumption. By conscientious landscaping, each of us can help relieve the demand for this critical resource and reduce our personal utility expenses.

Seven Xeriscape Principles

Xeriscaping is not limited to just yuccas and rock gardens. It is a philosophy that incorporates good gardening principles, and it can be practiced anywhere. The National Xeriscape Council, Inc., recommends the following principles:

1. Start with a good design. A master plan incorporates existing and future plants; soil, slope, and exposure; and your house and play areas into a design that meets your needs and conserves water.

2. Improve the soil. A plant needs a healthy root system to thrive and beautify your yard. Compacted, shallow, rocky, or sandy soil may not allow a plant to develop a root system that can sufficiently support luxuriant foliage growth. You can improve your soil by tilling in at least 2 inches of organic material, such as composted leaves, grass clippings, or dried manure. If you have shallow soil, till in 2 to 4 inches of loam topsoil. A proper soil is loose enough for roots to penetrate, has the proper pH for roots to absorb iron, and allows water to slowly percolate into the root zone.

3. Use mulch. A mulch covers the soil, prevents moisture loss, inhibits weed growth, and modifies extreme soil temperatures. Bark, wood chips, leaves, grass clippings, and colored gravel make good mulching materials.

Use 2 to 4 inches of mulch around trees and shrubs, in flowerbeds, and in landscaped areas. The mulching itself can be an attractive design element in your overall landscape plan.

4. Reduce lawn areas. Turf grass is necessary for outdoor recreation areas, and it dissipates heat and provides a cool space around your house or patio. But in arid locales, lawns guzzle water in the summer and require regular maintenance. To conserve water and save on utility bills, limit your lawn to small recreation and border areas around your house, and choose the grass best adapted to your climate and yard. Consider using wildflowers, groundcovers, trees, shrubs, and mulch for the majority of your landscape.

5. Water efficiently. Put the water where and when the plant needs it, and you can cut your water consumption, and water bill, by as much as 30 percent. Learn to tell when a plant needs water. Grass curls and lies flat. Leaves may droop, drop, or lose their shine. Learn to water as often as necessary to avoid drought stress, but without overwatering.

The way you water influences how much water a plant needs to thrive. Place the water in the root zone and water deeply. Shallow watering encourages a shallow root system, which requires more frequent watering since the upper portion of the soil dries out faster. Drip irrigation, soil basins built around plants, early- or late-day watering, and mulch all help to conserve water. Sprinkler systems used improperly can lose considerable water to evaporation and runoff.

6. Practice good maintenance. Maintenance keeps your plants healthy and attractive. Weeds, injured or dead limbs, and sickly plants detract from your landscape, increase your water bill, and can require costly replacement of plants. (See the chapter "Maintaining Your Landscape.")

7. Choose low-water-use plants adapted to your area. Decreasing elevation from mountaintop to desert, the amount of rainfall decreases linearly. Peaks in the Pecos Wilderness above Santa Fe receive 44 inches of annual precipitation while Yuma, in the low Sonoran desert, gets 4 inches. As one might expect, most Southwestern plants must be drought-tolerant to survive, but some are better adapted to drought than others. Some species grow only along streams and rivers or in cooler habitats with greater precipitation. They would quickly perish in the hot, arid desert or in an arid landscape setting.

Drought-Tolerant Plants for Xeriscaping

The following list, though not inclusive, delineates many species of trees, shrubs, vines, and groundcovers that will tolerate periods of drought. Refer to the "Native Plant Profiles" for more details.

Trees

Acacia farnesiana, huisache
Acacia greggii, catclaw acacia
Arbutus arizonica, Arizona madrone
Celtis laevigata var. *reticulata*, netleaf hackberry
Cercis canadensis var. *mexicana*, Mexican redbud
Chilopsis linearis, desert willow
Cupressus arizonica, Arizona cypress
Ebenopsis ebano, Texas ebony
Fraxinus cuspidata, fragrant ash
Fraxinus greggii, Gregg ash
Fraxinus velutina, Arizona ash
Juglans major, Arizona walnut
Juglans microcarpa, little walnut
Juniperus species, junipers
Leucaena retusa, goldenball leadtree
Olneya tesota, desert ironwood
Parkinsonia florida, blue palo verde
Parkinsonia hybrid, Desert Museum palo verde
Parkinsonia microphylla, foothills palo verde
Pinus cembroides, Mexican pinyon pine
Pinus edulis, New Mexico pinyon pine
Prosopis glandulosa, mesquite
Prosopis velutina, velvet mesquite
Prunus serotina var. *rufula* and var. *virens*, southwestern black cherry
Quercus arizonica, Arizona white oak
Quercus emoryi, Emory oak
Quercus grisea, gray oak
Quercus hypoleucoides, silverleaf oak
Quercus oblongifolia, Mexican blue oak
Quercus pungens, sandpaper oak
Quercus turbinella, shrub live oak
Rhus lanceolata, prairie flameleaf sumac
Robinia neomexicana, New Mexico locust
Sambucus nigra subsp. *canadensis*, Mexican elder
Sapindus saponana, soapberry
Ungnadia speciosa, Mexican buckeye

Shrubs

Acacia constricta, white-thorn acacia
Agave species, century plants
Aloysia gratissima, bee brush
Amorpha fruticosa, false indigo
Anisacanthus quadrifidus var. *wrightii*, flame anisacanthus
Anisacanthus thurberi, desert honeysuckle
Artemisia filifolia, sand sagebrush
Artemisia tridentata, big sagebrush
Baccharis sarothroides, desert broom
Bouvardia ternifolia, scarlet bouvardia
Buddleja marrubiifolia, woolly butterflybush
Caesalpinia gilliesii, desert bird of paradise
Calliandra conferta, fairy duster
Ceanothus greggii, desert ceanothus
Celtis pallida, desert hackberry
Cercocarpus montanus, mountain mahogany
Choisya dumosa, starleaf Mexican orange
Chrysactinia mexicana, damianita
Dalea formosa, feather dalea
Dalea frutescens, black dalea
Dasylirion species, sotols
Dodonaea viscosa, hopbush
Echinocereus species, hedgehog cacti
Encelia farinosa, brittle bush
Ephedra species, joint firs
Ericameria laricifolia, larchleaf goldenweed
Ericameria nauseosa, chamisa
Fallugia paradoxa, Apache plume
Fendlera rupicola, cliff fendlerbush
Ferocactus species, barrel cacti
Foresteria pubescens var. *pubescens*, desert olive
Fouquieria splendens, ocotillo
Garrya wrightii, silktassel
Hesperaloe parviflora, red yucca
Justicia californica, chuparosa
Justicia canadicans, jacobinia
Krascheninnikovia lanata, winterfat
Larrea tridentata, creosote bush
Leucophyllum frutescens, Texas ranger
Lycium species, wolfberry
Mahonia species, barberries
Mammillaria vivipara, pincushion cactus
Mimosa dysocarpa, velvet pod mimosa
Nolina species, beargrass
Opuntia species, cholla or prickly pear
Pachycereus schottii, senita cactus
Parthenium argentatum, guayule
Parthenium incanum, mariola
Psorothamnus scoparius, broom dalea
Purshia stansburiana, Mexican cliffrose
Rhus glabra, smooth sumac
Rhus microphylla, little-leaf sumac
Rhus ovata, sugar sumac
Rhus trilobata, three-leaf sumac
Rhus virens, evergreen sumac
Salvia greggii, autumn sage
Senna wislizeni, shrubby senna
Simmondsia chinesis, jojoba
Sophora secundiflora, Texas mountain laurel
Stenocereus thurberi, organ-pipe cactus
Tecoma stans, yellow trumpet flower
Vauquelinia californica, Arizona rosewood
Viguiera stenoloba, skeleton-leaf goldeneye
Yucca species

Vines

Campsis radicans, trumpet creeper
Clematis ligusticifolia, western virgin's bower
Maurandya antirrhiniflora, snapdragon vine
Parthenocissus quinquefolia, thicket creeper

Groundcovers

Artemisia ludoviciana, white sagebrush
Dalea greggii, Gregg dalea
Glandularia gooddingii, Goodding's verbena
Muhlenbergia rigens, deer grass
Phyla species, frogfruit
Sedum species, stonecrop

Given room to spread, wildflowers such as blackfoot daisy (*Melampodium leucanthum*) serve as an attractive groundcover.

Landscaping with
Groundcovers

Almost every landscape, whether small or large, private or commercial, has areas that receive no foot traffic but are also not suitable for trees, shrubs, or turf grass. A groundcover can turn a visually empty space into an eye-catching attraction. Groundcovers serve two general purposes, one utilitarian, the other aesthetic: They prevent erosion and cover unsightly bare spots, and they add an active or unifying element to a landscape design, a dimension of visual interest beyond what a cover of turf grass or crushed stone can provide.

A grassy lawn is desirable for play and entertaining, but many areas of turf serve no function other than contributing a tailored appearance to the yard—and anything is better than the bed of gravel that so many desert developers cover yards with in sprawling subdivisions. A border filled with low-profile plants provides visual relief to a wall, drive, sidewalk, or building front. Decorative groundcovers can also colorfully accent the area beneath open-branching shrubs and trees. A groundcover planting within a graveled area breaks the monotony and imparts a soft, cool feeling to the overall landscape. In cases where a tall plant would block the view in front of a window or

Sedum species offer a variety of options for groundcover use.

storefront, a vine or low-growing shrub can enhance the scene without obscuring the view.

Groundcovers also come to the rescue for areas that are difficult to maintain or have marginal growing conditions—such as shady sites or rocky, dry slopes—but where some type of planting would be beneficial. When used as an integral feature of a landscape design, groundcovers provide low-maintenance cover, as well as an extra touch of beauty.

Groundcover Qualities

For a plant to be both effective and attractive as a groundcover, it must exhibit special growth characteristics. In searching for native groundcovers, landscapers and propagators look for plants that have a low growth habit and dense foliage and can adapt to a wide variety of habitats. The plant must be able to survive and thrive in harsh environmental conditions, such as shade, heat, drought, and infertile soil. In addition, the ideal groundcover grows and spreads rapidly and has evergreen foliage.

Nature has endowed many plants with some of these basic characteristics, but precious few have them all. Unfortunately, plants that are adapted to habitats severely limited in soil nutrients, moisture, or light seldom grow rapidly or develop dense foliage. The task of the propagators is to find those plants that have most of the basic requirements.

Fortunately, many naturally low-growing shrubs, mat-forming wildflowers, and weakly climbing vines are suitable for use as groundcovers. Some species adapt to almost any situation, while others require a particular habitat. The best have evergreen leaves, attractive flowers, and/or decorative fruit.

Planting and Maintaining Groundcovers

Don't expect to set out a few recommended plants on an arid and rocky or compacted and shady site and get a dense cover of vegetation the next growing season. That a plant has the potential for thick growth doesn't mean it can

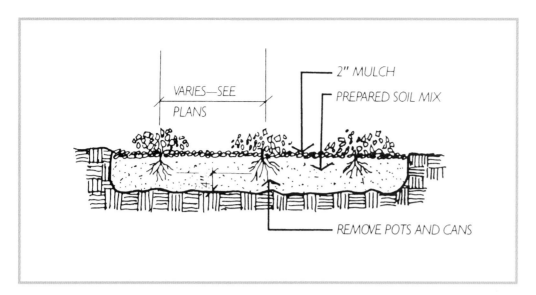

VARIES—SEE PLANS

2" MULCH

PREPARED SOIL MIX

REMOVE POTS AND CANS

With proper soil preparation and plant spacing, a groundcover will quickly fill in its garden spot.

achieve that growth under marginal conditions. You want the plant to thrive, not just survive. A plant can cope with less than the best if it has a robust root system. In many cases, soil preparation is the key to establishing a successful groundcover planting.

If you want a complete cover, you must first remove all the competing vegetation, especially grasses. Do it in the beginning, and you won't have to spend hours removing unsightly weeds later. You also may need to work some organic matter, such as peat, compost, or manure, into the upper 8 to 12 inches of soil to give the roots a healthy growing medium. Third, mulch between the new settings to hold in soil moisture and to reduce weed invasion. In one or two growing seasons, the plants should reach their potential.

Once established, a dense groundcover is not totally maintenance-free. Many plants begin to lose their vigor in two to four years, and bare spots develop. You may need to periodically replace plants to keep the cover complete. Other plants grow so vigorously that they need regular pruning to maintain a tailored appearance. A dense groundcover requires less attention than a lawn, but don't expect it to be totally maintenance-free.

Maybe you're not enamored with a groundcover that requires regular attention. Remember that a groundcover doesn't have to provide complete foliage cover, so if you're willing to excuse some bare spots, other low-maintenance options are available. Many low-growing deciduous shrubs have decorative foliage, flowers, or fruit through most of the year, and perennial wildflowers can provide a seasonal accent. A mixture of ornamental native shrubs and perennial wildflowers can give your landscape seasonal variety and an elegance far exceeding that of a solid planting of turf grass or dwarf junipers.

The dense foliage and purple flowers make giant four o'clock (*Mirabilis multiflora*) a useful and ornamental groundcover.

Opposite: Autumn sage (*Salvia greggii*) spreads quickly to cover garden areas with its pinkish blooms.

Native Plants Suitable for Groundcovers

Many native plants are suitable for use as groundcovers. The section on groundcovers in the "Native Plant Profiles" includes photos and descriptions of species whose primary landscape function is to provide groundcover, and which offer other attractive attributes for the garden. In addition, many shrubs, wildflowers, and vines can be used as groundcovers, and these are listed here; for a full description and photos, refer to the "Native Plant Profiles" later in the book.

Low-Growing Shrubs
Choisya dumosa, starleaf Mexican orange
Chrysactinia mexicana, damianita
Dasylirion species, sotols
Nolina species, beargrass
Rhus microphylla, little-leaf sumac
Rhus tridentate, prostrate three-leaf sumac
Salvia greggii, autumn sage

Perennial Wildflowers
Datura wrightii, sacred datura
Glandularia bipinnatifida, prairie verbena
Ipomoea leptophylla, bush morning glory

Linanthastrum nuttallii, nuttall gilia
Melampodium leucanthum, blackfoot daisy
Mirabilis multiflora, giant four-o'clock
Oenothera species, evening primrose
Psilostrophe tagetina, paperflower
Thymophylla pentachaeta, dogweed
Zinnia acerosa, desert zinnia
Zinnia grandiflora, plains zinnia

Vines
Clematis ligusticifolia, western virgin's bower
Lonicera arizonica, Arizona honeysuckle
Parthenocissus quinquefolia, thicket creeper

Thicket creeper (*Parthenocissus quinquefolia*) will rapidly cover walls and fences for both insulation and ornamental benefits.

Landscaping with Vines:

Upright Flower Beds and Hanging Gardens

How would you like to turn that nondescript fence in your yard into an upright flowerbed covered with fragrant blossoms? Why not transform your mailbox, gaslight, or porch column into a hanging garden of colorful flowers? Nature has supplied the perfect plants for such a conversion: vines. These versatile plants add natural beauty to your home landscape and require little maintenance.

Nature adapts every plant to a particular habitat and niche. Trees extend their arching limbs toward the sky, shrubs fill the spaces beneath the trees, and grasses and herbs cover the ground. In between, the vines twine in search of the sun. Many vines cling to their support with tendrils; some twist and twine around other objects; others cling with holdfasts.

Vines have other natural features that make them extraordinary landscaping plants. Adapted to growing in the dappled shadows beneath trees, most vines can tolerate both partial shade and full sun. They grow vigorously and are hardy, and many have ornamental foliage, flowers, and fruit. Wherever vines grow, they add natural beauty and visual interest.

Before buying a plant or turning a shovel of soil, you should determine how a vine will best fit into your yard. Do you want a dominant feature, a dense groundcover, or a graceful accent? Low-growing vines with slender stems provide a delicate touch, while high-climbing or thickly branching species rapidly become a major landscape element. Let's see how these special plants can beautify your landscape.

Vines As Dominant Features

Wire fences and rock or masonry walls can support vigorously growing, densely foliated vines such as trumpet creeper (*Campsis radicans*). The thick evergreen foliage turns an ordinary wire fence into an extraordinary privacy barrier covered with flamboyant yellow flowers in the spring. If you want scarlet spring and summer flowers, plant Arizona honeysuckle (*Lonicera arizonica*). You can enjoy brilliant shades of red and orange foliage in the autumn by planting a thicket creeper (*Parthenocissus quinquefolia*) along your fence or on an arbor. A slender-stemmed vine with dense foliage can turn a gaslight, a mailbox, or even an unsightly old stump into a prominent landscape feature in your yard. Most vines will overrun their supports, however, if not pruned periodically.

Vines As Accent Plants

An accent vine should complement but not obscure the object supporting it. Low-climbing vines with thin foliage are good for this. They bring visual interest and gracefully accent a wire fence without obscuring the view. A rock, rail,

The vibrant flowers of honeysuckle vines add a colorful accent to any landscape.

or lath fence forms the perfect backdrop for slender climbers, such as the unusual snapdragon vine (*Maurandya antirrhiniflora*). The small, delicate features complement mailboxes without overpowering them. A gaslight draped with the scarlet fruit of a balsam gourd (*Ibervillea lindheimeri*) becomes an eye-catching element of the landscape.

Don't forget that vines can work their magic on porch railings and columns, too. Vines will quickly cover chicken wire or a guide wire wrapped around a post. Some of my earliest memories are of playing on our front porch, shaded by a screen of jasmine growing on chicken wire stretched from the ground to the porch roof.

Customize Your Landscape

The next step after determining whether you need a dominant or accent planting is to choose the type of vine. Do you want a woody or herbaceous species, one with evergreen or deciduous leaves, or one with colorful flowers or fruit? For privacy and screen plantings, you'll want evergreens. In most other applications, deciduous and evergreen vines work equally well. Woody vines will densely cover a fence, porch column, or trellis. Twining vines and those with tendrils quickly climb on fences, trellises, and guide wires around posts, while those with holdfasts climb well on rock and masonry, although they may eventually damage the mortar. Avoid letting vines cover wooden buildings. They hasten decay and must be removed or destroyed when the surface requires painting.

The high-climbing species, such as trumpet creeper, develop thick, heavy branches and should be used only on fences or posts that can provide adequate support. Most low climbers have slender, twining branches that will not damage lath fences or trellises and are easier to contain.

Planting

Like any landscape addition, vines require careful planning and selection. For a dense cover along a fence, plant a high-climbing, thickly foliaged vine every 8 to 12 feet and low-climbing vines with slender stems every 3 to 4 feet. For variety, plant one section of your fence with a spring-blooming species and another with a summer or fall bloomer. Herbaceous perennial vines grow rapidly during the spring and summer and die back to the ground with the first freeze. The rootstock survives the winter and sprouts in the spring.

Nurseries offer a wide selection of woody vines, and you can choose herbaceous varieties from seed stores and catalogs, or you can gather your own seeds. Each vine listed in the "Native Plant Profiles" has flamboyant flowers, ornamental foliage, or colorful fruit and will provide generations of beauty in your yard. So, plant a vine and watch it twine!

Landscaping with Cacti

As the first European botanists crisscrossed the Americas, they encountered a bizarre family of plants unknown in the Old World. Unsure of the classification, they applied the Greek word *kaktos*, meaning "thistle." Modern botanists still argue about the proper organization of these puzzling plants. But one thing is constant: From the fifteenth century until the present, plant enthusiasts have found these unique plants irresistible. The demand for cacti was immediate, and it has increased through the centuries. Today, collectors annually strip tons of cacti from North and South American deserts to sell in souvenir shops and nurseries. With many species now either threatened or endangered, we are loving our native cacti to death. Fortunately, many cacti propagated from seeds and cuttings are available in the nursery trade. As a point of principle, be sure the cactus you buy wasn't collected from the countryside, either in the United States or Mexico. Our native plants belong in nature, too.

The Tucson Cactus and Succulent Society sponsors native cactus and succulent rescue operations, plant sales, field trips, nursery and garden visits, conventions and conferences throughout the year. The nonprofit organization holds monthly meetings that feature knowledgeable individuals who can educate you and help you understand more about these fascinating plants. Check their Web site (www.tucsoncactus.org) for a schedule of upcoming plant sales and activities.

Handle with Care

Cacti look tough, feel tough, and grow in a harsh environment, but they need tender care to survive in rock and xeriscape gardens. You see, cacti are specialists. They have adapted to marginal conditions with extremes of heat, light, and drought. Though cacti grow from 14,000-foot mountain peaks to torrid desert basins, most suffer if moved far from home. Many species have become so specialized to local conditions that they exist only in a single desert valley or on a particular geological outcropping. If you want your cacti to thrive, you must understand what makes them different from other landscape plants.

Cacti have drastically modified leaves, stems, and roots to catch, store, and conserve water in a desert environment. A netlike root system spreads out and rapidly soaks up moisture from fickle but usually torrential rains. To combat extended droughts, the thick succulent stems store water for long periods. Instead of normal leaves,

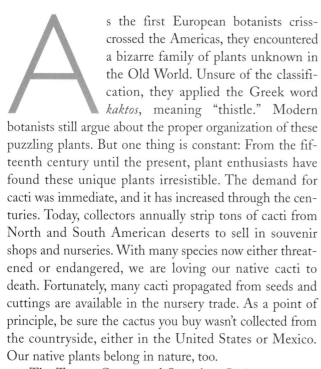

which lose considerable water, cactus leaves have evolved into rigid spines. This dense armament both shades and cools the plant and protects the succulent interior from thirsty desert creatures. With no leaves for photosynthesis, the green stems perform the task of food production. A thick, waxy epidermis covers cacti to further reduce water loss. Some cacti are so well adapted to their arid habitat that they transpire 6,000 times less water than ordinary plants. As a result of this reduced transpiration, many cacti grow at an extremely slow rate.

Overwatering: The Kiss of Death

Cacti roots soak up water as fast as possible, and the stems store and hold water as tenaciously as possible. In your garden, you want to find the magic line between watering enough to maximize growth and flowering, and overwatering, which can kill some cacti overnight. A root crown standing in water for 24 hours is susceptible to root rot and fungus invasion. A well-draining pot or garden is an absolute must. In the winter some cacti lose water to protect against frost and may appear shriveled. Don't water a wilted cactus unless you know the plant is stressed for water. The plant is probably just adapting to the overall environmental conditions. Texans have a saying, "Don't water your cactus until it rains in Presidio." Substitute Phoenix if you live in the Southwest, and your cacti will feel right at home.

Planting

Having the right soil mix for potted cacti or in a xeriscape garden is necessary for success. Potted cacti do well in a neutral soil, with an inch or so of granite gravel on the bottom of the pot for good drainage, then several inches of garden potting soil. Fill the remainder of the pot with coarse sand. For garden cacti, mix sand in with your garden soil if necessary to ensure proper drainage, and plant each cactus on a slightly elevated mound. Be sure your garden doesn't get regular runoff from lawn irrigation. Most of all, pay attention to the natural habitat of the cactus. Some species grow under desert shrubs and may benefit from some added leaf mulch.

Before transplanting a cactus or cutting, let it sit barerooted in a shady location for several days until the roots have thoroughly dried and calloused. Fungus easily invades fresh cuts or damaged roots.

Light Is Right

To bloom, cacti need heat and light. Many cacti do not begin photosynthesis until the temperature exceeds 75°F. Your cactus garden should receive more than a half-day of full sunlight to stimulate flowering and growth. The delicate flowers typically burst into bloom during the heat of the day, and many wither by nightfall. Both the spectacular flowers and the short blooming period represent adaptations that help the flower win a race against time. To ensure pollination, the flower must attract insects, thus the showy blossoms. Insects are active when the day is hottest, so the fragile flowers open in the afternoon. A bloom unpollinated during its first day may never get another chance. Many of the unprotected flowers become tidbits for the hungry critters active during the cool of the night. Night-blooming cacti, such as saguaro, usually have flowers on tall stems, out of reach of small herbivores, and they depend on bats or night-flying moths for pollination.

When your cacti burst into bloom, you can feel a sense of satisfaction for two reasons. First, the ephemeral flowers add a flamboyant, yet delicate, beauty to your yard. Second, you know that you have succeeded in creating a garden that duplicates the plant's natural requirements closely enough for it not just to survive, but to thrive and bloom.

Cacti are a fascinating combination of tough-looking spines and delicate flowers.

Below: Always remember to plant your cacti far from pathways and other areas of human contact.

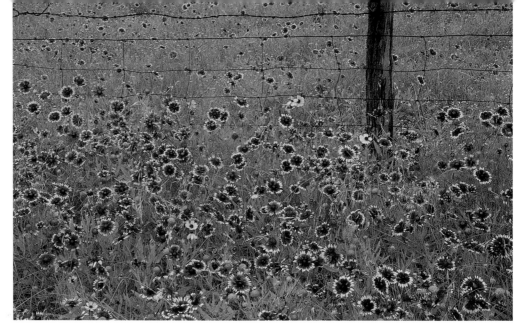

Wildflowers such as firewheel (*Gaillardia pulchella*) create colorful blankets throughout the Southwest.

Landscaping with Wildflowers

Nature seems to defy the logic of every conscientious gardener. Beautiful flowerbeds are the result of laborious hours of fertilizing; of fighting weeds, disease, and vermin; and of carefully mulching and watering the tender seedlings. Yet, without a gardener's care, patches of undisturbed ground across the countryside abound with a luxurious growth of wildflowers from early spring into fall.

The beauty radiating from nature's helter-skelter flower arrangements inspires every flower lover. Like magic, the stony mesas, open prairies, deserts, and woodlands burst forth with flower displays that make the most expert gardener envious. What a treat if we could have those unspoiled scenes of nature duplicated in our own yards!

Though you use the same gardening techniques for growing both domestic and native flowers, cultivating wildflowers has one basic goal that is different from formal flower gardening: You are trying to duplicate the conditions in the wild. The standard green-thumb skills and intuition are needed, as well as the ability to recognize the unique growing conditions that enable each species of wildflower to thrive. Traditionally, growers boast of their flower "gardens," but the wildflower enthusiast will want to show you his or her newly created wildflower "habitat."

The first step in cultivating wildflowers is to understand the microhabitat of your plot. Is the area exposed to warm morning, northeast sun or blazing, afternoon southwest sun? Does radiated heat from walkways, drives, walls, or landscape boulders add a few extra degrees of warmth to the plot? Do you need to mulch to keep roots cool and moist or add sand to increase drainage? Carefully scrutinize soil, light, and moisture conditions. What was the natural habitat before houses modified the environment? Don't expect moist woodland species to thrive on a sandy lawn.

Each species of wildflower grows within a certain range of environmental conditions. These conditions—the pH, texture, and composition of the soil, the slope, exposure, and moisture—define the flower's optimum habitat. The gardener must replicate the natural conditions as closely as possible if the favored plant is to grow successfully in the home plot.

The wildflower aficionado, before burying a seed or digging a plant, becomes well-acquainted with the flower's needs and the garden's microhabitat. A little homework will avoid the oft-repeated mistake, and resulting disappointment, of planting a shade-loving plant in full sunlight, or a plant requiring moisture and humidity in a hot, dry exposure. Choosing the species of wildflowers for your yard should receive as much consideration as planning the most formal landscape.

You can also create different microhabitats within your yard. An open lawn is ideal for sun-adapted plants, a tree-shaded corner for shade-tolerant species, or an enclosed entryway for moisture-loving flowers.

The quickest way to stock your garden is by purchasing seeds, seedlings, or bedding plants from a nursery. If this is your preferred course, beware of spectacular offers in almanacs and Sunday supplements. Avoid seed packs with general mixes of wildflower species from across the nation and around the world. They usually contain incompatible shade- and sun-loving plants. Many native seed sources offer mixes specifically designed for the different regions and elevations of the Southwest. You can also buy mixes for hummingbird and butterfly gardens and for seasonal color blends.

Planting Wildflowers from Seed

Whenever possible, you should purchase plants and seeds from a native plant nursery or arboretum in your area. Local garden clubs sometimes offer plant and seed exchanges from surplus plants in the members' yards. Or, you can collect your own seed, in permitted areas. Be aware, though, that seed or plant gathering on public land is generally prohibited. Planting seeds and stock from your region ensures that your landscape additions are adapted to your climate and gives you the satisfaction of re-establishing the botanical heritage that existed before urban sprawl engulfed the countryside.

Collecting Seed

Many wildflower lovers are not content with buying prepackaged seeds. Obtaining seeds and plants for a carefully prepared garden can be a year-round hobby. Discovering a specimen flower, marking it, and returning to collect the seeds adds to the sense of accomplishment of a successful garden. The timing of seed harvesting is critical, or the collector may find an empty seed pod on the prized flower. Remember, collecting plants or seeds on public property, including roadsides, is illegal.

A member of the sunflower family, black-eyed Susan (*Rudbeckia hirta*) readily reseeds itself to ensure colorful fall blooms year after year.

Penstemons offer a wide palette of colors for the garden.

Golden wave coreopsis (*Coreopsis tinctoria*) lives up to its name in springtime, showing off its bright golden flower heads.

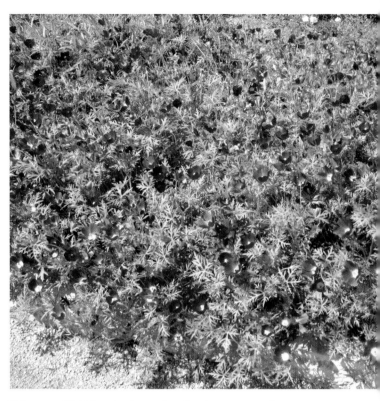

Winecup (*Callirhoe involucrata*) will paint your garden borders in bright purple hues in throughout the spring.

Many flowers have elaborate methods for dispersing their seeds. Numerous members of the sunflower family (Compositae) send their seeds floating in the breeze, while the dry pods of legumes (Leguminosae) split open, scattering their seeds on the ground. You can either pick the ripe pods and seed heads before they completely dry or place a muslin or paper sack over the flowers after the seeds have formed. After collecting, be sure to dry the seeds completely before storing them so they don't mold. Some seeds have succulent pulp that must be removed by rubbing on a screen. Sometimes you can clean small seeds in a blender at very low speed without damaging them.

Store the cleaned seeds in the refrigerator in jars, or in a cool, dry place safe from insects. Keep the seeds in paper bags (not plastic) to prevent molding, and plant within one year for best results.

Plants adapt to winter freezes by producing seeds that go through a dormant period. This dormancy prevents premature germination on warm fall days. After several months of cold weather, the inherent dormancy is broken, allowing the seeds to germinate as the soil warms up to 40°F. If you obtain seeds in the early spring, you can break the temperature dormancy by storing them in the refrigerator for two to eight weeks before planting.

When to Plant
Wildflowers naturally reseed themselves several weeks after blooming, in the spring for early-blooming species and in summer or fall for late bloomers. Generally, you will want to plant your seeds from late August through November, depending on the onset of winter. This allows the cooler temperatures to break any seed dormancy.

Other seeds need the fall rains to germinate, winter moisture to develop a root system, and spring rains to bloom.

Sowing the Seed
The first step in sowing the seed in your garden is to prepare a seedbed. Indiscriminately scattering seed is just setting the table for seed-eating insects and birds. Remove all vegetation just as you would when planting a vegetable garden. Rake the soil to break up the surface no more than an inch deep. Since some wildflower seeds are so small, you might want to mix your seeds with damp sand to give a more even distribution. After evenly scattering the seeds, lightly rake them into the soil, no deeper than two to four times their diameter. Firm up the soil and lightly water.

Watering and Waiting
All seeds need water to germinate, so you should water lightly three to four times a week to ensure optimum germination. If you live in higher elevations with hard winters, water the seedlings and the seedbed weekly until the first freeze if there are no fall rains. At lower elevations, moisten the seedbed weekly through December and January. This will ensure that spring-germinating seeds receive sufficient moisture. If you have a dry spring, supplemental watering will provide for optimum growth and blooming.

You may want to plant your seeds in a protected seedbed, cold frame, or peat pots and wait until the seedlings are well established before transplanting to your garden. You can start many species indoors from January to March, or four to six weeks before they are to be transplanted.

Natural Reseeding

Though annuals live only one growing season, and many perennials only a few, you can have a beautiful wildflower garden year after year by letting the flowers reseed themselves. After the flowers fade and the plants die, be sure to wait until the seeds have fallen before mowing or removing the old plant. Give the plants a good shake to dislodge all

For year-round appeal, dogweed (*Thymophylla pentachaeta*) gives you both attractive foliage and colorful flowers.

the seeds. If you have a naturalized area, leave the mowed stubble to cover and protect the seeds.

If you want a more dependable display of wildflowers, plant perennials along with the annuals. Most perennial wildflowers are herbaceous and die to the ground in the winter, but sprout from the roots with the first warm weather. They add color and beauty and may even spread to form flamboyant blankets of color and mixed bouquets that get prettier as the years pass. As a bonus, many bloom until the first frost.

Paint Your Yard with Perennial Flower Gardens

Imagine a flower garden—bordering your walk, decorating the corner of your yard, or edging your pool—that greets each season with a profusion of different-colored blooms. As the seasons progress, you have an ever-changing combination of flowers, from early-spring bloomers to fall ones that don't fade until the first frost.

Designing a perennial garden takes more forethought than just planting short flowers in the front and tall ones in the back. Half the fun is becoming the artist and arranging the blooming times and colors as though the garden were your canvas. Plant so that you will have a good balance of colors throughout the year. Use masses of each flower to create bold splashes, with adjacent colors complementing each other. Remember, your garden is a three-dimensional canvas. Mix naturally mounding plants with upright, sprawling, and cascading species so that they don't overrun one another. Don't forget foliage color, either. You can combine various shades of grays and greens for a delightful variation of hues.

Place species with attractive foliage—such as damianita (*Chrysactinia mexicana*), blackfoot daisy (*Melampodium leucanthum*), desert marigold (*Baileya multiradiata*), and dogweed (*Thymophylla pentachaeta*)—for a good year-round appearance and to cover the bare spots left when annuals and deciduous species die back. Avoid planting shrubby desert species, such as brittlebush (*Encelia farinosa*) and globemallow (*Sphaeralcea ambigua*), which respond to supplemental water by doubling and tripling in size, with penstemons, lupines, larkspurs, and other delicate species that are easily overcome by out-of-control neighbors.

Planting a perennial wildflower isn't the same as planting a tree. Many perennials live only a few seasons, and your flower garden will need periodic maintenance. You'll need to thin and cut back vigorously growing flowers and occasionally replace some plants, but no major replanting will be necessary. As a work-in-progress, your perennial garden will provide season after season of enjoyment as it evolves with your personal creative touch.

Bringing wildlife into the garden is one of the great attractions of landscaping with native plants. Hummingbirds flock to the blossoms of ocotillo in summer.

Landscaping to Attract Wildlife

There's good news and bad news when you create a well-designed native plant landscape. The assortment of food-producing, shelter-providing plants most likely will attract wildlife, and a yard that becomes a magnet for wildlife is good if you love birds and butterflies and plant accordingly. It's bad if rabbits and deer consider your tender new plants the best salad buffet in town. Fortunately, guidelines and programs are available to help you welcome the desirable birds and butterflies and protect your investment from nibbling intruders.

To me, the most compelling reason for landscaping with plants native to my area is to repair some of the environmental damage caused by urban growth. Habitat alteration is inevitable, but we can lessen the impact by preserving as much of the indigenous plant community as possible. If we maintain a diverse association of plants, our neighborhoods will attract and support a variety of birds, butterflies, squirrels, and other enjoyable wildlife.

Wildlife and urban development can be compatible. Many species of animals can coexist with humans if certain requirements are met. Like us, wildlife need food, shelter, water, and space to carry on daily, or nightly, activities. The animals most successful in cohabiting with humans are birds, butterflies, lizards, and small nocturnal mammals. They share our urban environment without getting in our way too much.

Put Out a Year-Round Welcome Mat

Many people go to extreme measures and great expense to attract birds to their yards. You can easily spend hundreds of dollars on birdhouses for wrens, chickadees, and other hole-nesting species. Maintaining feeders with varieties of seeds and suet can become a daily ritual. For those who love wildlife, having a yard full of birds is worth the trouble and expense. But with the proper selection of landscaping plants, you can let nature furnish most of the room and board, while you relax and enjoy the company.

As you design your landscape, consider the three primary requirements for attracting birds, butterflies, and other wildlife: food, water, and shelter. Select plants that provide a year-round supply of seeds, nuts, flowers, and fruit. Plants with tube-shaped flowers (particularly red) attract hummingbirds; acacias are famous nectar plants for honey bees; milkweeds, members of the sunflower and verbena families, and most other showy flowers attract butterflies. Trees and brushy shrubs offer nesting locations for

Left: A monarch butterfly enjoys some nectar from the aptly named butterfly weed (*Asclepias tuberosa*).

Below: A hummingbird zooms in on the flowers of an agave plant.

51

birds that build open nests, such as mockingbirds, cardinals, doves, thrashers, and jays. Providing a constant supply of clean water can be as easy as a dish or birdbath, or as elaborate as a fountain or flowing waterfall. With a diversity of plants in your yard that meet the habitat requirements of a variety of species, you can enjoy a year-round population of resident and migratory birds.

Unwelcome Wildlife

A creek, a wooded park, or even a vacant lot can be the home of an opossum, raccoon, ringtail cat, or skunk. At night they emerge and unobtrusively forage for food, often dining on rodents and reptiles, as well as gleaning spilled trash and uneaten dog and cat food. For five years, I had an opossum, skunk, and cat living under our house in perfect harmony with each other and us.

Wild mammals are usually considered vermin and reservoirs of disease for our domestic animals and are eradicated when possible. However, in most instances they are as harmless as the squirrels we enjoy in our trees. Snakes suffer a worse reputation. The few poisonous species have instilled such fear in humans that most people consider all snakes public enemies. The harmless snakes eat rodents, lizards, frogs, and toads and should be welcomed neighbors.

As subdivisions spread farther into the countryside and more and more desert and forests become streets and yards, wildlife either dies or adapts to the new environment. A number of small animals often find enough undisturbed habitat to survive and become habituated to urban living. But not all of our wildlife neighbors are welcome guests in your yards. Deer and rabbits often consider our prized landscape plants a tender item for their salad bowl.

You can fence off your garden plot and put wire cages around your saplings, but unless you have an eight-foot, deer-proof fence around your home lot, your landscape may become a herbivore buffet. Some plants come with their own defense, either inedible woody, woolly, or prickly foliage, or bitter-tasting, volatile oils. If you have a problem with unwelcome dinner guests, consider some of the deer- and rabbit-resistant plants listed in this chapter. Remember, no plant is deer-proof, just resistant. In a hot, dry summer when tender forbs are scarce, deer will feast on plants they normally wouldn't touch.

Wildscapes Program

The National Wildlife Federation sponsors a program with guidelines and specifications for establishing backyard habitats for wildlife (www.nwf.org/backyardwildlifehabitat).

Plants in the sunflower family (Asteraceae) provide a popular food source for butterflies.

The habitat restoration and conservation program helps rural and urban residents plan landscapes that provide wildlife habitats by planting native vegetation and installing birdbaths, ponds, and feeders. A properly designed backyard landscape provides places for birds, small mammals, and other wildlife to feed and drink, escape from predators, and raise their young.

Seed and Fruit Plants for Birds

The following plants are particularly suitable for supplying the food and shelter requirements of many bird species. Each plant's primary season for producing seed and fruit is indicated. Refer to the "Native Plant Profiles" for more details on the plants. Select the ones that fit your landscape design and are adapted to your landscape zone.

Trees	spring–summer	fall–winter
Acacia species	X	
Acer species	X	
Arbutus arizonica, Arizona madrone		X
Celtis species, hackberries		X
Cercis species, redbud		X
Chilopsis linearis, desert willow		X
Fraxinus species, ashes	X	
Juglans species, walnuts		X
Juniperus species, junipers		X
Pinus species, pines	X	X
Prosopis species, mesquite		X
Prunus serotina, black cherry	X	
Prunus virginiana, chokecherry	X	
Quercus species, oaks		X
Rhus species, sumacs		X
Sambucus mexicana, Mexican elder		X
Washingtonia species, palms	X	

Shrubs	spring–summer	fall–winter
Agave species, century plants	X	
Amorpha fruticosa, false indigo		X
Dasylirion species, sotols		X
Fouquieria splendens, ocotillo	X	
Hesperaloe parviflora, red yucca	X	
Justicia species, chuparosa	X	
Lycium species, wolfberries	X	X
Mahonia species, barberries	X	
Nolina species, beargrass		X
Rhus species, sumacs		X
Ribes aureum, golden current	X	
Yucca species	X	

Vines	spring–summer	fall–winter
Parthenocissus inserta, Virginia creeper		X
Parthenocissus quinquefolia, thicket creeper	X	

Flowering Plants That Attract Hummingbirds

Flowers	spring–summer	summer–fall
Aquilegia species, columbines	X	
Castilleja species, paintbrushes	X	X
Delphinium species, larkspurs	X	
Ipomoea leptophylla, bush morning glory		X
Ipomopsis aggregata, skyrocket		X
Lobelia cardinalis, cardinal flower		X
Lupinus species, lupines	X	
Mimulus species, monkey flowers	X	X
Mirabilis multiflora, giant four-o'clock		X
Monarda species, beebalms	X	X
Penstemon species, beard tongues	X	X
Salvia species, sages		X
Sphaeralcea species, globemallows	X	

Trees, Shrubs, Vines	spring–summer	summer–fall
Agave species, century plants		X
Amorpha fruticosa, false indigo	X	
Anisacanthus thurberi, desert honeysuckle	X	X
Bouvardia ternifolia, scarlet bouvardia	X	X
Buddleja marrubiifolia, woolly butterflybush	X	
Calliandra conferta, fairy duster	X	
Campsis radicans, trumpet creeper vine		X
Chilopsis linearis, desert willow		X
Ebenopsis ebano, Texas ebony	X	
Echinocereus triglochidiatus, claret cup cactus	X	
Fouquieria splendens, ocotillo		X
Hesperaloe parviflora, red yucca		X
Justicia californica, chuparosa	X	X
Justicia candicans, jacobinia	X	X
Leucophyllum frutescens, Texas ranger	X	
Lycium species, wolfberries	X	
Robinia neomexicana, New Mexico locust	X	
Salvia greggii, autumn sage	X	X
Tecoma stans, yellow trumpet flower	X	X
Ungnadia speciosa, Mexican buckeye	X	
Yucca species	X	

Deer- and Rabbit-Resistant Plants

Trees
Be sure to cage all saplings and small trees until foliage is above the forage line (about 6 feet high).

Chilopsis linearis, desert willow
Rhus lanceolata, flameleaf sumac
Sapindus saponaria var. *drummondii*, western soapberry
Ungnadia speciosa, Mexican buckeye

Shrubs
Agave species, century plants
Anisacanthus thurberi, desert honeysuckle
Aster species
Cactus species
Caesalpinia gilliesii, bird of paradise
Chrysactinia mexicana, damianita
Dalea frutescens, black dalea
Dasylirion species, sotols
Ericameria nauseosa, chamisa
Eysenhardtia texana, kidneywood
Fallugia paradoxa, Apache plume
Garrya wrightii, silktassel
Hesperaloe parviflora, red yucca
Juniperus species, junipers
Larrea tridentata, creosote bush
Leucophyllum species, cenizos
Lycium species, wolfberries
Mahonia species, barberries
Mimosa borealis, fragrant mimosa
Rhus aromatica, aromatic sumac
Rhus virens, evergreen sumac
Salvia greggii, autumn sage
Sophora secundiflora, Texas mountain laurel
Tecoma stans, yellow trumpet flower
Yucca species

Wildflowers
Achillea species, yarrows
Baileya multiradiata, desert marigold
Coreopsis species
Datura wrightii, sacred datura
Delphinium species, larkspurs
Gaillardia pulchella, Indian blanket
Glandularia bipinnatifida, prairie verbena
Helianthus maximiliani, Maximilian sunflower
Liatris punctata, blazing star
Linum species, flaxes
Lobelia cardinalis, cardinal flower
Lupinus species, lupines
Melampodium leucanthum, blackfoot daisy
Monarda citriodora, lemon beebalm
Pectis angustifolia, limoncillo
Psilostrophe tagetina, paperflower
Rudbeckia hirta, black-eyed Susan
Salvia farinacea, mealycup blue sage
Senna species
Solidago species, goldenrods
Thymophylla pentachaeta, dogweed
Verbesina enceliodies, golden crownbeard
Viguiera dentata, goldeneye
Zinnia acerosa, desert zinnia
Zinnia grandiflora, plains zinnia

Vines and Groundcovers
Campsis radicans, trumpet creeper (browsed, but vigorous new growth develops)
Clematis species (browsed, but vigorous new growth develops)
Dalea greggii, Gregg dalea
Muhlenbergia lindheimeri, Lindheimer muhly
Phyla species, frogfruit
Pteridium aquilinum, bracken fern

Plants That Attract Butterflies

M any native flowers provide nectar for adult butterflies, while others are beneficial for attracting butterfly larva. Not all the plants listed here are covered in this book; species that are featured in the "Native Plant Profiles" are indicated with an asterisk. The others are native or naturalized plants, or common garden plants.

Abelia species
 nectar (tiger swallowtail)
Achillea millefolium, milfoil*
 larva (painted lady)
Agalinis pulchella, purple gerardia
 larva and nectar (buckeye)
Ageratina, boneset
 nectar (common wood nymph, gulf fritillary, monarch, queen, red admiral, zebra longwing)
Ambrosia, ragweeds
 larva and nectar (bordered patch)
Amorpha canescens, lead plant
 larva (dogface)
Amorpha fruticosa, false indigo*
 larva (dogface)
Anethum graveolens, dill
 larva (black swallowtail)
Antirrhinum, snapdragon
 nectar (buckeye)
Apocynum, dogbane
 nectar (snout butterfly)
Aristolochia, Dutchman's pipe
 larva (pipevine swallowtail)
Artemisia vulgaris, mugwort
 larva and nectar (painted lady)
Asclepias ovalifolia, milkweed
 nectar (common wood nymph, giant swallowtail, morning cloak, queen, question mark, red admiral, tiger swallowtail, variegated fritillary); larva (monarch, queen)
Asclepias tuberosa, butterfly weed*
 nectar (black swallowtail, tiger swallowtail, variegated fritillary)
Aster species
 nectar (black swallowtail, buckeye, gulf fritillary, painted lady, question mark, red admiral, spicebush swallowtail, sulphurs, pearl crescent); larva (sulphurs)
Bicuculla cucullaria, Dutchman's breeches
 larva (black swallowtail)
Buddleja, butterflybush*
 nectar (giant swallowtail, gulf fritillary, pipevine swallowtail, tiger swallowtail)
Calycanthus, spicebush
 larva (spicebush swallowtail)
Celtis, hackberry*
 larva (hackberry butterfly, morning cloak, question mark, snout butterfly)
Cephalanthus occidentalis, button bush
 nectar (common wood nymph, painted lady)

Chamaecrista fasciculata, partridge pea
 larva (cloudless giant sulpher)
Chrysanthemum, daisies
 nectar (bordered patch)
Cirsium, thistles
 nectar (black swallowtail, common wood nymph, painted lady, pipevine swallowtail); larva (painted lady)
Clematis species*
 nectar (common wood nymph)
Coreopsis species*
 nectar (buckeye)
Cornus, dogwood
 nectar (snout butterfly)
Croton argenteus, silver croton
 larva (goatweed butterfly)
Croton capitatus, woolly croton
 larva (goatweed butterfly)
Croton monanthogynus, one-seed croton
 larva (goatweed butterfly)
Cruciferae, mustards
 larva (great southern white, long-tailed skipper); nectar (long-tailed skipper)
Ebenopsis ebano, ebony*
 larva (sulphurs)
Fraxinus, ash*
 larva (tiger swallowtail, two-tailed swallowtail)
Helianthemum, frostweed
 nectar (monarch)
Helianthus, sunflower*
 nectar (bordered patch, monarch); larva (bordered patch)
Iva axillaris, poverty weed
 nectar (great purple hairstreak)
Lantana species*
 nectar (black swallowtail, cloudless giant sulpher, giant swallowtail, gulf fritillary, julia, monarch, pipevine swallowtail, spicebush swallowtail, sulphurs, zebra longwing)
Laurus nobilis, sweet bay
 larva (spicebush swallowtail)
Lepidium sativum, pepper grass
 larva (great southern white)
Liatris, gayfeather*
 nectar (painted lady)
Linaria, toadflax
 nectar (buckeye)
Linum, flax*
 nectar (variegated fritillary)
Linum rigidum, stiff-stem flax
 larva (variegated fritillary)

Lobelia cardinalis, cardinal flower*
     nectar (cloudless giant sulpher, pipevine swallowtail, spicebush swallowtail)
Lonicera, honeysuckle*
     nectar (giant swallowtail, tiger swallowtail)
Lupinus, lupines*
     larva (sulphurs)
Malva, mallow
     larva (painted lady)
Malvaviscus arboreus var. *drummondii*, Turk's cap
     nectar (cloudless giant sulpher)
Matelea reticulata, milkweed vine
     larva (monarch)
Monarda species*
     nectar (spicebush swallowtail)
Passiflora, passion flower and passion vine
     larva (gulf fritillary, julia, variegated fritillary, zebra longwing)
Persea borbonia, red bay
     larva (spicebush swallowtail)
Petroselinum crispum, parsley
     larva (black swallowtail)
Phlox species*
     nectar (black swallowtail, pipevine swallowtail, spicebush swallowtail)
Phyla, frogfruit*
     nectar (buckeye, queen); larva (buckeye)
Plantago, plantain
     nectar (buckeye)
Populus, cottonwood*
     larva (morning cloak, tiger swallowtail, great purple hairstreak)
Prosopis glandulosa, mesquite*
     larva (great purple hairstreak)
Prunus, wild cherries*
     larva (red admiral, tiger swallowtail, pale swallowtail)
Prunus mexicana, Mexican plum
     nectar (great purple hairstreak); larva (tiger swallowtail)
Ptelea, hop tree
     larva (giant swallowtail)
Ruellia species
     larva (buckeye, common wood nymph); nectar (buckeye)
Salix, willow
     larva (morning cloak, tiger swallowtail)
Salvia, sage*
     nectar (dogface, spicebush swallowtail, tiger swallowtail)
Salvia misella, tropical sage
     nectar (sulphurs)
Sassafras albidum, sassafras
     larva (spicebush swallowtail)
Sedum, stonecrop*
     larva (variegated fritillary)

Senna species*
     larva (cloudless giant sulpher)
Solidago, goldenrod
     nectar (cloudless giant sulpher, great purple hairstreak, monarch, morning cloak, snout butterfly)
Sphaeralcea, globemallow*
     larva (painted lady)
Thymophylla pentachaeta, dogweed*
     larva (sulphurs)
Trifolium, clover
     nectar (black swallowtail, variegated fritillary); larva (dogface, sulphurs)
Ulmus americana, American elm
     larva (morning cloak)
Ulmus crassifolia, cedar elm
     larva (question mark)
Verbena species*
     nectar (dogface, spicebush swallowtail, buckeye)
Viguiera, goldeneye*
     nectar (common wood nymph, zebra longwing)
Viola, violet*
     larva (variegated fritillary)
Viscum album, mistletoe
     larva (great purple hairstreak)
Zanthoxylum fagara, lime prickly ash
     larva (giant swallowtail)
Zinnia grandiflora, zinnia*
     nectar (monarch)
decaying wood
     nectar (goatweed butterfly)
dung
     nectar (hackberry butterfly)
fruit juice
     nectar (goatweed butterfly)
fruit tree blossoms
     nectar (black swallowtail)
grasses
     larva (common wood nymph)
legumes
     larva and nectar (long-tailed skipper)
mud
     nectar (question mark)
nettles
     larva (question mark, red admiral)
pellitory
     larva (red admiral)
rotting fruit
     nectar (hackberry butterfly)
tree sap
     nectar (goatweed butterfly, hackberry butterfly, question mark)

Trees

Acacia greggii
Catclaw acacia

Native Distribution: desert washes, grasslands, mesas; below 5,000 feet; California to Texas, Nevada, and Utah, Mexico.
Landscape Zone: 1–6.
Size: shrubby, 15–30 feet.
Leaves: deciduous.
Flower: April–October; creamy yellow spikes.
Fruit: 5-inch flat pods.
Soil: sandy, alkaline, well draining.
Exposure: full sun, partial shade.
Temperature Tolerance: cold hardy to 0°F.
Water: drought tolerant, 8 inches/year minimum.
Propagation: scarified seeds.
Profile: This shrubby acacia makes a delightful single- or multi-trunked ornamental tree reaching 30 feet, but you'll have to prune it to the desired shape. You'll also have to isolate this bad boy, with its vicious thorns. In the wild it often forms impenetrable thickets of thorny, waist- to head-high shrubs, so don't plant where human contact is probable. On the plus side, blossoms cover the tree in the spring and continue blooming to a lesser extent into fall. Its fragrant flowers and twisted, flat pods accent mixed plantings and make it an appealing specimen plant for a small area. The feathery foliage and irregular crown provide filtered shade.

Top: *Acacia greggii* flowers

Above: *Acacia greggii*

Acacia farnesiana (Acacia smallii)
Huisache or sweet acacia

Native Distribution: hillsides, desert grasslands; up to 2,000–4,000 feet; southern California to Florida, Mexico.
Landscape Zone: 1–2.
Size: 15–25 feet tall, vase-like shape, multiple trunks.
Leaves: deciduous.
Flower: February–May; round, golden, fragrant.
Fruit: round seed pods, 2–3 inches long.
Soil: adaptable; well or slow draining.
Exposure: full sun.
Temperature Tolerance: 20°F.
Water: drought tolerant, 8 inches/year minimum.
Propagation: scarified seeds.
Profile: In the spring, the barren limbs of huisache turn into golden wands and perfume the air with a profusion of flowers. Its fernlike foliage and rounded crown cast dense shade as the tree matures. Lower branches tend to droop and require pruning. The tree's

Acacia farnesiana

moderate size makes it appropriate for small areas unsuitable for a large tree. You can trim huisache into a densely foliated shrub or sheared hedge. The numerous slender branches have pairs of pin-like thorns, making it an effective physical-barrier hedge. In the northern extremes of its range, hard freezes nip flower production, cause limb loss, or cause the tree to freeze to the ground. Huisache has been planted ornamentally since the 1600s.

Acacia farnesiana flowers

Acer grandidentatum
Bigtooth maple

Native Distribution: hillsides, canyons, Ponderosa-Oak to Spruce-Fir woodlands; 4,500–8,000 feet; Arizona to Texas, north to Montana, Mexico.
Landscape Zone: 3–7.
Size: to 50 feet.
Leaves: deciduous, brilliant fall color.
Fruit: spring; winged seeds on female trees.
Soil: rich, well draining.
Exposure: full sun.
Temperature Tolerance: cold hardy to −20°F.
Water: drought tolerant, 16 inches/year minimum.
Propagation: freshly gathered seeds, but extremely poor viability.
Profile: Bigtooth maple, the western counterpart of the eastern sugar maple

(*Acer saccharum*), rates as one of the premier landscape trees in the Southwest. In the autumn, the leaves paint the landscape with hues of red, orange, and gold. Its large crown provides cool shade for yards, walkways, parking lots, and the southwest sides of buildings. Bigtooth maples grow as much as three feet per year. Four-year-old specimens can reach eight feet tall. The trees should thrive in areas with at least 16 inches of rain, cold winters, and about a 225-day growing season. For their autumn colors to develop fully, bigtooth maples require cold nights and sunny days in the fall. To get the best color display, be sure the trees you buy come from your area. Poor seed viability limits availability in the trade, but some nurseries have the tree in quantity. For a small space, choose the Rocky Mountain maple, *Acer glabrum*, usually a multiple-stemmed shrubby tree 10–20 feet tall, which has similar habitat requirements.

Acer grandidentatum fall color

Acer glabrum

Arbutus arizonica
Arizona madrone

Native Distribution: foothills, sunny slopes, Pinyon-Juniper to Pine-Oak woodlands; 4,000–7,000 feet; Arizona south of the Mogollon Rim, southwestern New Mexico, Mexico.
Landscape Zone: 2–7.
Size: 15–45 feet.
Leaves: evergreen.
Flower: April–September; clusters of tiny, creamy blooms.
Fruit: fall; ornate red berries.
Soil: adaptable; well draining.
Exposure: full shade, partial sun.
Temperature Tolerance: cold hardy to 0°F.
Water: drought tolerant, 16 inches/year minimum.
Propagation: seeds, cuttings.
Profile: Few trees in the Southwest have the ornamental beauty of the

Upper left: *Arbutus arizonica*

Left: *Arbutus arizonica* foliage

madrone. The vibrant, shiny leaves form a dense crown, accented in the spring by clusters of creamy white flowers and in the fall by bright red berries. Wildlife love the succulent fruit. In the spring, the smooth white bark peels away in paper-thin layers to reveal stylish pinkish-red new bark. The twisting multiple trunks and ornate bark make this tree a classic landscape choice. With its evergreen foliage, abundant flowers, and colorful fruit, a madrone will enliven small front and side yards, patios, and commercial plantings. Seedlings may take years to become fully established, so buy container saplings if possible. Well-draining soil is more important than soil type. Don't use fertilizers that contain copper, since madrones have a symbiotic relationship with root fungi that are killed by the element. The Texas madrone, *Arbutus xalapensis*, ranges well into the mountains of New Mexico and is equally ornamental.

Celtis laevigata var. reticulata (Celtis reticulata)
Netleaf hackberry

Native Distribution: upper desert to oak woodlands, canyons, streams, bottomlands; 1,500–7,000 feet; California to Texas, north to Washington, Mexico.
Landscape Zone: 1–7.
Size: 30–40 feet tall.
Leaves: deciduous.
Fruit: fall; round fleshy red drupes.
Soil: adaptable; well draining.
Exposure: full sun, partial shade.
Temperature Tolerance: cold hardy to −20°F.
Water: drought tolerant, 12 inches/year minimum.
Propagation: seeds.
Profile: Many people consider these fast-growing trees a weed, but hack-

Celtis laevigata var. reticulata

Celtis laevigata var. reticulate foliage and berry

berries definitely have a place in the landscape. They grow almost anywhere, provide abundant shade, and produce tiny fruit that make excellent forage for birds. The trunk has distinctive, warty growths, and the leaves turn yellow in fall, but don't expect a color pageant. Use this tree for quick-growing, deciduous shade over your roof in the summer, for confined areas and side yards, as a curb planting, or in naturalized areas. The shrubby desert hackberry, *Celtis pallida* (see shrub section), is extremely drought tolerant and can be trimmed into an attractive, dense shrub or multi-trunked tree up to 15 feet high.

Cercis orbiculata (Cercis occidentalis)
Western or California redbud

Native Distribution: rocky hillsides, mountains, and canyons; below 6,000 feet; California, Arizona, Utah, Nevada.

Landscape Zone: 1–6.

Size: 15–30 feet.

Leaves: deciduous.

Flower: February–April; tiny, red.

Fruit: 2- to 3-inch pods.

Soil: adaptable; well draining.

Exposure: full sun, partial shade.

Temperature Tolerance: cold hardy.

Water: moderately drought tolerant, 12–35 inches/year minimum, depending on variety.

Propagation: stratified, scarified seeds.

Profile: The redbud greets spring with a blaze of color. Before the leaves emerge, tiny scarlet blossoms cover the bare limbs. The glory lasts for only two weeks, though, and then the petals blanket the ground like red snow. Redbuds grow rapidly and have an upright-rounded to flat-topped crown that provides moderately dense shade. They are perfect for adding spring color to a limited space, such as a side yard, patio, or isolated corner. Use them as a border along long drives or as a focal plant in a landscape island. In Phoenix and low-desert areas, redbuds need a few below-freezing nights to induce spring flowering, and they may sunburn if planted in southern exposures.

Mexican redbud, *Cercis canadensis* var. *mexicana*, grows in the mountains of New Mexico and west Texas. Several forms of redbud are available, including ones with double, pink, or white flowers and red leaves. Be sure to purchase one that is adapted to your area.

Cercis orbiculata flowers

Cercis orbiculata

Chilopsis linearis
Desert willow

Native Distribution: desert washes, grasslands, foothills, and mesas; 1,500–5,000 feet; California to Texas, Nevada, Utah, Mexico.
Landscape Zone: 1–3.
Size: 10–25 feet.
Leaves: deciduous.
Flower: April–August; clusters of orchid-like, pink to lavender, 1 1/2-inch-long blossoms.
Fruit: 4-to 12-inch seed pods.
Soil: adaptable; well draining.
Exposure: full sun, partial shade.
Temperature Tolerance: heat tolerant, cold hardy to 0°F.
Water: drought tolerant, 12 inches/year minimum.
Propagation: fresh seeds, semi-hardwood and dormant cuttings.
Profile: This premier, fast-growing plant brings spectacular trumpet-shaped flowers and bright green, willow-like foliage to your yard. Clusters of up to five blossoms dangle from the branch tips all summer. You'll need to prune desert willow to develop the shape you desire. Direct its growth as a large shrub with many branches and thick foliage for background, wind-break, screen, or specimen plantings. You can also train it into a small tree with an upright form and single or multiple trunks. Horticulturists have developed a number of cultivars with flower colors ranging from the natural pinkish-purple to deep pink, burgundy, and white. Since flowers grow on new wood, pruning in the dormant season encourages profuse blooming. Desert willow is used in shelter-belt plantings as far north as Kansas. It freezes to the ground, but recovers rapidly and regains its height.

Upper left: *Chilopsis linearis*

Left: Shrubby *Chilopsis linearis*

Cupressus arizonica
Arizona cypress

Native Distribution: mountain canyons and slopes; 3,000–8,000 feet; California to Texas, Mexico.
Landscape Zone: 2–7.
Size: 20–50 feet tall, 20 feet wide.
Leaves: evergreen.
Fruit: 1-inch cones.
Soil: adaptable; well draining.
Exposure: full sun.
Temperature Tolerance: cold hardy to −15°F.
Water: drought tolerant, 10–12 inches/year minimum.
Propagation: cuttings.
Profile: The grayish-green, juniper-like foliage and classic Christmas tree shape make Arizona cypress a popular yard tree throughout the Southwest. When planted close together, younger specimens make a striking head-high or taller border hedge or background planting. Use a row planting as a sun screen, to provide visual privacy, or as a windbreak. As the tree matures, it develops a rounded crown, often with

spreading branches. You can remove lower limbs to reveal the scaly red bark and shape the plant into a large shade tree. At lower elevations, it benefits from occasional deep watering in the summer. Growing rapidly when young, Arizona cypress specimens can live 700 years. Various varieties and forms have been segregated, including silver-, gray-, green-, and blue-foliated varieties and compact, dwarf, and pyramid-shaped forms.

Cupressus arizonica

Cupressus arizonica foliage and fruit

Ebenopsis ebano (Pithecellobium flexicaule)
Texas ebony, ape's earring, ebano

Native Distribution: loamy alluvial soils, near streams; south Texas, Mexico.
Landscape Zone: 1.
Size: 15–30 feet.
Leaves: evergreen.
Flower: May–August; fragrant, creamy, cylindrical spikes.
Fruit: 4- to 6-inch woody pods.
Soil: adaptable; deep, well draining.
Exposure: full sun, partial shade.
Temperature Tolerance: cold hardy to 25°F.
Water: drought tolerant.
Propagation: scarified seeds.
Profile: Though its native range in the United States is restricted to south Texas, many Southwestern landscapers rate Texas ebony on their top-10 lists for desert landscaping, so I'm including

it by default. You'll find the deep green foliage, zigzag branching, and profuse, fragrant flowers a delightful addition to your yard or patio planting. The dense evergreen foliage and rounded crown provide year-round shade. You can also prune Texas ebony into a dense shrub. The thick growth of thorny, zigzag branches makes a good sheared security hedge. A hedge planted around the Visitors Center at Santa Ana National Wildlife Refuge in south Texas grew four feet tall and extremely dense within four years. The bean pods of Texas ebony may remain on the tree for over a year. It suffers leaf and twig damage at freezing temperatures and in hard freezes may die back to the ground. The abundant woody pods can cause considerable ground litter.

Ebenopsis ebano

Fraxinus cuspidata

Native Distribution: rocky mountain slopes; 2,400–7,000 feet; Arizona to Texas, Mexico.
Landscape Zone: 1–3.
Size: 10–20 feet.
Leaves: deciduous.

Fraxinus cuspidata flowers

Flower: April–May; 2- to 4-inch clusters of showy white flowers.
Fruit: clusters of winged seeds.
Soil: moderate to well draining, slightly acidic igneous soil or slightly alkaline limestone.
Exposure: full sun, partial shade.
Temperature Tolerance: cold hardy to 0°F.

Fraxinus cuspidata
Fragrant ash

Water: drought tolerant, 16 inches/year minimum.
Propagation: fresh or stratified seeds.
Profile: As the leaves of fragrant ash emerge in the spring, bundles of feathery white flowers cover the tree and droop gracefully from the branch tips. This is our only ash with showy flowers. The small size makes it adaptable to yards or commercial plantings where large trees are unsuitable. It makes an attractive specimen plant or addition to a patio or courtyard. In mass plantings, fragrant ash is a colorful companion and compatible in size and habitat with western redbud, goldenball leadtree, and Mexican buckeye.

Fraxinus velutina (Fraxinus pennsylvanica subsp. velutina)
Arizona or velvet ash

Fraxinus velutina foliage and flowers

Below: *Fraxinus velutina*

Native Distribution: mountain streams, canyons; 3,000–7,000 feet; California to Texas, Nevada, Utah, Mexico.
Landscape Zone: 1–4.
Size: 30–50 feet.
Leaves: deciduous, 3–5 leaflets per leaf.
Flower: not significant.

Fruit: 1-inch-long, winged seeds on female trees.
Soil: adaptable.
Exposure: full sun.
Temperature Tolerance: heat tolerant, cold hardy to 0°F.
Water: drought tolerant, 8 inches/year minimum.
Propagation: seeds.
Profile: For decades, so many new houses came with a six-foot-tall Arizona ash sapling in the front yard that overuse spoiled much of the tree's appeal. One aspect of landscaping with native plants is to restore the natural diversity found in nature, rather than producing a neighborhood of cloned houses with cloned landscape designs. With the rant out of the way, I have to admit that the 'Fan-Tex' or 'Rio Grande' ash, a grafted cultivar of Arizona ash, has a lot to recommend for medium- to large-scale landscapes. It reaches 35 feet, has a dense round canopy, and holds a lush appearance longer that the species type. It's the best form to use for residential yards, parking lots, and street plantings, although like most ash species, it is susceptible to borers.

Juglans major
Arizona walnut
Juglans microcarpa
Little walnut

Native Distribution: streambeds, ravines, upper desert grasslands, oak woodlands; 2,000–7,000 feet; Arizona to Texas, Mexico.
Landscape Zone: 2–6.
Size: 15–45 feet.
Leaves: deciduous.
Fruit: fall; 1/2- to 1-inch-diameter nuts.
Soil: alkaline, well draining.
Exposure: full to partial shade.
Temperature Tolerance: heat tolerant, cold hardy to 0°F.
Water: drought tolerant, 16–24 inches/year minimum.
Propagation: seeds.
Profile: These two trees are so closely related that some botanists consider them varieties of a single species, but they do have different growth charac-

Juglans microcarpa

teristics. Little walnut often has a shrubby appearance with multiple trunks. It reaches about 20 feet, with trunks that spread from the base to form a pleasing shade tree. Arizona walnut grows to 45 feet from a single trunk with a rounded canopy of dark green leaves. Both species grow rapidly,

live long, and provide sweet, but hard-shelled, nuts for wildlife and human consumption. The Arizona walnut grows better at higher elevations and should be used there; in low, desert settings, it needs occasional irrigation. Both bear good crops every two to three years.

Juniperus deppeana
Alligator juniper

Native Distribution: hills, mesas, Pinyon-Oak and Ponderosa woodlands; 4,500–8,000 feet; Arizona to west Texas, Mexico.
Landscape Zone: 3–7.
Size: 25–50 feet.
Leaves: evergreen, scale-like, blue-gray.
Fruit: winter; 1/4- to 1/2-inch, berry-like cones on female trees.
Soil: adaptable; well draining.
Exposure: full sun.
Temperature Tolerance: heat tolerant, cold hardy to 0°F.
Water: drought tolerant, 16 inches/year minimum.
Propagation: seeds.
Profile: Unlike most junipers, this tree has an upright stature with a stout trunk and a rounded crown. Reddish brown, berry-like fruit accent the bluish green foliage, and the checkered bark resembles the back of an alligator,

hence the tree's common name. The thick, evergreen foliage and pyramid shape make alligator juniper suitable for windbreaks and screen plantings along fences, drives, or property lines, or as a specimen plant. The lower branches often grow almost to the ground, but you can remove them for a

more open appearance. You also can prune it into an attractive hedge or shrub. The male trees produce mildly allergenic pollen in the spring.

Right: *Juniperus deppeana* bark

Juniperus deppeana

Juniperus scopulorum

Juniperus scopulorum
Rocky Mountain juniper

Native Distribution: mesas and mountain slopes; 5,000–9,000 feet; Arizona to Texas, north to Canada.
Landscape Zone: 1–7.
Size: to 35 feet.
Leaves: evergreen, scale-like.
Fruit: winter; 1/4- to 1/3-inch, bright blue, berry-like cones on female trees.
Soil: adaptable; well draining.
Exposure: full sun.
Temperature Tolerance: cold hardy.
Water: drought tolerant, 16 inches/year minimum.
Propagation: stratified seeds, cuttings.
Profile: *Juniperus scopulorum* is one of the most commonly planted junipers in the western United States. Horticulturists have developed numerous varieties to fit almost any landscape need. You can choose forms with silver, green, gray, or bluish foliage; a pyramid, round, or columnar shape; and erect or weeping branches. The size varies from a 35-feet-tall tree to a medium-sized shrub, or a 10-inch groundcover. Be sure to select the variety compatible with your landscape design and climate. As with all junipers, Rocky Mountain juniper should be planted in an area large enough for the mature tree, because heavy pruning destroys the natural shape. The male trees produce a mildly allergenic pollen. At lower elevations (3,000–8,000 feet), select one-seed juniper, *Juniperus monosperma*, which has similar landscape qualities. It is the common plant in Pinyon-Juniper woodlands covering northern Arizona and New Mexico.

Leucaena retusa

Leucaena retusa
Goldenball leadtree

Native Distribution: dry, rocky, hillsides; 1,500–5,500 feet; New Mexico to west Texas, Mexico.
Landscape Zone: 1–3.
Size: 15–25 feet.
Leaves: deciduous.
Flower: April–October; yellow, round, 1 inch.
Fruit: 3- to 10-inch pods.
Soil: adaptable; well draining.
Exposure: full sun, partial shade.

Leucaena retusa flowers

Temperature Tolerance: cold hardy to 0°F.
Water: drought tolerant, 12 inches/year minimum.
Propagation: seeds, cuttings.
Profile: Few trees can give your yard more beauty and visual interest than the goldenball leadtree. From spring through summer, 1-inch flower balls cover the tree with a profusion of lemon-yellow color. The tree's feathery, bright green foliage casts moderate shade, allowing you to plant flowers and shrubs under it. Goldenball leadtree grows rapidly, often with multiple trunks, and a typical specimen of 15 feet has a crown spread of 10 feet. The moderate size of this tree makes it suitable for planting near buildings, along drives and walks, in courtyards, and in other areas of limited space. With its long summer bloom, goldenball leadtree is compatible in a colorscape design with early bloomers such as western redbud, Mexican buckeye, desert bird of paradise, and fairy duster.

Olneya tesota
Desert ironwood

Native Distribution: desert washes; below 2,500 feet; Arizona, California, Mexico.

Landscape Zone: 1–3.

Size: 15–30 feet.

Leaves: evergreen, bluish, compound, 2 inches long with 3/4-inch leaflets, pair of 1/2-inch thorns at base of leaves.

Flower: May–June; lavender, pea-like in small clusters.

Fruit: 2 1/2-inch-long brown pods.

Soil: well draining.

Exposure: full sun.

Temperature Tolerance: hardy to 20°F.

Water: drought tolerant.

Propagation: scarified seeds.

Profile: This hardy tree of the Sonoran Desert adds a gray-green color component your landscape. With its smooth gray bark, ornate branching, and airy gray foliage, desert ironwood is an eye-catching, small-scale tree for courtyard, xeriscape, and cactus gardens. As a specimen plant, it accents a garden wall, fence, or side yard. You'll probably have to prune the lower limbs through the years to create an attractive trunk. The prickly thorns on the branches make this a plant you don't want to brush up against, so trim it up or keep it in the background. The flowers cover the tree with lavender hues in the spring but are short-lasting. For extended color, plant with palo verde species, desert willow, acacias, ocotillo, or goldenball leadtree.

Top: *Olneya tesota*

Right: *Olneya tesota* flowers

Parkinsonia microphylla

Native Distribution: desert washes, valleys; below 4,000 feet; southern New Mexico to California, Mexico.
Landscape Zone: 1–3
Size: 15–25 feet tall and wide.
Leaves: deciduous in cold and drought; 1/2- to 1-inch spines on twigs.
Flower: March–May; abundant, yellow.
Fruit: 2- to 3-inch-long seed pods.
Soil: sandy, well draining.
Exposure: full sun.
Temperature Tolerance: hardy to 10°F.
Water: drought tolerant, 8 inches/year minimum.
Propagation: scarified seeds.

Parkinsonia florida (Cercidium floridum)
Blue palo verde

Profile: The fast-growing blue palo verde is one of the most popular landscape trees in Phoenix and Tucson, and for good reason. From March through July (depending on moisture), lemon-yellow flower clusters obscure the branches. Once you see a blue palo verde in full bloom, you'll know why it was designated the state tree of Arizona. The graceful, spreading shape and smooth, bluish-green trunk and limbs add to the tree's ornamental effect, though the limbs have 1-inch prickles. This truly drought-tolerant plant loses its tiny leaves during dry summers, but the dense array of slender branches still provide filtered shade. The similar foothills, or little-leaf, palo verde, *Parkinsonia microphylla*, has equal landscape value and blooms a few weeks after the blue palo verde. The Desert Museum palo verde, a three-way hybrid between blue and foothills palo verde and Texas palo verde (*Parkinsonia aculeate*), is thornless and has larger, showier yellow flowers that bloom well into the summer.

Parkinsonia florida

Picea pungens
Colorado blue spruce

Native Distribution: Spruce-Fir forests; 7,000–11,000 feet; New Mexico, Arizona, north to Wyoming.
Landscape Zone: 2–7.
Size: 70–100 feet.
Leaves: evergreen needles.
Fruit: 3- to 4-inch-long cones.
Soil: clay, loam, well draining.
Exposure: full sun.
Temperature Tolerance: cold hardy.
Water: drought tolerant above 7,000 feet.
Propagation: seeds.

Profile: With more than a dozen varieties of this popular conifer to choose from, you can select the exact size, shape, and color best suited for your landscape. Foliage colors include dark green and various shades of bluish green, gold, yellow, and silver. The size and shape vary from the natural tall-pyramid form to compact and symmetrical, flat-topped, dwarf, and weeping forms. Some varieties grow rapidly, while others take 10 years to grow 10 feet. Blue spruce is widely planted outside its optimum growing area. It survives, but may suffer from heat and drought stress and need occasional deep watering. It is often planted as a living Christmas tree.

Picea pungens

Pinus edulis
New Mexico or Colorado pinyon pine

Native Distribution: mesas, hillsides, mountain slopes; 4,000–7,000 feet; California to west Texas, north to Wyoming, Mexico.
Landscape Zone: 2–6.
Size: 10–25 feet.
Leaves: evergreen, 1- to 2-inch needles.
Fruit: 2-inch-long cones with edible nuts.
Soil: variable, dry, alkaline, well draining.
Exposure: full sun, partial shade.
Temperature Tolerance: cold hardy to −20°F.
Water: drought tolerant, 16 inches/year minimum.
Propagation: fresh seeds.
Profile: This small-proportioned pine adds a distinctly Southwestern sense of place to yards and patios throughout the Arizona-New Mexico highlands. Pinyons accent and add year-round greenery to bare walls and corners of buildings, and they even can be used as large container plants. They provide an attractive focal plant in mixed plantings with other western species, such as Apache plume, fern bush, and mountain mahogany. Younger specimens have dense foliage and a pyramid shape, resembling a 10- to 15-foot-tall Christmas tree. Pinyons grow slowly, and with age (probably decades) they develop an open, rounded canopy. New Mexico pinyon and the similar Mexican pinyon (*Pinus cembroides*) are both available in the nursery trade. *Pinus edulis*, the state tree of New Mexico, comes from the highest elevations and is the most cold tolerant of the pinyon pines. Mexican pinyon is more heat tolerant and survives well as far north as the Rocky Mountains. Both languish in desert conditions, so avoid them in Phoenix. Due to the decade-long drought, pinyons have been particularly hard hit by bark beetles in New Mexico.

Pinus edulis foliage and cones

Right: *Pinus cembroides*

Populus fremontii
Arizona or Fremont cottonwood

Native Distribution: stream banks and bottomlands; below 6,500 feet; California to west Texas.
Landscape Zone: 2–6.
Size: 40–90 feet.
Leaves: deciduous.
Fruit: copious cottony seeds on female trees.
Soil: adaptable; deep, moist, well draining.
Exposure: full sun.
Temperature Tolerance: cold hardy.
Water: requires regular moisture.
Propagation: fresh seeds, semi-hardwood cuttings.
Profile: First the good news: Cottonwoods grow quickly into tall, picturesque trees that bear gold foliage in the fall. Now the bad news: They need regular irrigation and female trees throw a snowstorm of cottony, wind-blown seeds, so be sure you plant a male. They are also relatively short-lived (30–60 years) and have an invasive root system. The water-greedy roots invade sewer pipes, rob water from your lawn, and heave pavement. If you have an average-sized yard, you don't have room for a cottonwood unless it's on your back property line. But if you have acreage or a sizeable yard and want a large shade tree, this is a good choice. When planted in moist soil, a cottonwood can grow into an attractive shade tree in four to five years, but they eventually outgrow your ability to water them in Phoenix or Tucson. Several varieties exist, so plant the one best suited to your landscape zone.

Populus fremontii

Populus tremuloides
Quaking aspen

Populus tremuloides

Native Distribution: Ponderosa Pine and Spruce-Fir forests; above 6,000 feet; Southwest mountains and northern United States, Canada.
Landscape Zone: 6–7.
Size: 20–60 feet.
Leaves: deciduous, yellow fall colors.
Flower: spring; 2-inch catkins.
Fruit: small, cottony seeds.
Soil: moist, sandy, well draining.
Exposure: cool, full sun or partial shade.
Temperature Tolerance: cold hardy, but not heat tolerant.
Water: needs moisture, 20 inches/year minimum.
Propagation: seeds, root cuttings.

Profile: Few trees can match the ornate qualities of quaking aspen. With smooth white bark, leaves that whisper with the wind, and brilliant golden fall colors, an aspen is hard to resist. No wonder I've seen it planted, and struggling to survive, in hot, dry yards in Albuquerque. This fast-growing beauty needs moist, cool soil to keep its roots healthy. With a northern exposure and lots of mulch, an aspen might survive at lower elevations, but it would be stressed. If you live in Santa Fe, Prescott, or Flagstaff, plant it in the cooler exposures of your yard, but at lower, hotter elevations, avoid the temptation.

Prosopis glandulosa
Honey mesquite
Prosopis velutina
Velvet mesquite

Prosopis glandulosa

Prosopis glandulosa flowers

Native Distribution: brushlands, prairies, hills; below 4,500 feet; California to Texas, Mexico.
Landscape Zone: 1–3.
Size: 15–30 feet.
Leaves: deciduous.
Flower: May–June; 2-inch fragrant yellow spikes.
Fruit: 4- to 8-inch pods.
Soil: adaptable; deep, well draining.
Exposure: full sun.
Temperature Tolerance: heat tolerant, cold hardy to 0°F.
Water: drought tolerant, 8 inches/year minimum.
Propagation: fresh or scarified seeds, root cuttings.
Profile: Ranchers might shake their heads in disbelief at the notion of planting thorny mesquites in city yards. Although despised on rangeland, mesquite is prized as an arid-climate landscape tree for small- and medium-scale designs. The abundance of yellow spring flowers, the open crown, airy foliage, and twisted, often multiple, trunks of these two species add western charm to a yard, patio, or xeriscape garden. The bright green, drooping leaves provide light shade, allowing you to plant sun-loving shrubs and wildflowers beneath them. You can water them to speed growth, but once a mesquite sinks its taproot, it can survive the driest summer. The roots may penetrate 60–150 feet deep looking for water, so don't plant one near a septic system or pool. A thornless variety exists, and hybrid crosses between native and South American species are available. The native screwbean mesquite, *Prosopis pubescens*, has ornate, twisted seed pods and similar landscape uses. It grows in floodplains and needs more water than its super drought-tolerant relatives.

Prunus serotina var. *rufula* and var. *virens*
Southwestern black cherry

Prunus serotina

Native Distribution: canyons, mesas, hillsides; 4,500–9,000 feet; Arizona to Texas, Mexico.
Landscape Zone: 3–7.
Size: 30 feet.
Leaves: deciduous, yellow fall color.
Flower: March–April; white clusters of tiny flowers.
Fruit: 3/8-inch, red-to-black drupes.
Soil: adaptable; well draining.
Exposure: full sun, partial shade.
Temperature Tolerance: heat tolerant, cold hardy.
Water: drought tolerant, 16 inches/year minimum.
Propagation: double-stratified seeds, cuttings.
Profile: The southwestern black cherry combines three worthy landscape virtues: attractive spring flowers, good shade in the summer, and colorful autumn foliage. In the spring, 4-inch tassels of tiny flowers cover the tree in dense clusters, followed by 3/8-inch red fruit that turns to black. The lustrous dark green summer foliage provides dense shade, and in the fall, the leaves turn brilliant hues of yellow. The leaves may persist through the winter. Thirty-three species of birds and numerous animals enjoy the bitter cherries, but the leaves are toxic to livestock. A number of varieties of black cherry grow across North America, so be sure you get one native to the Southwest.

Prunus virginiana var. *demissa* and var. *melanocarpa*
Common or western chokecherry

Native Distribution: dry, rocky slopes, woods, moist areas; 4,500–9,000 feet; California to Texas, north into Canada.
Landscape Zone: 2–7.
Size: shrubby to 20 feet tall.
Leaves: deciduous.
Flower: April–July; 3- to 6-inch clusters of white flowers.
Fruit: July–September; red-to-black 1/2-inch drupes.
Soil: adaptable; well draining.
Exposure: full sun, partial shade.
Temperature Tolerance: cold hardy to −20°F.
Water: moderately drought tolerant, 16 inches/year minimum.
Propagation: fall-sown or spring-stratified seeds, cuttings.
Profile: Widely used for ornamental planting and erosion control, chokecherry has dark green, lustrous leaves; abundant spring flowers; and attractive bundles of red-to-black fruit that ripen in the fall. You can trim this versatile plant into a shrub or let it grow as a small tree. It spreads by root suckers and forms dense thickets in the wild. Use it as an accent for patios or small yards and in mass plantings. You can choose dwarf and full-sized varieties, with broad to narrow leaves and black-to-amber-to-yellow fruit. About 40 species of birds and numerous small animals eat the fruit.

Above: *Prunus virginiana*

Left: *Prunus virginiana* flowers

Native Plant Profiles

Oaks

n the Southwest, oaks occur primarily in the Pinyon-Juniper vegetation zone, 4,500–6,000 feet in elevation. Gambel oak, along with ponderosa pine, is a major component or the Pine-Oak, or Transition, Zone, at 6,500–8,000 feet.

If your landscape is suitable in habitat and space for an oak, you should consider the following factors in selecting a species: mature size, evergreen or deciduous, fall color, leaf size and color, and crown shape. Gambel oak produces brilliant fall color; gray oak and Mexican blue oak add blue-gray tones to your yard; and silverleaf oak has lustrous green leaves with striking silver-felt undersides. The statuesque Arizona white oak is perfect if you want a full-sized evergreen. The other species described here will fit well in a city yard or where the design calls for a medium- to small-scale tree.

Nurseries and government agencies in desert landscape zones 1 and 2 often recommend the drought-tolerant plateau live oak (*Quercus fusiformis*), a native of the rocky Edwards Plateau of Texas. It resembles the coastal live oak (*Quercus virginia*) and is often referred to by that name. This slow-growing evergreen survives summers in Phoenix and winters in Albuquerque. Several other species of Texas and California oaks are also available in the nursery trade. Since adding an oak to your landscape is a major investment of both dollars and the time required for the tree to mature, why not choose one specifically adapted to your area through thousands of years of natural selection?

Quercus arizonica
Arizona white oak

Native Distribution: widespread in canyons, mountain slopes, Pinyon-Juniper and Ponderosa Pine woodlands; 5,000–7,500 feet; Arizona to west Texas, Mexico.
Landscape Zone: 3–6.
Size: 20–40 feet.
Leaves: evergreen.
Fruit: acorns.
Soil: well draining.
Exposure: full sun, partial shade.

Temperature Tolerance: cold hardy.
Water: drought tolerant, 16 inches/year minimum.
Propagation: fresh acorns.
Profile: The Arizona white oak is one of the most attractive trees that grows in the Southwest highlands. With an irregular crown and spreading limbs, it is a smaller version of the plateau live oak of west Texas and the coastal live oak of the southern states. The open, spreading branching yields an informal, airy feel compared to the shaped look of trees with dense, rounded canopies. The graceful profile and bluish-green leaves of this drought- and heat-tolerant tree add class to any home or commercial landscape. It grows slowly, so it won't outgrow your design any time soon.

Quercus emoryi
Emory oak

Native Distribution: moist canyons, valleys, mountains, Chaparral, Oak-Pinyon, and Ponderosa Pine forests,; 3,000–8,000 feet; Arizona, New Mexico, Texas, Mexico.
Landscape Zone: 2–6.
Size: 20–40 feet.
Leaves: partially evergreen, shiny, holly-like.
Fruit: acorns.
Soil: igneous, well draining.
Exposure: full sun, partial shade.
Temperature Tolerance: heat tolerant, cold hardy.
Water: drought tolerant, 16 inches/year minimum.
Propagation: fresh acorns.
Profile: This drought- and heat-tolerant oak is one of the prominent trees in the southern reaches of the Oak-Pinyon Belt. As a medium-sized landscape tree with a rounded crown, it adds the classic charm of an evergreen oak to your yard. The shiny, holly-like leaves complement small-leafed shrubs, such as silktassel, desert sumac, shrubby senna, and buffaloberry. Emory oak is medium to slow growing and apparently always grows in nature on igneous-derived acidic soils. If you have alkaline, limestone soil, plant sandpaper oak instead.

Left: *Quercus emoryi* foliage   Above: *Quercus emoryi*

73

Quercus gambelii

Quercus gambelii
Gambel oak

Native Distribution: mountain slopes in Pinyon-Juniper, Ponderosa Pine, and Spruce-Fir forests; 4,500–8,000 feet; Arizona to west Texas, Utah, Colorado, Mexico.
Landscape Zone: 2–7.
Size: shrubby to 30 feet.
Leaves: deciduous with fall colors.
Fruit: acorns.
Soil: adaptable; well draining.
Exposure: full sun, partial shade.
Temperature Tolerance: cold hardy; subject to heat stress at low elevations.
Water: drought tolerant, 16 inches/year minimum.
Propagation: fresh acorns.
Profile: In lower elevations across its range, Gambel oak forms shrubby thickets, and at higher elevations it is a major woodland component with ponderosa pine, bigtooth maple, and quaking aspen. This adaptable oak brings fall hues of yellow, orange, and red to your yard. The small size suits it well for city yards, courtyards, or as an anchor for a large landscape island. You can use it alone as a specimen tree or as an accent for a mixed planting. It grows slowly and develops a rounded crown with a dense canopy of deeply lobed, dark green leaves. Don't plant a Gambel oak in a hot location in the lower range of its altitude zone or it might suffer heat stress and leaf-spot diseases. It survives well in Albuquerque, where temperatures cool off at night.

Native Distribution: dry, rocky mountain slopes, Pinyon-Juniper to Ponderosa Pine forests; 4,500–7,800 feet; Arizona to west Texas, Mexico.
Landscape Zone: 2–6.
Size: 15–25 feet.
Leaves: deciduous to almost evergreen, gray-green.
Fruit: acorns.
Soil: adaptable; acid or alkaline, well draining.

Quercus grisea
Gray oak

Exposure: full sun, partial shade.
Temperature Tolerance: cold hardy.
Water: drought tolerant, 16 inches/year minimum.
Propagation: fresh acorns.
Profile: You can add subtle shades of gray-green to your yard with this handsome medium-sized tree. Its neutral gray-colored leaves complement other gray-foliated species, such as blue spruce, silvery buffaloberry, big sagebrush, and chamisa. Gray oak has a rounded crown and is suitable for landscapes with limited area. Its drought tolerance and adaptability to both acidic and alkaline soils make gray oak a useful landscape tree over a wide range of the Southwest.

Above: *Quercus grisea* foliage

Right: *Quercus grisea*

Quercus hypoleucoides
Silverleaf oak

Native Distribution: canyons and mountain slopes in Oak-Juniper woodlands; 4,000–8,500 feet; southern Arizona to west Texas, Mexico.
Landscape Zone: 2–6.
Size: 15–40 feet.
Leaves: deciduous to almost evergreen.
Fruit: acorns.
Soil: igneous, well draining.
Exposure: full sun, partial shade.
Temperature Tolerance: cold hardy.
Water: drought tolerant, 16 inches/year.
Propagation: fresh acorns.

Profile: The dark green, lance-shaped leaves with silver undersides make this medium-sized tree a striking specimen in any landscape setting. It gives a regal accent to a group planting or courtyard. The narrow crown provides moderate shade. Under harsh environmental conditions in nature, silverleaf oak remains shrubby, so it would probably survive marginal conditions in the landscape, but without developing its classic shape. Hopefully, this attractive tree will become more available in the nursery trade.

Quercus hypoleucoides foliage

Quercus oblongifolia
Mexican blue oak

Native Distribution: foothills, mesas, mountain slopes; 4,500–6,000 feet; southern Arizona, New Mexico.
Landscape Zone: 2–6.
Size: 25 feet.
Leaves: evergreen, bluish.

Fruit: acorns.
Soil: well draining.
Exposure: full sun, partial shade.
Temperature Tolerance: cold hardy.
Water: drought tolerant, 16 inches/year minimum.

Propagation: fresh acorns.
Profile: Though not widely available, this small oak has superb landscaping qualities. Its rounded crown and spreading, contorted branches provide year-round shade for your yard. With distinctive bluish-green leaves, Mexican blue oak provides a vivid color contrast with sugar sumac, greenleaf manzanita, and Arizona rosewood. Its neutral color blends well with rock gardens and adobe or masonry walls. As an extra color bonus, the young leaves have a reddish blush in the spring. This species is closely related to gray oak, *Quercus grisea.*

Quercus oblongifolia

Quercus pungens

Native Distribution: dry hills, mountains, Chaparral Belt to Pinyon-Juniper woodlands; 2,500–6,500 feet; Arizona to west Texas, Mexico.
Landscape Zone: 2–6.

Quercus pungens
Sandpaper Oak

Size: 15–20 feet, shrubby.
Leaves: evergreen, shiny green, holly-like with prickly margins.
Fruit: acorns.
Soil: adaptable, well draining.
Exposure: full sun, partial shade.
Temperature Tolerance: heat and cold tolerant.
Water: drought tolerant, 16 inches/year minimum.
Propagation: fresh acorns.
Profile: Throughout much of its native range, sandpaper oak forms shrubby thickets, but in the proper habitat, it can grow into a handsome tree with a rounded crown. Its tolerance to dry, rocky soil and its small, bright green leaves with ornately toothed margins make sandpaper oak a perfect choice for much of the Southwest. The small size makes it adaptable for city lots and courtyards as a specimen tree, hedge, or as a focal point in a mixed planting. The species' shiny green leaves contrast well with gray-foliated plants such as Texas ranger, woolly butterflybush, sagebrush, and brittlebush; its holly-like leaves mirror the prickly leaves of barberries, yuccas, and agaves. The shrub live oak, *Quercus turbinella*, also has a shrubby habit and is used in similar landscape applications. It grows at higher elevations, 4,500–8,000 feet, from the Chaparral Belt to the Ponderosa Forests.

Rhus lanceolata
Prairie flameleaf sumac

Native Distribution: prairies, limestone hills, mountains; New Mexico to central Texas and north into Oklahoma, Mexico.

Landscape Zone: 1–5.
Size: 10–30 feet.
Leaves: deciduous, red fall color.
Flower: spring; dense clusters of white blossoms.
Fruit: fall; hard red drupes.
Soil: adaptable; calcareous to neutral, well draining.
Exposure: full sun, partial shade.
Temperature Tolerance: highly heat tolerant, cold hardy to −10°F.
Water: drought tolerant, 16 inches/year minimum.

Propagation: scarified seeds, semi-hardwood cuttings.
Profile: If you want a fast-growing, medium-sized tree that provides spring, summer, and fall color, this may be just the plant for you. In the spring and summer, large bundles of white flowers decorate the plants, followed by attractive grape-like clusters of red seeds in the fall. The leaves turn brilliant hues of red and orange in the autumn. Because of its moderate size, flameleaf sumac can be used in mass plantings, along sidewalk easements, as a border plant for walls and property lines, and in confined areas. You can prune it heavily to get the desired shape. I wanted a thick-branching screen to shade the southwest side of my house, so I pruned my flameleaf sumac back each winter. In three years' time, the dense, multi-trunked plant was taller than my roof and was sending out root suckers 30 feet into my lawn—so beware if you don't want a *Rhus* thicket in your yard. The fruit has a pleasant tart flavor and makes a refreshing drink when soaked in water. Some people are allergic to the oil in the plant.

Rhus lanceolata fruit

Rhus lanceolata

Robinia neomexicana
New Mexico or rose locust

Top: *Robinia neomexicana*

Left: *Robinia neomexicana* flowers

Native Distribution: shrublands, mountain slopes, Chaparral Belt to Spruce-Fir forests; 4,000–8,500 feet; California to west Texas, Colorado to Nevada.
Landscape Zone: 2–7.
Size: 12–20 feet.
Leaves: deciduous, 1/2-inch-long paired thorns at the nodes.
Flower: April–August; clusters of delicate, rose, pea-like flowers.
Fruit: fall; 2- to 4-inch-long bean pods.
Soil: adaptable; well draining.
Exposure: full sun, partial shade.
Temperature Tolerance: cold hardy.
Water: drought tolerant, 12 inches/year minimum.
Propagation: scarified seeds, root cuttings.
Profile: If you see a New Mexico locust when it's covered with showy pink blossoms in the spring and through the summer, you'll know why it's a popular accent plant in the Southwest, even though it's armed with thorns. Its small size adapts it to courtyard, patio, and mixed plantings, but its paired thorns limit use where human contact is expected. In the fall, the flat, thin bean pods dangle from the limbs. In the wild, New Mexican locust spreads aggressively by root suckers and forms thorny thickets. You can prune it into a single- or multi-trunked tree, and control suckering by mowing or limiting water. Use this fast-growing tree for erosion control, as a windbreak, or as a screen planting. Once established, it's difficult to eradicate.

The introduced black locust, *Robinia pseudoacacia*, widely used in landscaping, is larger and has showy white flowers, but I don't recommend it as a landscape plant. Its sparse branching, thorns, and open profile make it unattractive and a poor shade tree, and its weedy root suckers make it hard to control.

Sambucus nigra subsp. canadensis (Sambucus mexicana)
Mexican elder

Native Distribution: desert, chaparral, and mountain drainages; 1,000–5,000 feet; California to west Texas, Mexico.
Landscape Zone: 1–3.
Size: 10–20 feet.
Leaves: evergreen, deciduous in drought conditions.
Flower: September–June; flat-topped clusters of yellowish white blooms.
Fruit: fall; 1/4-inch diameter, bluish black, in clusters.
Soil: adaptable; deep, moist, poor or well draining.
Exposure: full sun, partial shade.
Temperature Tolerance: cold hardy.
Water: drought tolerant, 16 inches/year minimum.
Propagation: scarified, stratified seeds, softwood cuttings.
Profile: This plant reverses the seasons and gives character to your landscape in the winter. As cool weather arrives, Mexican elder develops lush foliage. In the spring, bundles of creamy flowers cover the limbs, followed by clusters of berries. In a typical Phoenix summer, it sheds its leaves. For year-round foliage color, plant it with Texas ebony, mesquite, and desert willow. This fast-growing plant develops a rounded crown with dense foliage, but you'll have to use your pruning shears to train it into a handsome tree. In the wild it often grows as a large-spreading shrub, making it an excellent choice for windbreak or screen plantings in your landscape. This plant normally grows along desert waterways, so give it a few good drinks during the summer. Supplemental water accelerates the growth of young plants and greatly improves fall foliage.

Top: *Sambucus nigra* subsp. *canadensis* flowers
Right: *Sambucus nigra* subsp. *canadensis*

Sapindus saponaria var. drummondii (Sapindus drummondii)
Western soapberry

Native Distribution: along streams, grasslands in Pinyon-Juniper belt; 2,400–6,000 feet; Arizona, southern New Mexico, east to Louisiana, north to Kansas, Mexico.

Landscape Zone: 1–6.

Size: 15–30 feet.

Leaves: deciduous, fall color.

Flower: May–August; showy white panicles.

Fruit: clusters of amber berries on female trees.

Soil: widely adaptable; well draining.

Exposure: full sun, partial shade.

Temperature Tolerance: cold hardy to –10°F.

Water: drought tolerant, 8–16 inches/year minimum.

Propagation: scarified, stratified seeds.

Profile: If you want a plant that has abundant spring flowers, brilliant autumn color, and will grow almost anywhere, consider the soapberry. Despite its unglamorous name, the tree has high landscaping value. In the spring, 5- to 10-inch cascading clusters of cream-colored blossoms decorate the branch tips. The showy flowers contrasted against the light green foliage make a colorful addition to any setting. Fall weather paints the leaves with striking shades of gold and yellow. The amber fruit remains on the tree all winter. Soapberries grow moderately fast, reaching 30 feet in rich soil, with an erect shape and a rounded crown. Its moderate size suits home lots, side yards, or business fronts. The deciduous foliage provides moderate shade, which becomes denser as the tree increases in size. Put some berries in a jar, mash them slightly, fill with water and shake, and you'll see how the tree got its name. Though toxic, the berries have been used in past times as a cleansing agent.

Sapindus saponaria var. *drummondii* flowers and foliage

Sapindus saponaria var. *drummondii*

Ungnadia speciosa
Mexican buckeye

Native Distribution: rocky slopes and stream banks of the Chihuahuan Desert; New Mexico, Texas, Mexico.
Landscape Zone: 1–6.
Size: 8–15 feet.
Leaves: deciduous.
Flower: March–April; small pink blossoms.
Fruit: three-chambered pods with black seeds.
Soil: adaptable; well draining.
Exposure: full sun, partial shade.
Temperature Tolerance: cold hardy to 0°F.
Water: drought tolerant, 16 inches/year minimum.
Propagation: fresh seeds.
Profile: You'll know spring has arrived when clusters of small pink flowers decorate the limbs of the Mexican buckeye. The fragrant blossoms appear with the new leaves and accent the barren limbs. Mexican buckeye is a fast-growing large shrub or small tree. You can use it as a specimen plant for small lawns, side yards, and patios, or to accent entryways, walks, and drives. Its size and early blooming make it an ideal companion for redbud and New Mexico locust in mass or border plantings. The tree is densely foliated, with shiny, dark green leaves. Cinnamon-colored, three-lobed seed pods dangle like ornaments from the limbs in the winter. Each pod contains three black, round, poisonous seeds. With colorful flowers, lustrous foliage, and ornate seed pods, Mexican buckeye gives your landscape visual interest throughout most of the year.

Ungnadia speciosa flowers

Ungnadia speciosa

Washingtonia filifera
California fan palm

Native Distribution: oases, canyons, moist areas in desert scrublands; 2,500 feet; southeastern California, Baja Mexico; Arizona has five native groves in La Paz and Yavapai Counties.
Landscape Zone: 1–2.
Size: 30–60 feet.
Leaves: evergreen, gray-green fronds with stringy tips.
Flower: May–June; white, 3/8-inch-long flowers in 12-inch clusters.
Fruit: fall; 1/2-inch long, oval.
Soil: adaptable; well draining.
Exposure: full sun, partial shade.
Temperature Tolerance: cold hardy to 15°F.
Water: drought tolerant.
Propagation: seeds.
Profile: In nature, this picturesque palm with a stout trunk grows only in isolated groves around desert oases and in moist, protected canyons. In cultivation, it adorns landscapes from southern California to Florida. The fan palm's tall, stately profile topped with fan-shaped fronds is the icon of the sun-drenched, freeze-free climate that makes the Southwest one of the fastest-growing regions in the nation. Planted alone or in clusters, these palms cast feathery shadows across pools, patios, and courtyards and line streets, entry drives, and business properties. They add grace and elegance, but not without maintenance. Every one of the heavy, woody fronds must be removed by hand while standing on a tall ladder, or the thatch will surround the trunk like a bushy skirt. California fan palms grow fast from seed, up to 15 feet in 10 years, and will often sprout in close proximity to the parent tree. They require occasional deep watering. The similar Mexican fan palm, *Washington robusta*, is also widely used in cultivation. It has a slender, 12-inch-diameter trunk and glossy, green fronds, but it suffers leaf damage at 20°F.

Washingtonia filifera

Washingtonia robusta

79

Shrubs and Small Trees

Acacia constricta

Acacia constricta
White-thorn acacia

Native Distribution: desert scrub, desert grasslands; 2,500–5,000 feet; Arizona to west Texas, Mexico.
Landscape Zone: 1–3.
Size: 3–18 feet.
Leaves: deciduous, compound, 1 to 2 inches long with 3–6 paired leaflets per leaf; thorns straight, paired at twig nodes, 1 1/2 inches long.
Flower: May–August; yellow, dense, round heads, 1/2-inch diameter.
Fruit: woody seed pods, 2–5 inches long.
Soil: sandy, sandy loam, limestone, well drained.
Exposure: full sun, partial shade.
Temperature Tolerance: cold hardy to 5°F.
Water: drought tolerant.
Propagation: fresh seeds.

Profile: The fragrant, butter-ball flowers and airy, spreading shape of *Acacia constricta* add color and texture to mixed plantings. This thicket-forming shrub naturally grows with ocotillo, yucca, prickly pear, agave, and catclaw acacia, so it will feel right at home in a xeriscape or cacti garden. It adds a splash of color when planted in landscape islands with desert hackberry, ironwood, and brittlebush. An abundance of stiff, sharp thorns make white-thorn acacia an effective barrier hedge. The thorns tend to diminish in size with age. *Acacia constricta* var. *paucispina* has few to no thorns and grows at higher elevations, but should do well throughout southern Arizona and New Mexico. Quail enjoy the seeds and honey bees the flowers.

Native Distribution: sandy, gravelly hills, deserts, mesas, mountain slopes; Southwest U.S., Mexico.
Landscape Zone: 1–6.
Size: 2–6 feet in diameter.
Leaves: evergreen, sword-like with vicious thorns.
Flower: June–August; yellow clusters on 6- to 15-foot stalks.
Soil: adaptable; well draining.
Exposure: full sun.
Temperature Tolerance: extremely heat tolerant, cold hardy to 10–20°F.
Water: drought tolerant, 8 inches/year minimum.
Propagation: fresh seeds, root suckers.
Profile: The classic agaves add a distinctive desert accent to any landscape. The perfectly symmetrical rosette of grayish-green leaves creates a natural focal point for cactus gardens or a commanding accent for a corner planting. The stiff, viciously armed leaves have needlelike thorns at the tips and

Agave species
Century plant or agave

catclaw teeth along the edges. For this reason, avoid planting them along walks or entryways where human contact, especially by children, is probable. Several Mexican species have leaves without catclaws on the edges, but all are thorn tipped. The terminal thorns can be clipped, but that diminishes the ornamental appeal. Agaves grow rapidly for 8 to 25 years and then send up a tall flowering stalk and die; by that time most species will be surrounded by offshoots.

With a dozen Southwest species and numerous cultivars, century plants come in all sizes, so be sure to choose one compatible with your landscape. Mexican species tend to be frost sensitive, while some native species survive at elevations up to 9,000 feet. *Agave americana* is the largest native; its leaves grow up to 6 feet long. Many horticultural varieties exist, including ones with yellow-and-white-striped leaves. For medium-sized plants, *Agave parryi* subsp. *parryi* (*A. scabra*) grows 3 to 5 feet tall and wide, and *A. palmeri* forms compact rosettes to 4 feet wide. If you need a plant for confined areas, *A. parryi* subsp. *neomexicana* forms a rounded rosette 2 feet across, with 1-foot leaves, and is cold tolerant to 0°F. *Agave murpheyi* and the mat-forming *A. schottii* have leaves 1/2 inch wide and 1 foot long. For a different look, *A. toumeyana* produces a 2-foot-wide rosette of narrow, dark green leaves lined with white, treadlike fibers. *Agave utahensis*—a high-desert, freeze-tolerant species—has a small rosette and sends up a bottle-brush flower stalk instead of the classic candelabra.

Photos opposite

Clockwise, from top left: *Agave* in bloom
Green and blue *Agave* plants
Agave americana
Agave landscaping

Aloysia gratissima
Bee brush or white brush

Native Distribution: grasslands, canyons, limestone hillsides; 1,000–4,000 feet; California to east Texas, Mexico.
Landscape Zone: 1–3.
Size: 3–10 feet.
Leaves: deciduous.
Flower: March–November; spikes of vanilla-scented white flowers.
Soil: adaptable; limestone, poor or well draining.
Exposure: full sun, partial shade.
Temperature Tolerance: extremely heat tolerant, cold hardy to 10°F.
Water: drought tolerant.

Propagation: fresh seeds, softwood cuttings.
Profile: The fragrant flowers of bee brush perfume your yard throughout the spring and in fall following heavy rains. The small, white flowers, with their distinct vanilla aroma, densely cover erect spikes on the branch tips. You can use this slender, intricately branched plant as a background along a wall or fence, in a mass planting, or pruned into an upright profile. Though shaggy, its stature adds structure to mixed plantings of white-thorn acacia, fragrant mimosa, and three-leaf sumac. It also makes a good deciduous companion for evergreens such as Arizona rosewood, barberries, and creosote bush. You may have to prune it back heavily every few years to keep it dense and encourage flowering. A similar species, *Aloysia wrightii*, grows at elevations of 1,500–6,000 feet and has the same landscape applications in landscape zones 2–6 as *A. gratissima*. Butterflies feast on the nectar and birds on the seeds of both species.

Aloysia gratissima

Right: *Aloysia gratissima* flowers

Amelanchier utahensis
Serviceberry

Native Distribution: dry, open slopes, mountainsides, canyons, Pinyon-Juniper woodlands, Ponderosa Pine forests; 2,000–7,500 feet; California to Texas, north to Montana.
Landscape Zone: 2–6.
Size: 6–15 feet.
Leaves: deciduous.
Flower: April–May; showy, white, 3- to 6-inch clusters.
Fruit: June–July; sweet, blueberry-like, edible.
Soil: well draining.
Exposure: full sun; not shade tolerant.
Temperature Tolerance: moderately heat tolerant, cold hardy to −20°F.
Water: drought tolerant.
Propagation: fall-planted seeds or stratified in spring to break dormancy.

Profile: Do you have a dry, southwest exposure that needs a boost? Plant a serviceberry and you'll be the first on your block with a blooming tree in spring. In April, showy clusters of white blossoms cover the bare limbs. For a medley of colors, plant serviceberry with other early bloomers, such as redbud, desert ceanothus, and Stansbury cliffrose. The leaves turn shades of yellow and red in fall, and the ornate gray bark and intricate branching give the tree year-round ornamental value. At least 35 species of birds feast on the summer berries, and deer devour the leaves. Country churches used to decorate their services with the flowers of *Amelanchier*, hence the common name.

Amelanchier utahensis

Amorpha fruticosa
False indigo

Native Distribution: woodlands, canyons, stream banks; 2,500–7,000 feet; California to Texas, north to Wyoming, eastern United States.
Landscape Zone: 2–6.
Size: 4–10 feet.
Leaves: deciduous.
Flower: May–June; purple spikes.
Soil: adaptable; well draining.
Exposure: full sun, partial shade.
Temperature Tolerance: cold hardy.
Water: drought tolerant.
Propagation: scarified seeds, softwood and hardwood cuttings.
Profile: The distinctive 6-inch spikes of yellow-tipped, deep purple flowers make false indigo an attractive addition to your landscape. The yellow stamens extend just beyond the purple petals, providing a dramatic contrast of colors. You can prune this plant into a multi-stemmed specimen or a clumped shrub. Its attractive foliage and flowers add interest to background plantings along a fence or wall, to entry gardens, or to mixed groupings. The bright green leaves and purple flowers make a striking companion with other small-leafed species, such as fairy duster, fragrant mimosa, little-leaf sumac, and daleas. This widespread plant has many varieties, including a white-flowering form, one with crispy-looking leaves, one with variegated leaves, and a dwarf form that is not cold hardy. Butterflies love the flowers.

Amorpha fruticosa

Anisacanthus thurberi
Desert honeysuckle or chuparosa

Native Distribution: canyons, hills; 2,500–5,500 feet; Arizona, Texas, Mexico.
Landscape Zone: 1–6.
Size: 3–5 feet.
Leaves: deciduous.
Flower: June–October; red-orange, tube shaped, 1–2 inches long.
Soil: adaptable; well draining.
Exposure: full sun, partial shade.
Temperature Tolerance: heat tolerant, cold hardy to 10°F, root hardy to 0°F.
Water: drought tolerant, 12–16 inches/year minimum.
Propagation: fresh seeds, cuttings.
Profile: The orange-to-red tubular flowers of desert honeysuckle add brilliant color to your yard from June through the first frost. The hotter and drier it gets, the more these heat- and drought-tolerant shrubs bloom. They have irregular branches with narrow olive-green leaves. You should cut the plant back every winter to rejuvenate flower and foliage growth. These colorful shrubs make striking specimen plants if planted alone, and I've also seen them used as informal low hedges. Although densely foliated, desert honeysuckle doesn't shear well into a shaped hedge. The small size suits borders along walks and patios or in plantings in front of windows. The honeysuckle-like flowers attract hummingbirds throughout the summer. The variety from the Chihuahuan Desert, Mexican fire anisacanthus (*Anisacanthus quadrifidus* var. *wrightii*), is widely available and has identical landscape applications.

Anisacanthus thurberi

Left: *Anisacanthus quadrifidus* var. *wrightii*

Arctostaphylos patula

Greenleaf manzanita

Arctostaphylos patula flowers

Native Distribution: open, dry hillsides from chaparral to pine-oak woodlands; 7,000–8,500 feet; California, Arizona, Colorado, north to Canada.
Landscape Zone: 3–7.
Size: 3 feet.
Leaves: evergreen, leathery, 1–1 1/2 inches.
Flower: March–May; white to pink, bell-shaped, 1/4 inch long, in clusters.

Fruit: summer; 1/4-inch-diameter, apple-like pomes.
Soil: adaptable; coarse, well draining.
Exposure: full sun, light shade.
Temperature Tolerance: cold hardy to 0˚F.
Water: drought tolerant.
Propagation: scarified seeds, sprouting, layering.
Profile: With sinuous red stems, evergreen leaves, and blueberry-type flowers, the only thing missing with this

wonderful shrub is easy availability. Greenleaf manzanita's leathery, green to bluish leaves point upward toward the sun to give the rounded shrub a well-manicured appearance. The low, bushy plant only reaches three feet high, perfect for border hedges and foreground plantings. The pointleaf manzanita, *Arctostaphylos pungens*, grows 3 to 10 feet tall and makes a dramatic accent plant for patios, pool areas, or landscape islands. You can prune the lower limbs to show off the spectacular red bark of the gnarled trunks. It grows throughout Arizona and New Mexico at elevations of 3,500–8,000 feet. Most manzanitas thrive in cool summers, so avoid planting in desert valleys. Nurseries sell numerous species and varieties of manzanita, from head-high shrubs to knee-high plants. Wildlife relish the fruit.

Arctostaphylos patula

Artemisia filifolia
Sand sagebrush

Native Distribution: desert grass-lands, sandy hills; 2,500–6,500 feet; Arizona to west Texas, Mexico.
Landscape Zone: 2–6.
Size: 4–6 feet.
Leaves: evergreen, 1 1/2–3 inches long, threadlike.
Flower: August–November; minute, on spikes; allergenic pollen in fall.
Soil: sandy, gypsum, calcareous, well draining.
Exposure: full sun, partial shade.
Temperature Tolerance: cold hardy to 0°F.
Water: drought tolerant, 8 inches/year minimum.
Propagation: seeds.
Profile: Look out your window in Albuquerque and you'll probably see sand sagebrush; this bush thrives in sandy locations that would stifle most other plants. Like wands of grass, the fil-ament-like leaves add a dynamic element to a yard as they rustle in the breeze. The silky, fine-textured leaves add a bluish sil-ver accent to group plantings or xeriscape gardens. You can use sand sagebrush as an informal hedge or a background planting along a fence or wall. The ash-colored leaves complement other gray plants and provide a striking contrast with green-foliated shrubs. It will even-tually occupy a 4-foot-square area and may need cutting back to maintain dense foliage. Most people, except those sensitive to the allergenic pollen com-mon to all artemisias, consider the minute flowers insignificant.

Artemisia filifolia

Artemisia tridentata
Big sagebrush

Native Distribution: deserts to timberline in arid soils; 1,500–10,000 feet; western United States; Canada, Mexico.
Landscape Zone: 1–7.
Size: 3–8 feet.
Leaves: evergreen, 1/2 to 1 3/4 inches long, silvery, hairy, wedge-shaped with three lobes.
Flower: fall; minute on spikes; allergenic pollen.
Soil: adaptable; well draining.
Exposure: full sun.
Temperature Tolerance: cold hardy to –30°F.
Water: drought tolerant, 10 inches/year minimum.
Propagation: seeds.
Profile: Though big sagebrush is prob-ably the most common range plant in the western United States, it deserves a place in our city landscapes. Its aro-matic leaves produce the refreshing desert aroma that fills the air after thunderstorms. In your yard, the small, three-lobed, grayish-green leaves will contrast well with pinyons and junipers and complement winterfat, barberry, and daleas. Big sagebrush grows rapidly if water is available. You may occa-sionally have to cut it back to maintain dense branching and foliage. As with all artemisias, the wind-blown pollen may cause allergic reactions in sensi-tive people.

Artemisia tridentata

Baccharis sarothroides

Baccharis sarothroides
Desert broom

Native Distribution: sandy hillsides, washes, streams; 1,000–5,500 feet; southwestern New Mexico to southern California, Mexico.
Landscape Zone: 1–6.
Size: 3–9 feet.
Leaves: evergreen, 1/4 to 1 1/2 inches long, green stems.
Flower: August–September; heads of small, white flowers on female plants.
Fruit: fall–winter; showy white seed heads.
Soil: sandy, rocky, well draining.
Exposure: full sun, partial shade.
Temperature Tolerance: cold hardy to 10°F.
Water: drought tolerant.
Propagation: seeds.

Profile: Desert broom is a large, bushy evergreen with brilliant green stems. The dense array of slender branches creates a thick, rounded profile. Use it to screen a fence, for a privacy hedge, or as a background or windbreak. For mass coverage, plant on 4- to 5-foot centers. In the fall, white flower heads cover the branch tips of the female plants as though they had been dusted with snow; they also produce copious amounts of seed that sprout vigorously. You are better off choosing a male plant and avoiding the seed litter. If the shrub becomes woody, prune in the winter. Limiting water after the plant is established encourages dense growth. The bright-green desert broom contrasts well with gray-foliated plants such as woolly butterfly-bush, sagebrush, brittlebush, and Texas ranger. Several hybrids are available that are smaller and more rounded.

Bouvardia ternifolia (Bouvardia glaberrima)
Scarlet bouvardia

Bouvardia ternifolia

Native Distribution: rocky slopes, mountain canyons; 3,000–7,500 feet; Arizona to west Texas, Mexico.
Landscape Zone: 1–6.

Bouvardia ternifolia flowers

Size: 1–3 feet.
Leaves: deciduous.
Flower: June–September; clusters of red, 1- to 2-inch-long, trumpet-shaped blooms.
Soil: well drained, neutral to acid; becomes chlorotic in alkaline soils.
Exposure: full sun, partial shade.

Temperature Tolerance: moderately cold hardy to 20°F.
Water: drought tolerant, 16 inches/year minimum.
Propagation: seeds, softwood cuttings.
Profile: Throughout the summer and fall, bundles of slender, scarlet flowers crown the branch tips of this delightful shrub. Its small size and brilliant flowers adapt it to a host of applications. Scarlet bouvardia will beautify your patio, pool, and entryway gardens, or you can plant it in a container. Use it as a colorful foreground shrub for terraced, corner, and mixed plantings. Bouvardia is a compatible companion for fairy duster, fragrant mimosa, daleas, and barberries. Pruning the dead flowers helps maintain a compact shape. Cultivars offer flower colors ranging from pale pink to red. Hummingbirds love the brilliant flowers.

Buddleja marrubiifolia
Woolly butterflybush

Native Distribution: desert canyons, arroyos; 1,800–3,000 feet; west Texas, Mexico.
Landscape Zone: 1–3.
Size: 2–4 feet.
Leaves: semi-evergreen, gray.
Flower: spring–fall; 1/2-inch round heads of tiny orange flowers.
Soil: limestone, well draining.
Exposure: full sun.
Temperature Tolerance: heat tolerant, cold hardy to 15°F.
Water: drought tolerant, 12 inches/year minimum.
Propagation: seeds, softwood and hardwood cuttings.
Profile: Landscapers across the Southwest love this Chihuahuan Desert native. Gumball-sized clusters of red-to-orange flowers decorate woolly butterflybush throughout the summer, and the gray, velvet-covered leaves last into the winter. Use this densely branched shrub for border plantings, landscape islands, pool and patio designs, and containers. It makes a commanding focal plant for mixed plantings of small shrubs, or as a foreground accent with larger species. For a striking combo, plant woolly butterflybush with Texas ranger and prune so that their limbs intertwine; the contrasting flowers will seem to bloom from one plant. The ashen foliage and the bright flowers of woolly butterflybush create a striking contrast, especially when mixed with green-foliated species such as hopbush, damianita, creosote bush, and desert broom. Pruning in the early spring helps to keep a dense shape and promote flowering, since this species blooms on new wood. Butterflies and hummingbirds love the flowers.

Buddleja marrubiifolia flowers

Buddleja marrubiifolia

87

Caesalpinia gilliesii
Desert bird of paradise

Native Distribution: roadsides, vacant lots, dry hills, washes; native to Argentina, Uruguay; naturalized throughout the desert Southwest from California to west Texas, Florida, Mexico.
Landscape Zone: 1–2.
Size: 5–10 feet tall, 4–6 feet wide.
Leaves: deciduous, evergreen in frost-free climates, fern-like leaflets.
Flower: spring and early summer, then sporadically; yellow, 4–5 inches long, showy with long, red stamens.
Fruit: curly, fuzzy pods, persistent on branches unless removed.
Soil: adaptable; well draining.
Exposure: full sun.
Temperature Tolerance: extremely heat tolerant, root hardy to 5°F, twig damage and leaf loss at 25°F.
Water: extremely drought tolerant.
Propagation: seeds.
Profile: Originally introduced from South America, this plant was too tough to die in the Southwestern deserts, and it spread from west Texas to California. Flamboyant spikes of airy yellow flowers with long, red stamens burst into bloom to provide summer color in a xeriscape garden or patio planting. The tropical, fern-like leaves and multiple, slender trunks complement mesquite, nolina, yuccas, and ocotillo. This large, irregular shrub can be trained to 15-foot tree, but it looks best as an informal shrub. An occasional deep watering encourages blooming. The seeds and the green seed pods are toxic.

The closely related *Caesalpinia mexicana* has yellow flowers and broader leaflets. It freezes back as a herbaceous perennial at 18°F. It can be shaped into a 10-foot tree. The widely used *C. pulcherrima* has red flowers and spines, and it is severely damaged by freezing. Prune it to 12 inches in the winter, and by summer it grows into a 6-foot, airy bush covered with flowers.

Top: *Caesalpinia gilliesii*

Above: *Caesalpinia pulcherrima*

Right: *Caesalpinia gilliesii* flowers

Calliandra conferta
Fairy duster

Native Distribution: grasslands, hills, dry plains; below 5,000 feet; California to west Texas, Mexico.

Landscape Zone: 1–3.

Size: 4 feet.

Leaves: semi-evergreen, compound, fern-like leaflets.

Flower: spring, fall; clusters of pink heads with 1-inch, tassel-like stamens.

Soil: adaptable; coarse, well draining.

Exposure: full sun, light shade.

Temperature Tolerance: heat tolerant, root hardy to 5°F.

Water: very drought tolerant, 10 inches/year minimum.

Propagation: seeds.

Profile: When rose to pink tassels cover the slender limbs of this loose shrub, you'll know why its got its name. In the early spring, fairy duster turns a mass planting into a colorful pompom rally. With extra water, it can carry its unusual flowers into the summer with another burst of blooms in the fall. Use fairy duster as a low border or foreground planting, landscape island accent, or to draw attention to a patio or courtyard garden. The puffball blooms and lacy leaflets match well with mesquite, acacias, daleas, fragrant mimosa, yuccas, and joint fir. Baja fairy duster, *Calliandra californica*, with a similar growth habit and native to Baja California, has 2-inch red flowers. It suffers twig damage at 25°F. If you enjoy hummingbirds, plant a fairy duster in your yard.

Calliandra californica flowers

Calliandra californica

Ceanothus greggii
Desert ceanothus

Native Distribution: dry hills, rocky slopes, scrublands, Pinyon-Juniper woodlands; 2,000–7,000 feet; California to west Texas, Nevada, Utah, Mexico.
Landscape Zone: 2–4.
Size: 1–7 feet.
Leaves: semi-evergreen, leathery, 1/4–1 inch long.
Flowers: March–June; white to bluish, 3/8-inch-long petals in clusters.
Soil: adaptable; well draining.
Exposure: full sun.
Temperature Tolerance: heat tolerant, cold hardy to 0°F.
Water: drought tolerant.
Propagation: spring-sown seeds, softwood cuttings.
Profile: With dense clusters of fragrant, creamy, lilac-like flowers, desert ceanothus adds spring color to a xeriscape garden, landscape island, or mixed planting. The intricately branching, grayish-white shrub forms a rounded profile. Use it as an informal hedge along a fence or rock wall or in border plantings where it receives full sun and reflected heat. Deep watering in the spring encourages profuse blooming. The shrub's small leaf structure matches well with bee brush, false indigo, chamisa, and desert honeysuckle. The similar Fendler's ceanothus, *Ceanothus fendleri*, grows from 5,000 to 10,000 feet and is suitable for landscape zones 6 and 7. Deer browse these shrubs.

Left: *Ceanothus greggii* flowers
Below: *Ceanothus greggii*

Celtis pallida
Desert hackberry

Native Distribution: deserts, canyons, dry hills; 1,500–3,500 feet; Arizona to central Texas, Mexico.
Landscape Zone: 1–3.
Size: 8–20 feet.
Leaves: evergreen, dark green, 1 1/2 inches long.
Fruit: 1/4-inch, round, yellow to orange drupes.
Soil: adaptable; well draining.
Exposure: full sun, partial shade.
Temperature Tolerance: heat tolerant, evergreen to 20°F, cold hardy to 0°F.
Water: drought tolerant, 12 inches/year minimum.
Propagation: fall-sown seeds.
Profile: This dense, informal shrub is perfect for landscapes designed to repair the habitat for wildlife. The spiny, zigzag branches and thick foliage provide excellent cover for birds, and the hard fruit is a major source of fall forage for birds, rabbits, and other small mammals. With its rich green leaves, this sprawling shrub makes an effective border screen, corner plant, or neutral background for a showy accent planting. If you're designing for wildlife, mix desert hackberry with wolfberry, bee brush, barberries, and sumacs to create a real wildlife buffet. Desert hackberry also hosts honey bees and the caterpillars of empress leilia and snout butterflies.

Above and right: *Celtis pallida*

Cercocarpus montanus
Mountain mahogany

Native Distribution: rocky canyons, mesas, dry mountain slopes, Juniper-Pinyon woodlands; 3,000–9,500 feet; California to central Texas, north to Montana, Mexico.
Landscape Zone: 2–7.
Size: 5–15 feet.
Leaves: almost evergreen, wedge-shaped, 1-inch long.
Fruit: summer–fall; 1- to 3-inch feathery, spiral tail on seeds.
Soil: adaptable; well draining.
Exposure: full sun.
Temperature Tolerance: heat tolerant, cold hardy to −30°F.
Water: drought tolerant, 12 inches/year minimum.
Propagation: scarified, stratified seeds, softwood cuttings.
Profile: If you want a densely foliated, almost evergreen shrub with an interesting fall display, plant a mountain mahogany. Just when many plants are fading, this shrub is coming into its most beautiful

Cercocarpus montanus

Left: *Cercocarpus montanus* seed heads

season. As the seeds begin to mature, they develop a twisted, feathery tail, and by September they almost obscure the leaves. You can shape the plant into a compact shrub or hedge suitable for screen, border, or foundation plantings. When planted alone, mountain mahogany attractively accents open areas or landscape islands. Given time and proper pruning, this slow-growing plant will become a small, multi-trunked tree with ornate, shaggy, reddish bark.

Botanists recognize seven botanical varieties within this confusing species, each with slightly different forms and distribution, but all have excellent landscape applications. The curl-leaf mountain mahogany, *Cercocarpus ledifolius*, is a distinct species that also has exceptional landscape value. It has evergreen leaves with white undersides.

Chamaebatiaria millefolium
Fernbush

Native Distribution: dry, rocky slopes, sagebrush chaparral, Pinyon-Juniper woodlands; 4,000–8,000 feet; Arizona north to Idaho.
Landscape Zone: 2–7.
Size: 3–6 feet.
Leaves: mostly evergreen.

Flower: July–November; clusters of 1/2-inch, creamy flowers.
Soil: adaptable; well draining.
Exposure: full sun, partial shade.
Temperature Tolerance: cold hardy.
Water: drought tolerant, 15 inches/year.

Propagation: stratified seeds.
Profile: At first glance, you might think this densely foliated shrub is some kind of fern. Its leaves look like tiny fronds, but the woody branches and dense spikes of small, white flowers will change your mind. The unusual leaves and profuse flowers of fernbush add a midsummer accent to your landscape at a time when a blooming shrub is most welcome. The shrub is large and dense enough to use for screen, background, or border plantings, or as a specimen plant. The texture of the leaves complement Fremont barberry, big sagebrush, mountain mahogany, and pinyon pine—plants that share its habitat requirements. Extra water will help it develop dense foliage. Fernbush is abundant and commonly planted from the South Rim of the Grand Canyon to Santa Fe, but it will survive in cool microhabitats in Albuquerque.

Chamaebatiaria millefolium

Chamaebatiaria millefolium flowers

Choisya dumosa
Starleaf Mexican orange

Choisya dumosa flowers and foliage

Native Distribution: sandy and rocky slopes, desert grasslands, oak woodlands; 3,000–7,000 feet; Southeast Arizona to central Texas, Mexico.

Landscape Zone: 2–7.

Size: 3 feet.

Leaves: evergreen.

Flower: June–October; 1-inch clusters of white flowers.

Soil: adaptable; limestone, igneous, well draining.

Exposure: full sun.

Temperature Tolerance: extremely heat tolerant, cold hardy to 0°F.

Water: drought tolerant, 16 inches/year minimum.

Propagation: stratified fresh seeds, hardwood and semi-hardwood cuttings.

Profile: I predict that someday this member of the citrus family (Rutaceae) will be as popular in Southwest landscapes as Texas ranger and century plants. *Choisya dumosa* has a compact form, highly aromatic evergreen leaves, and showy flowers from April through September—a combination that brings year-round interest for your yard. Use this low-growing, intricately branched plant to accent cactus and xeriscape gardens, group plantings, as a border plant along drives and walks, and in a container for patios and pools. Starleaf Mexican orange grows 2 to 3 feet in height, which makes it ideal as a shrubby groundcover or for stabilizing a rocky slope. With its low, rounded profile, it complements mixed plantings of larger shrubs and adds winter color when used with deciduous species. The olive-green leaves provide color variety when planted with gray-leafed species such as agaves, winterfat, or big sagebrush. This plant of many uses absolutely requires well-draining soil.

Below: *Choisya dumosa*

Chrysactinia mexicana

Chrysactinia mexicana
Damianita

Native Distribution: limestone hills, slopes; 2,000–6,000 feet; New Mexico through central Texas, Mexico.
Landscape Zone: 1–4.
Size: 1- to 2-foot mound.
Leaves: evergreen, needle-like, aromatic.

Flower: April–September; yellow, profuse.
Soil: sand, loam, limestone, alkaline, well draining.
Exposure: full sun.
Temperature Tolerance: extremely heat tolerant, cold hardy to 0°F.
Water: drought tolerant, 12 inches/year minimum.
Propagation: fall-sown or stratified seeds, hardwood and semi-hardwood cuttings.
Profile: Any plant that can bloom profusely during the heat of summer in Phoenix is a favorite of mine. From spring through September, damianita is completely covered by showy, lemon-yellow flowers. A compact rounded sub-shrub, it forms dense clumps 1 to 2 feet high and wide. The spherical shape and mass of golden blooms make it an outstanding choice for borders along walkways, in patios and poolside gardens, as a foreground plant, or to accent a desert garden. In mass plantings it stabilizes dry, rocky slopes and provides brilliant color. And the highly aromatic leaves add an extra zest to your yard. With a long flowering season, this perennial evergreen contributes color to your landscape throughout the year.

Dalea formosa flowers, with plumes
Right: *Dalea frutescens* flowers and foliage

Dalea formosa
Feather dalea
Dalea frutescens
Black dalea

Native Distribution: dry hills, deserts flats, mesas, Pinyon-Juniper woodlands; 2,000–6,500 feet; Arizona to central Texas, Colorado, Oklahoma, Mexico.
Landscape Zone: 1–4.
Size: 2–4 feet.
Leaves: deciduous.
Flower: 1/2-inch purple, pea-like flowers on spikes. *Dalea formosa*: March–June, with feathery plumes; *Dalea frutescens*: July–October, without plumes.
Fruit: seeds with feathery tails.
Soil: adaptable; well draining.
Exposure: full sun.

Temperature Tolerance: heat tolerant, cold hardy to 0°F.
Water: drought tolerant, 8 inches/year minimum.
Propagation: fresh seeds, semi-hardwood cuttings.
Profile: Feather dalea, or purple dalea, as *Dalea formosa* is sometimes called, is true to its species name: *formosa* is Latin for "beautiful." Richly colored blossoms and feathery flower cups combine to make it one of the most valuable ornamental shrubs of the Southwest. From March to June, and often again in wet Septembers, masses of the small blooms completely cover the shrub. The deep purple blossom has a yellow throat surrounded by feathery plumes. Tiny grayish green leaves punctuate the attractive flowers. This shrub has rigid zigzag branches and a naturally rounded shape. Black dalea, *D. frutescens*, is similar in shape, flower, and landscape applications. The leaflets are slightly larger and brighter green than those of feather dalea, but black dalea's flowers lack the ornate feathery plumes. It makes up for the loss by adding color to your landscape when you need it most. As a fall bloomer, it's the perfect addition for a year-round colorscape. The purple flowers of the 'Sierra Negra' cultivar provide a blaze of fall color. Use daleas as low border shrubs or as foreground accents in a xeriscape garden or mixed planting. Or plant them in mass for a groundcover with a dramatic splash of color. Both species grow moderately fast, and winter pruning encourages a compact shape. Overwatering or over-fertilizing produces weak growth.

Dasiphora floribunda (Potentilla fruiticosa)
Shrubby cinquefoil

Native Distribution: mountain grasslands, forests; 6,000–10,000 feet; New Mexico to California, north to Alaska, east to New Jersey, Canada.
Landscape Zone: 3–7.
Size: 2–3 feet.
Leaves: usually evergreen, 5 leaflets, 3/4 inch long.
Flower: June–September; 1 inch wide, yellow, rose-like.
Soil: adaptable; moist to well draining.
Exposure: full sun to shade.
Temperature Tolerance: cold hardy.
Water: regular water, 20 inches/year minimum.
Propagation: seeds.
Profile: This delightful little shrub graces your landscape with bright yellow flowers from summer through fall.

The five-petaled, rose-like blossoms decorate the leafy stems like drops of golden paint. The five-fingered leaves crowd the intricately branching limbs to create a densely foliated shrub. The long blooming season, showy flowers, and attractive foliage make this plant a good choice for almost any landscape or colorscape design. But shrubby cinquefoil prefers cool climates. In Albuquerque, it reportedly tends to die out from heat stress and suffers from spider mites. Popular around the world, shrubby cinquefoil comes in numerous varieties, including those with small or large heights, various foliage tints, and flowers in red, orange, white, or shades of yellow.

Dasiphora floribunda flowers

Dasiphora floribunda

Dasylirion leiophyllum
Dasylirion wheeleri
Sotol or desert spoon

Dasylirion

Above: *Dasylirion* seed head

Right: *Dasylirion*

Native Distribution: limestone hills, desert grasslands; 3,000–6,000 feet; Arizona to central Texas, Mexico.
Landscape Zone: 1–6.
Size: 2–4 feet tall, 3–6 feet wide.
Leaves: evergreen, narrow, 3–4 feet long with spines on margin.
Flower: May–August; creamy spikes on 10- to 15-foot stalks.
Fruit: reddish seed heads.
Soil: sandy, rocky, well draining.
Exposure: full sun.
Temperature Tolerance: heat tolerant, cold hardy to 0°F.
Water: drought tolerant, 8 inches/year minimum.
Propagation: fresh seeds.
Profile: Sotols give your home or commercial landscape a distinctive Southwest flavor. The dense rosette of blue-green leaves adds texture and balance to a xeriscape or cactus garden and provides a foliage complement to agaves, yuccas, chollas, and prickly pears. In summer, when the bloom stalk displays its rusty seed head, a sotol becomes a dominant focal point. The plant's low stature makes it an ideal foreground accent in front of windows, on patios, or other places where you don't want a visual barrier. Given time, sotols develop a short, stout trunk. Sharp teeth line the blade-like leaves, so keep the plants away from children's play areas. Various Mexican species are also available, but they are more sensitive to frost.

Dodonaea viscosa
Hopbush

Native Distribution: desert hills, canyons; 2,000–5,000 feet; Arizona, Florida.
Landscape Zone: 1–2.
Size: 12–15 feet tall, oval shaped.
Leaves: evergreen, narrow, 4–8 inches long.
Fruit: April–September; showy 1/2- to 1-inch disks with three rounded wings; flowers insignificant.
Soil: sandy, rocky, well draining.
Exposure: full sun, light shade.
Temperature Tolerance: heat tolerant, cold hardy to 15°F.
Water: drought tolerant, 8 inches/year minimum.
Propagation: seeds.
Profile: Also called varnish-leaf because of its shiny foliage, the versatile hopbush ranges through tropical Africa, Australia, China, India, and into Arizona and its sister sunshine state, Florida—so it feels right at home in Phoenix and Tucson. Densely foliated with narrow, waxy, evergreen leaves, hopbush can serve as an ideal hedge or privacy screen when planted on 5- to 8-foot centers. By early spring, clusters of winged seed disks decorate the shrub. They add color to your yard as they mature from green to yellow, pink, and finally red. In addition to its use as hedges or screens, hopbush can be planted as a specimen by a pool or patio without fear of invasive roots. Use it to enliven a fence or wall, or as a backdrop for a landscape island. The assortment of available cultivars offers variety in leaf color and hardiness. The red-leafed 'Purpurea' makes a dramatic statement, but it is only cold hardy to 25°F. Quail and doves eat the seeds of hopbush.

Top: *Dodonaea viscosa*

Right: *Dodonaea viscosa* in fruit

Encelia farinosa
Brittlebush

Native Distribution: Sonoran and Mojave deserts, sandy or gravel hills; below 3,000 feet; Arizona, California, Utah, Nevada.
Landscape Zone: 1–2.
Size: mounds 2–4 feet tall and wide.
Leaves: evergreen, but drought-deciduous, gray-green to silver, woolly, 2–4 inches long.
Flower: November–May, after rain; yellow, 2 inches wide on long stems.
Soil: sandy, rocky, well draining.
Exposure: full sun.
Temperature Tolerance: heat tolerant, limbs cold hardy to 25°F, roots hardy to 15°F.
Water: drought tolerant, 8 inches/year minimum.
Propagation: seeds, easily transplanted.
Profile: In wet springtimes, brittlebush floods Arizona's desert hills with

Above: *Encelia farinosa*

Left: *Encelia farinosa* flowers

waves of brilliant yellow. Plant this durable shrub in the hottest, driest spot in your yard and watch it burst into bloom after winter and spring rains. Bright yellow, daisy-like flowers borne on 6-inch stems obscure the ash-colored leaves. When not in bloom, the plant's rounded mound of silver foliage adds variety to a cactus or xeriscape garden or a mass planting.

Mix it with palo verde, huisache, mesquite, or ironwood for understory interest, or use it as a foreground plant with agaves, chollas, yuccas, daleas, jojobas, and desert bird of paradise. Brittlebush goes dormant and loses it leaves in extreme drought, but you should irrigate only sparingly. If given excess water, it will take over your garden, so keep your shears handy.

Ephedra

Native Distribution: sandy, rocky plains, hills; below 6,000 feet; California to Texas, Mexico.
Landscape Zone: 1–6.
Size: 1–6 feet.
Leaves: minuscule, scale-like.

Ephedra stems and flowers

Flower: spring; tiny, in stem nodes, red to yellow according to species.
Fruit: summer; tiny cones on female plants.
Soil: sandy, rocky, well draining.
Exposure: full sun.

Ephedra species
Joint fir or Mormon tea

Temperature Tolerance: heat tolerant, cold hardy to 0–10°F.
Water: drought tolerant, 8 inches/year minimum.
Propagation: fresh or stratified seeds.
Profile: The smooth, green-to-yellowish, pencil-like stems of these densely branching plants provide eye-catching focal points in your cactus or xeriscape garden or for patio or pool plantings. In the absence of leaves, the broom-like stems carry on photosynthesis and give the plant its green color. Male and female plants are separate and have slightly different-colored flowers, but the blooms are too small to make much difference. Ephedras complement beargrass, sotol, prickly pear, ocotillo, and yucca. They add year-round green to mixed plantings with deciduous shrubs. A dozen species and varieties of *Ephedra*, all with similar landscape applications, grow in Arizona and New Mexico. Some are adapted to low deserts, some to high deserts, so pick one from your area.

Ericameria laricifolia

Ericameria laricifolia
Larchleaf goldenweed or turpentine bush

Native Distribution: desert slopes, grasslands, mesas; 3,000–6,000 feet; California to Texas, Utah, Nevada, Mexico.
Landscape Zone: 1–6.
Size: 2–4 feet.
Leaves: evergreen, needle-like, 1/16-inch wide, 3/4 inch long.
Flower: August–December; heads of 1/2-inch, golden flowers.
Soil: limestone, well draining.
Exposure: full sun.
Temperature Tolerance: extremely heat tolerant, cold hardy to 0°F.
Water: drought tolerant, 8 inches/year minimum.
Propagation: seeds.
Profile: The compact shape, dense branching, and attractive fall flowers make this close relative to chamisa a perfect colorscape choice. An array of bright yellow flowers crowns the stiff, erect branches of larchleaf goldenweed from August through December. The flowers and dark green leaves make an attractive border for your walk or drive or a foreground accent in a mixed planting. For year-round color, plant this shrub with spring-blooming yuccas, Texas ranger, fragrant mimosa, verbenas, and lupines. The Aguirre clone, collected in south-central New Mexico, has especially showy flowers and rich, green foliage. The aromatic leaves give *Ericameria laricifolia* its other common name, turpentine bush. A trim after blooming keeps the foliage dense.

Ericameria nauseosa (Chrysothamnus nauseosus)
Rabbitbrush or chamisa

Native Distribution: dry soils, mesas, plains; 2,000–8,000 feet; California to Texas, north to Canada, Mexico.
Landscape Zone: 3–7.
Size: 2–5 feet.
Leaves: semi-evergreen, needle-like, 2 1/2 inches long.
Flower: July–October; clusters of showy, rayless, yellow flowers.
Soil: adaptable; alkaline, well draining.
Exposure: full sun, partial shade.
Temperature Tolerance: cold hardy, requires cool summers.
Water: drought tolerant, 8 inches/year minimum.
Propagation: fresh seeds, hardwood cuttings.
Profile: With bluish-green leaves, woolly white stems, and fall yellow flowers, chamisa accents your landscape throughout the year. The slender, erect stems grow from a woody base and are densely covered with the narrow, ashen leaves. You can plant chamisa in mass as an unsheared hedge along fences or drives for fall color. With mixed species, it provides a striking contrast with evergreens such as barberries, starleaf Mexican orange, and pinyon pine. For a bouquet of fall colors, plant it with red yucca, winterfat, and feather dalea. You may have to prune this fast-growing plant back in the winter to keep it full and to encourage blooming. Chamisa is one of the most abundant plants from Santa Fe north.

Ericameria nauseosa

Fallugia paradoxa
Apache plume

Native Distribution: dry, rocky slopes, chaparral, hills; 4,000–8,000 feet; California to central Texas, Mexico.
Landscape Zone: 3–7.
Size: 3–8 feet.
Leaves: evergreen, lobed, 3/4 inch long.
Flower: April–October; 1 inch, rose-like, white.
Fruit: summer–winter; showy, tassel-like seed heads.
Soil: adaptable; well draining.
Exposure: full sun.
Temperature Tolerance: heat tolerant, cold hardy to −30°F.
Water: drought tolerant, 8 inches/year minimum.
Propagation: fresh seeds, layering, root suckers.
Profile: With snow-white flowers, feathery seed tassels, evergreen foliage, and a well-rounded shape, Apache

Fallugia paradoxa flowers

plume contributes year-round to high-desert landscapes. The fragrant flowers bloom continually until October, and the pink feathery plumes almost obscure the shrub much of the year, making it a great component of a colorscape design. The seed heads resemble miniature feather dusters, and they reminded early settlers of the head-dress worn by the Apaches. Use this ornamental shrub as a specimen, for a backdrop along a fence, or in a mass planting. It forms dense clumps, making it suitable for hedges and screens. Apache plume grows rapidly and flowers the first or second year from seed. Prune in the winter, since it flowers on

Fallugia paradoxa

new spring growth. You may need to cut it back severely every few years. An occasional deep watering in the summer encourages flowering.

Fendlera rupicola
Cliff fendlerbush

Fendlera rupicola

Native Distribution: rocky slopes and canyons, desert shrub, Pinyon-Juniper woodlands; 3,000–7,000 feet; Arizona to Texas, Nevada to Colorado, Mexico.
Landscape Zone: 2–6.
Size: 4–6 feet.
Leaves: deciduous, 1 3/4 inches long.
Flower: March–June; 3/4 inch, white.
Soil: adaptable; well draining.
Exposure: full sun, partial shade.
Temperature Tolerance: heat tolerant, cold hardy to 0°F.
Water: drought tolerant, 12 inches/year minimum.
Propagation: stratified seeds, softwood cuttings.
Profile: In the spring, this intricately branching shrub will dazzle your yard with showy masses of snow-white flowers. The fragrant blossoms have four delicate, pink-tinged petals, and they profusely cover the branch tips. Use cliff fendlerbush as a specimen shrub or in background or mixed plantings. The showy flowers add color when mixed with junipers, pinyon pine, joint fir, silktassel, and mountain mahogany. Moderate pruning after blooming keeps it from getting too rangy. The specific name *rupicola* means "rock loving," so be sure you plant it in loose, well-draining soil. The variety *falcata* has larger flowers, up to 1 1/2 inches across.

Forestiera pubescens var. pubescens
(Forestiera neomexicana)
New Mexican privet, New Mexican olive, or desert olive

Forestiera pubescens var. pubescens

Native Distribution: hillsides, mesas, valleys; 2,000–7,000 feet; California to Texas, Nevada to Oklahoma.
Landscape Zone: 2–6.
Size: 6–20 feet tall, 8 feet wide.
Leaves: deciduous, 1 inch long, yellow fall color.
Flower: March–May; insignificant.
Fruit: summer; 1/4 inch, oval, bluish, on female plants.
Soil: adaptable; well draining.
Exposure: full sun.
Temperature Tolerance: cold hardy to 10°F.
Water: drought tolerant.
Propagation: seeds, cuttings, layers.
Profile: This ornate shrub goes by many names, and it fits many applications. With ornate gray bark, multiple trunks, and airy branching, it is most striking when pruned into a 10- to 20-foot-tall tree for a patio, courtyard, or specimen planting. You can let it grow into an informal screen or background, or shear it into a hedge. In group plantings, the small glossy leaves direct attention to companion plants such as dalea, fairy duster, red yucca, and bird of paradise. In the fall, New Mexican privet commands its own attention with a colorful display of dense yellow foliage. Birds and small wildlife enjoy the fruit, but you need plants of both sexes to produce fruit, so plant several at a time.

Fouquieria splendens
Ocotillo

Native Distribution: desert slopes, flats; below 5,000 feet; California to Texas, Nevada, Mexico.
Landscape Zone: 1–2.
Size: 6–15 feet.
Leaves: briefly after rain.
Flower: March–June; clusters of red flowers.
Soil: rocky, calcareous or igneous, well draining.
Exposure: full sun.
Temperature Tolerance: cold hardy to 10°F.
Water: drought tolerant, 8 inches/year minimum.
Propagation: fresh seeds, cuttings.
Profile: Ocotillo is one of the strangest plants of the arid West, and one that was used in Southwest landscapes for centuries before Europeans arrived. Numerous thorn-covered, wand-like branches sprout from a short stem or root crown. The branches are barren during most of the year, but after a rain, tiny green leaves sprout and cover the plant. In the spring, clusters of scarlet, bell-shaped flowers crown each waving branch tip. The intense contrast between the spiny branches and the brilliant flowers adds flair to any landscape design. The airy structure of the plant accents without dominating a group planting, providing a good balance in a xeriscape garden. Interestingly, one of the earliest landscape uses of ocotillo was as a living fence. When planted in a trench and woven together with wire, the thorny branches sprout and grow into a fence impenetrable to predators and humans alike. In humid climates, ocotillo is prone to rot and will seldom flower. Most mature plants for sale come from the wild, so be sure yours has been rescued from a bulldozer, not stripped from natural areas. Nurseries sometimes carry the shrubby Mexican species, *Fouquieria diquetii*. Its wands branch more than those of *F. splendens*, and it is more frost sensitive.

Above: *Fouquieria splendens* flowers

Left: *Fouquieria splendens* as a fence

Fraxinus greggii
Gregg ash

Native Distribution: dry, rocky hills, washes; 1,200–5,000 feet; southern Arizona to Texas, Mexico.
Landscape Zone: 1–4.
Size: 10–15 feet.
Leaves: evergreen.
Fruit: summer; 1/2-inch-long winged seeds.
Soil: limestone, well draining.
Exposure: full sun, partial shade.
Temperature Tolerance: heat tolerant, cold hardy to 10°F.
Water: drought tolerant, 8 inches/year minimum.
Propagation: fresh or stratified seeds.
Profile: The compact, upright shape and evergreen foliage make Gregg ash a good choice if you want a small tree or large shrub. You can plant it in a large planter box to accent pools and patios, or use it as a specimen plant. With year-round foliage color, this ash makes a good component for a row planting or visual screen. In group plantings, its foliage, size, and habitat are compatible with Texas mountain laurel, Mexican buckeye, and Arizona rosewood. Its rich, green foliage contrasts well with gray-foliated shrubs such as Texas ranger, woolly butterflybush, brittlebush, and sagebrush.

Fraxinus greggii

Garrya wrightii
Wright silktassel

Garrya wrightii

Garrya wrightii foliage

Native Distribution: dry hills and canyons, chaparral, Pinyon-Juniper-Oak woodlands; 3,000–8,000 feet; Arizona to Texas, Mexico.
Landscape Zone: 2–6.
Size: 3–10 feet.
Leaves: evergreen, light green, 2 inches long.
Fruit: summer; 1/4-inch purple drupes on female plants.
Soil: adaptable; well draining.
Exposure: full sun.
Temperature Tolerance: heat tolerant, cold hardy to 10–20°F.

Water: drought tolerant, 12 inches/year minimum.
Propagation: scarified, stratified seeds, semi-hardwood cuttings.
Profile: Silktassel is evergreen, fast growing, densely foliated, and drought and heat tolerant. The only thing lacking is showy flowers and fruit, but sometimes you can't have everything. When used alone as a specimen plant, silktassel develops a full, symmetrical shape, growing to 10 feet. The lustrous green leaves contribute year-round color to a mixed planting with deciduous species. It makes an ideal visual screen or privacy hedge, or you can prune it into a medium-sized background or boundary hedge. It's a suitable companion for mountain mahogany, desert ceanothus, pinyon pine, junipers, and gray oak. Quinine bush (*Garrya flavescens*) is a similar species with fuzzy, gray-green leaves. It has the same habitat requirements and landscape applications as Wright silktassel.

Hesperaloe parviflora
Red yucca

Native Distribution: limestone hills of central and west Texas, Mexico.
Landscape Zone: 1–6.
Size: 2–4 feet across.
Leaves: evergreen, sword-like.
Flower: May–October; spikes of 1-inch, pink-to-red flowers on 4- to 8-foot stalks.
Soil: adaptable; well draining.
Exposure: full sun, partial shade.
Temperature Tolerance: extremely heat tolerant, cold hardy to 0°F.
Water: drought tolerant, 16 inches/year minimum.
Propagation: seeds.
Profile: The much-loved red yucca grows on almost every block in Albuquerque, Tucson, and Phoenix, but you'll have to go to west Texas to find it in the wild. The small size, symmetrical rosette of leaves, and graceful

Left:
Hesperaloe parviflora flowers

Right:
Hesperaloe parviflora

arching flower stalk give this yucca-like plant an artistic, picturesque shape. *Hesperaloe parviflora* is the perfect accent for a xeriscape garden, and it provides a natural focal point for small landscape islands, patios, or poolsides. But that's not all: This versatile plant can surround a tree or lamppost, serve as a groundcover, or be planted in a container. The abundant coral flowers decorate nodding stalks and provide color until the first freeze. The flowers also attract hummingbirds. Unlike those of true yuccas, the long, stiff leaves of red yucca are thornless, making it safe to use as a border

plant along walks and drives. The yellow-flowered cultivar *H. parviflora* 'Yellow' is also available. Giant hesperaloe, *H. funifera*, is a larger, white-flowered species native to west Texas and Mexico.

Justicia californica
Chuparosa
Justicia candicans (Jacobinia ovata)
Jacobinia or red justicia

Native Distribution: dry soils of deserts, washes, rocky foothills and slopes; 1,000–2,500 feet; Arizona, California, Mexico.

Landscape Zone: 1–2.

Size: 3–4 feet.

Leaves: drought-deciduous, oval, 1 inch long.

Flower: periodically all year; 1 1/2 inches long, tube-shaped, red.

Soil: adaptable; alkaline, well draining.

Exposure: full sun.

Temperature Tolerance: heat tolerant, twig damage at 28°F, root hardy to 20°F.

Water: drought tolerant, 10 inches/year minimum.

Propagation: seeds.

Profile: With their red tubular flowers, these sister plants in the Acanthus family are a must for desert humming-

bird gardens. The flamboyant flowers are in bloom for much of the year, and they cover the rounded shrubs, especially if given regular deep watering. The long bloom period complements a colorscape design and creates a striking palette in a landscape island or xeriscape garden. Combine with creosote bush, larchleaf goldenweed, damianita, or the yellow clone of red yucca. Jacobinia tolerates light shade, while chuparosa prefers full sun. Any freeze-damaged limbs should be pruned in spring after the last frost. The widely used Mexican honeysuckle, *Justicia spicigera*, is shade tolerant and has orange flowers. At higher elevations, you are better off planting another hummingbird magnet from the same family: desert honeysuckle, *Anisacanthus thurberi*.

Justicia californica flowers

Justicia candicans

Krascheninnikovia lanata

Krascheninnikovia lanata
(Ceratoides lanata, Eurotia lanata)
Winterfat

Native Distribution: dry soils of deserts, mesas, open slopes; 2,000–7,000 feet; California to west Texas, north to Canada.
Landscape Zone: 2–6.
Size: 1–3 feet tall.
Leaves: evergreen.
Fruit: fall–winter; showy, cottony seed heads along the stems on female plants.

Soil: adaptable; alkaline, well draining.
Exposure: full sun, intolerant of shade.
Temperature Tolerance: heat tolerant, cold hardy to –30°F.
Water: drought tolerant, 5–20 inches/year.
Propagation: stratified seeds, softwood cuttings.
Profile: Numerous erect, slender branches grow from the woody base of this ornate addition to your garden. Woolly hairs densely cover the narrow, bluish-green leaves that crowd the stems. From September through December, plumes of fluffy white seeds cover the female plants. The seed plumes remind me of miniature sticks of cotton candy, especially when they glow in the afternoon sun. The dried plumes make an attractive addition to flower arrangements. Use this fast-growing shrub as a color accent with evergreen plants such as starleaf Mexican orange, barberry, and ephedra. The spreading root system and low profile make winterfat a good choice for a groundcover in hot, arid locations. You'll probably need to trim it back before it begins its spring growth, to keep it thick. Winterfat requires climates with cold nights to thrive. Across its native range from the Southwest deserts to Canada, it serves as an important winter forage for mule and white-tailed deer, Rocky Mountain elk, bighorn sheep, pronghorn, rabbits, and ground squirrels.

Lantana urticoides (Lantana horrida)
West Indian lantana

Native Distribution: sandy, rocky soils; Texas to Mississippi, Mexico; naturalized west to California.
Landscape Zone: 1–6.
Size: 2–6 feet.
Leaves: deciduous.
Flower: spring–winter; 1-inch heads of orange and red flowers.
Fruit: black drupes; poisonous to humans.
Soil: adaptable; well draining.
Exposure: full sun, partial shade.
Temperature Tolerance: extremely heat tolerant, cold hardy to 10–20°F.

Water: drought tolerant, 12 inches/year minimum.
Propagation: fresh seeds, softwood and semi-hardwood cuttings.
Profile: The multicolored flowers of this fast-growing shrub provide brilliant colors for your yard from the heat of summer to the first frost. Each flower head is a miniature bouquet of tiny yellow blossoms surrounded by bright orange blooms. Lantanas grow into sprawling shrubs up to 6 feet tall, but typically are 2 to 3 feet tall. As a low shrub, they are suitable for groundcovers, slope and curb plantings, or terraced landscapes. You can use them as colorful surround plants for trees and posts, in a mixed planting, or as a container plant pruned into a poodle shape or other imaginative forms. You'll need to cut them back severely every winter if planted in rich soil, or they will take over your garden. Prune damaged limbs that freeze during hard winters. Numerous horticultural varieties of lantana occur in the nursery trade, including many dwarf and trailing forms.

Lantana urticoides

Lantana urticoides flowers

Larrea tridentata
Creosote bush

Native Distribution: sandy scrublands, mesas of Chihuahuan, Mojave, and Sonoran deserts; below 3,500 feet; California to west Texas, north to Utah, Mexico.
Landscape Zone: 1–3.
Size: 3–6 feet.
Leaves: evergreen, resinous, 3/8 inch long.
Flower: spring–winter; yellow, 1/2 inch.
Fruit: fuzzy capsules.
Soil: adaptable; alkaline, well draining.
Exposure: full sun.
Temperature Tolerance: extremely heat tolerant, cold hardy to 0–10°F.
Water: drought tolerant, 4 inches/year minimum.
Propagation: scarified seeds soaked in water.
Profile: Creosote bush grows in the hottest, driest deserts in the Southwest. When given the advantages of a landscape setting, this normally open-branching shrub develops into a densely foliated specimen plant with a rounded profile. Lemon-yellow flowers or fuzzy seeds accent the plant throughout most of the year. Use as a screen or border hedge, or to accent a cactus garden. In xeriscapes or mixed plantings, its green foliage complements Texas ranger, daleas, woolly butterflybush, brittlebush, and Apache plume. When mass planted, creosote bushes add more than looks to your yard. After a rain, they perfume the air with that invigorating desert aroma. Extra water in the summer speeds up growth, but overwatering kills. Creosote bush clones itself with root suckers, so the plant survives long after the main plant dies. The clones may be the earth's oldest living organisms. One specimen in the Mojave Desert, known as "King Clone," is estimated to be 11,700 years old.

Above: *Larrea tridentata* flowers

Below: *Larrea tridentata*

Leucophyllum frutescens
Texas ranger

Native Distribution: desert flats, limestone hills; 1,000–4,500 feet; New Mexico to west Texas, Mexico.
Landscape Zone: 1–2.
Size: 4–8 feet.
Leaves: evergreen, silver, 1/4 to 3/4 inch long.
Flower: anytime, especially after rain; 1 inch, purple, pink, or white.
Soil: alkaline, well draining.
Exposure: full sun.
Temperature Tolerance: extremely heat tolerant, cold hardy to 5°F.
Water: drought tolerant, 8 inches/year minimum.
Propagation: seeds, cuttings.
Profile: When Southwest landscapers discovered Texas ranger, they thought they'd found heaven. Few plants offer as many premier landscape qualities. It has striking silvery to gray-green evergreen foliage, spectacular purple flowers, and a long blooming season. It grows rapidly with dense foliage and survives harsh or marginal conditions with minimal maintenance, although it will not tolerate high humidity. With a naturally erect, rounded shape, Texas ranger makes an ideal specimen plant or component of a mass or mixed planting. It even can be sheared into a formal shrub or hedge. If it gets too rangy, prune severely during the winter to promote dense growth. With many variations of size and flowers and foliage color available, be sure to choose one suitable for your landscape requirements. *Leucophyllum frutescens* 'Green Cloud' and 'Green Leaf' grow vigorously to 6–8 feet tall and have green foliage; 'White Cloud' has white flowers. For borders and foreground plants, choose the low-growing, 3- to 4-foot 'Compacta' or 'Silverado' cultivars. 'Silver Cloud' and 'Thunder Cloud' have deep purple flowers and silver foliage and reach 4 feet in height.

Above: *Leucophyllum frutescens*

Right: *Leucophyllum frutescens* flowers

Lonicera albiflora

Lonicera albiflora
White honeysuckle

Native Distribution: prairies, mountain canyons, rocky slopes, sandy soils; Arizona, New Mexico; Texas, Oklahoma, Mexico.
Landscape Zone: 2–4.
Size: 4–9 feet.
Leaves: semi-evergreen.
Flower: March–May; clusters of creamy, tube-shaped flowers 1/2 to 2/3 inch long.
Fruit: late fall; orange-to-red berries.
Soil: adaptable; alkaline, well draining.
Exposure: full to partial shade.
Temperature Tolerance: heat tolerant, cold hardy to 0–10°F.
Water: drought tolerant, 16 inches/year minimum.
Propagation: fresh or stratified seeds, softwood or semi-hardwood cuttings.

Profile: Creamy, funnel-shaped flowers cover this bushy evergreen shrub in the early spring, and colorful red berries follow in October and November. The flower clusters and scarlet fruit nestle tightly against paired olive-green leaves. Its twining, arching branches and rounded shape make white honeysuckle suitable for foundation plantings, informal hedges, and mass plantings. The shrub grows thick enough for background plantings and barrier hedges, or you can trim it into a densely foliated small shrub. And you have the luxury of planting it in shady locations. You'll probably have to prune it yearly, with severe pruning every few years to keep the foliage dense. The berries attract birds, and deer browse the foliage. White honeysuckle grows at lower elevations than the red-flowering vine, Arizona honeysuckle (*Lonicera arizonica*).

Lycium fremontii

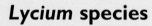

Lycium pallidum foliage and fruit

Fruit: summer; 3/8-inch, red, juicy berries.
Soil: adaptable; well draining.
Exposure: full sun, partial shade.
Temperature Tolerance: heat tolerant, cold hardy to 0–10°F.
Water: drought tolerant, 8 inches/year minimum.
Propagation: fresh seeds, semi-hardwood cuttings.
Profile: If you want to attract wildlife, wolfberry's dense, thorny branches and small, juicy fruit provide a great habitat for birds and small mammals. Though

Native Distribution: deserts to dry mountain slopes; 500–7,000 feet; California to west Texas, Mexico.
Landscape Zone: 1–6.
Size: 3–9 feet tall.
Leaves: evergreen, drought-deciduous, 1–3 inches long.

Lycium species
Wolfberry or desert thorn

not particularly ornamental, this thicket-forming shrub with 2- to 4-inch spines makes a good a barrier or background hedge. The small flowers, red berries, bluish-green leaves, and arching limbs add a wildscape look to desert gardens or mixed plantings. Wolfberry maintains lush foliage when given occasional water; otherwise, it responds to drought by dropping its leaves. Nine species of *Lycium*, with variations in cold hardiness, grow across Arizona and New Mexico, so choose one from your area. *Lycium pallidum* grows at 3,500–7,000 feet, *L. andersonii* below 6,000 feet, and *L. berlanderii* and *L. fremontii* below 3,000 feet. Ironwood, palo verdes, acacias, desert hackberry, and daleas make good companion plants at low elevations. The wolfberry species from higher elevations grow well with mountain mahogany, Apache plume, junipers, and oaks. Besides providing important forage for animals, wolfberry—a member of the tomato family (Solanaceae)—was a traditional food source for Southwestern Indians.

Mahonia fremontii (Berberis fremontii)
Fremont barberry
Mahonia haematocarpa (Berberis haematocarpa)
Red barberry
Mahonia trifoliolata (Berberis trifoliolata)
Agarita

Native Distribution: *Mahonia fremontii*: Pinyon-Juniper woodlands; 4,000–7,000 feet; New Mexico to California. *Mahonia haematocarpa*: desert grasslands to oak woodlands; 3,000–5,000 feet; California to Texas. *Mahonia trifoliolata*: desert grasslands, hills; 500–3,000 feet; Arizona to central Texas.

Landscape Zone: *Mahonia fremontii*, 2–6; *M. haematocarpa*, 2–4; *M. trifoliolata*, 2.

Size: 3–6 feet.

Leaves: evergreen, holly-like.

Flower: February–April; clusters of small yellow blooms.

Fruit: May–August; edible, red berries.

Soil: adaptable; alkaline, well draining.

Exposure: full sun, partial shade.

Temperature Tolerance: heat tolerant, cold hardy to 0–15°F.

Water: drought tolerant, 16 inches/year minimum.

Propagation: fall-sown or stratified seeds.

Profile: In late winter and early spring, clusters of lemon-yellow flowers accent the spiny, holly-like leaves of these three similar barberries. By May, bright red berries create a wildlife buffet. The ornamental evergreen leaves, fragrant flowers, and colorful fruit make these *Mahonia* species premier landscape shrubs for most Southwest cities. Use these low-maintenance shrubs as specimen plants, garden accents, or for borders along drives. The ornate leaves with prickly lobes and the plant's dense branching make barberries good barrier hedges and cover for birds. The blue-green, prickly leaves naturally contrast silver-leafed shrubs, such as Texas ranger, brittlebush, and woolly butterflybush, and with spiny plants such as yuccas, sotols, and agaves. The leaves of Fremont and red barberry often turn mottled hues of yellow and red in the winter. The various species grow at different altitudes with corresponding cold hardiness, so be sure to choose the one suited to your area. The tart fruit of *Mahonia* makes a tasty jelly.

Mahonia haematocarpa foliage and fruit

Mahonia trifoliolata

Mahonia trifoliolata foliage and flowers

Mimosa dysocarpa
Velvet pod mimosa

Mimosa dysocarpa

Native Distribution: canyons, limestone hills; 2,500–6,500 feet; Arizona to Texas.
Landscape Zone: 1–4.
Size: 3–6 feet.
Leaves: deciduous, compound, lacy.
Flower: May–September; fragrant, 2-inch, pink spikes.
Fruit: 1- to 2-inch-long, fuzzy pods.
Soil: adaptable; well draining.
Exposure: full sun, light shade.
Temperature Tolerance: heat tolerant, cold hardy to 15°F.
Water: drought tolerant, 8 inches/year minimum.
Propagation: scarified seeds, semi-hardwood cuttings.
Profile: At first, you may think that only a diabolic landscaper would recommend a plant armed with vicious catclaw thorns—but people love roses, so why not mimosas? When this compact, rounded shrub blooms, you'll understand the attraction. Pink cylinders of pompom flowers cover the plant and perfume the air. Use velvet pod mimosa to accent a xeriscape or cactus garden, against a masonry wall, or under an open-canopy tree, such as mesquite, palo verde, or huisache. It adds color to combinations with chollas, prickly pears, agaves, and nolinas. Periodic trimming maintains dense branching and encourages flowering. The variety *Mimosa dysocarpa* var. *wrightii* has been described as having mostly thornless branches, which would do well in the nursery trade. Two other widespread species have similar habitat requirements and landscape applications: the compact fragrant mimosa, *M. borealis*, and the open-branching catclaw mimosa, *M. aculeaticarpa* var. *biuncifera*. Both have round, puff-ball flowers. Quail enjoy mimosa seeds.

Mimosa borealis

Nolina texana
Beargrass or sacahuista

Native Distribution: slopes, ravines, brushlands, 3,500–5,000 feet; California to central Texas; Mexico.
Landscape Zone: 1–6.
Size: 3–4 feet tall and wide.
Leaves: evergreen, wiry, grass-like, 2–4 feet long.
Flower: March–July; large panicles of creamy white flowers on 1- to 2-foot-tall stalks.
Soil: sandy, rocky, loam, well draining.
Exposure: full sun, partial shade.
Temperature Tolerance: extremely heat tolerant, cold hardy to 15°F.

Water: drought tolerant, 8 inches/year minimum.
Propagation: seeds, plant division.
Profile: Beargrass looks like a rounded clump of thick-bladed grass, until it sends up its short, yucca-like flower stalk. Covered with a mass of tiny, creamy flowers, the 2-foot-tall flower stalks nestle among the wiry leaves, creating an eye-catching contrast in color and texture. The compact shape, symmetrical profile, and arching, spreading leaves make beargrass an ideal focal plant for a xeriscape or cactus garden.

Its stiff, grass-like leaves complement thick-bladed plants such as yuccas and agaves. You can plant beargrasses on 3- to 4-foot centers for a groundcover or to stabilize rocky slopes. Beargrass is particularly attractive in a planter or along a ledge, with its long leaves dangling over the edge. The similar *Nolina macrocarpa* has a 3-foot bloom stalk and is cold hardy to −15°F. The larger, more dramatic bigelow nolina, *N. bigelovii*, sends up an 8-foot flower stalk and develops a short trunk and is suitable for landscape zones 1–2.

Nolina texana

Parthenium incanum
Mariola

Native Distribution: rocky desert grasslands, mesas; 2,000–6,500 feet; Arizona to west Texas, Nevada, Utah, Mexico.
Landscape Zone: 1–6.
Size: 2 feet high, 3 feet wide.
Leaves: evergreen, gray, 3/4 inch long.
Flower: spring–fall; flat-topped, 2- to 3-inch-wide clusters of tiny white flowers.
Soil: adaptable; well draining.
Exposure: sun.
Temperature Tolerance: extremely heat tolerant, cold hardy to 10°F.
Water: drought tolerant, 8 inches/year minimum.
Propagation: scarified, stratified seeds.

Profile: With ornate silvery leaves and a compact profile, this small, rounded shrub makes a beautiful foreground accent in a xeriscape garden, a ground-cover for slopes or rocky areas, or a border along a walk or drive. Mariola will bloom all summer if you give it an occasional drink. Its neutral color contrasts well with starleaf Mexican orange, damianita, joint fir, and other green-leafed species. You'll want to trim the dead flower stems to keep the plant neat looking, and prune the bush back every few years to keep it dense. The larger and closely related guayule, *Parthenium argentatum*, grows in Texas and Mexico and is often used in similar landscape applications.

Parthenium argentatum flowers and foliage

Parthenium incanum

Psorothamnus scoparius (Dalea scoparia)
Broom dalea

Native Distribution: high desert scrublands; 3,000–6,000 feet; Arizona to west Texas, Mexico.

Landscape Zone: 2–6.

Size: 1–4 feet high and wide.

Leaves: minute.

Flower: May–June, August–September; clusters of purple, 1/2-inch blooms.

Soil: sandy, well draining.

Exposure: full sun.

Temperature Tolerance: heat tolerant, cold hardy to 15°F.

Water: drought tolerant, 8 inches/year minimum.

Propagation: fresh seeds.

Profile: This rapid-growing, low-mounding shrub makes up for its almost nonexistent leaves with profuse flowering. The small, intensely purple blooms cover the dense maze of broom-like, gray branches in spring and fall. Use this unusual, eye-catching plant as a groundcover in sandy areas, as a texture element in xeriscape gardens, or as a seasonal accent in a color-scape scheme. For a splash of color, combine broom dalea with damianita, dogweed, giant four-o'clock, or brittle-bush. Its pencil-like branches complement joint fir, red yucca, beargrass, and sand sagebrush. Seasonal deep watering encourages profuse flowering.

Psorothamnus scoparius flowers

Below: *Psorothamnus scoparius*

Purshia stansburiana (Cowania mexicana var. stansburiana)
Stansbury or Mexican cliffrose

Native Distribution: dry slopes and mesas, desert grasslands, Pinyon-Juniper and Ponderosa Pine forests; 3,000–8,000 feet; New Mexico to California, north into Idaho, Mexico.
Landscape Zone: 2–6.
Size: 1–6 feet.
Leaves: evergreen.

Flower: April–July; 1 inch, creamy.
Fruit: seeds with feathery tails.
Soil: limestone soils, well draining.
Exposure: full sun, partial shade.
Temperature Tolerance: heat tolerant, cold hardy.
Water: drought tolerant, 12 inches/year minimum.

Propagation: stratified seeds.
Profile: From spring through summer, cliffrose is a mass of fragrant snowy flowers. The rose-like, 1-inch blooms crowd the branches and accent the dark green foliage. When the flowers go to seed, feathery plumes cover the shrub. The evergreen foliage, showy flowers, and ornamental seeds make cliffrose a year-round attraction in your landscape. Use it as a screen or in a mixed planting, or plant it alone to accent the corner of your yard, a pool, or patio. You can prune this intricately branched, densely foliated plant into formal or informal designs, but I like its natural gnarled shape best. Cliffrose is popular from Albuquerque north. It grows slowly and can develop into a picturesque small tree with brown shredding bark. The summer flowers and small leaves make it an attractive companion plant for fernbush, golden currant, three-leaf sumac, barberries, and Apache plume.

Purshia stansburiana

Purshia stansburiana flowers

Rhus glabra
Smooth sumac

Rhus glabra foliage

Native Distribution: moist or dry woods, Pinyon-Juniper to Ponderosa Pine forests; 5,000–8,000 feet; throughout United States, Canada, Mexico.
Landscape Zone: 3–7.
Size: 3–10 feet.
Leaves: deciduous, red fall color.
Flower: June–August; large clusters of white flowers.
Fruit: fall–winter; clusters of hard, red drupes.
Soil: adaptable; well draining.

Exposure: full sun, partial shade.
Temperature Tolerance: cold hardy to –20°F.
Water: drought tolerant, 16 inches/year minimum.
Propagation: scarified, stratified seeds, semi-hardwood cuttings.
Profile: The showy *Rhus glabra* has the longest, most ornamental leaves of the sumacs. In the spring and summer, large bundles of white flowers decorate the shrubby tree, followed by attractive grape-like clusters of red seeds. Come autumn, the dark green leaves turn brilliant hues of red and orange. This fast-growing plant spreads by root suckers and will form a thicket if naturalized in an unmowed area. Because of its moderate size, smooth sumac is good for background plantings or as a three-season specimen plant. You easily can prune it into a small tree for confined areas. Birds and small mammals relish the seeds, which can be made into a tart lemonade-like drink. Some people are allergic to the oil on the fruit and leaves. Numerous varieties are available, including one with yellow fruit and a dwarf form.

Rhus glabra fruit

Rhus microphylla
Little-leaf sumac or desert sumac

Native Distribution: desert grasslands, Chaparral, Pinyon-Juniper woodlands; 3,500–6,000 feet; Arizona to central Texas, Mexico.
Landscape Zone: 2–7.
Size: 1–6 feet tall and wide.
Leaves: deciduous, compound with 5–9 tiny leaflets, 1/2–1 1/2 inches long.
Flower: March–May, before the leaves; white, in small clusters.
Fruit: July–August: hard, red drupes.
Soil: adaptable; well draining.
Exposure: full sun, partial shade.
Temperature Tolerance: heat tolerant, cold hardy to –10°F.
Water: drought tolerant, 12 inches/year minimum.
Propagation: scarified, stratified seeds, cuttings.
Profile: The thick foliage and intricate branching of *Rhus microphylla* make this versatile shrub an ideal specimen, background, or companion plant, or as a hedge. The dense array of tiny leaves provide a neutral-green backdrop for colorful accent plants such as fragrant mimosa, catclaw acacia, creosote bush, or yuccas and agaves. You can shear little-leaf sumac into a low or head-high hedge for foundations, borders, backgrounds, or visual barriers. If you use it as a hedge, you may want to combine with evergreens, such as smooth sumac, buffaloberry, or jojoba, since this shrub is deciduous. Spherical clusters of minute, white flowers emerge in the spring before the leaves, and the decorative red fruit provides abundant ornamental color during the summer. Birds and other wildlife feed on the fruit.

Above: *Rhus microphylla* fruit

Right: *Rhus microphylla*

Rhus ovata
Sugar sumac

Rhus ovata

Native Distribution: shrubland, Chaparral; 3,000–5,000 feet; Arizona, California, Mexico.
Landscape Zone: 1–4.
Size: 8–15 feet tall and wide.
Leaves: evergreen, 2–4 inches long.
Flower: March–May; clusters of creamy flowers.
Fruit: hard, red drupes.
Soil: adaptable; well draining.
Exposure: full sun, afternoon shade.
Temperature Tolerance: heat tolerant, cold hardy to 0°F.
Water: drought tolerant, 12 inches/year minimum.
Propagation: scarified, stratified seeds, cuttings.

Profile: Give this evergreen sumac a place in the sun and admire the results. In the spring, red twigs highlight the shiny green leaves, and clusters of creamy flowers cover the branches. By late summer, red berries replace the flowers and attract a host of birds and small mammals. This naturally rounded shrub needs little attention other than an occasional deep watering in summer and a seasonal trim. Sugar sumac makes a handsome patio or pool specimen and provides year-round foliage texture when mixed with deciduous plants in a landscape island, screen planting, or hedge. Accent it with daleas, fairy duster, desert ceanothus, Fremont barberry, scarlet bouvardia, and mimosas.

Rhus trilobata
Skunkbush or three-leaf sumac

Temperature Tolerance: heat tolerant, cold hardy to −20°F.
Water: drought tolerant, 10 inches/year minimum.
Propagation: scarified, stratified seeds, cuttings.
Profile: This three-season shrub delights your yard with showy flowers, colorful fruit, vibrant foliage, and fall colors. Skunkbush starts spring with showy spikes of yellowish flowers that develop into clusters of red fruit, which are relished by wildlife. The dense, green foliage gives a striking contrast with gray-leafed species all summer, and in the autumn the three, dark green leaflets provide a showy display of red and orange. You can prune skunkbush into a moderately compact rounded form for background or specimen plantings, or plant it in mass for groundcover and erosion control. It grows fast and spreads by rhizomes to form thickets. It naturally grows in association with mountain mahogany, manzanita, catclaw acacia, mimosa, nolina, silktassel, junipers, and pinyon pine. Crushed leaves have a tart scent described as sweet by some and skunk-like by others.

Above: *Rhus trilobata*

Left: *Rhus trilobata* fruit

Native Distribution: grassland, shrubland, Chaparral, pine forests; 2,500–7,500 feet; widespread California to Texas, north into Canada, Mexico.
Landscape Zone: 2–6.
Size: 3–8 feet tall and wide.
Leaves: deciduous, red and orange fall color.
Flower: March–June, before the leaves; yellowish clusters.
Fruit: hard, red drupes.
Soil: adaptable; well draining.
Exposure: full sun, partial shade.

Rhus virens
Evergreen sumac

Native Distribution: rocky hills; 2,000–5,000 feet; Arizona to central Texas, Mexico.
Landscape Zone: 1–4.
Size: 4–10 feet tall and wide.
Leaves: evergreen, colorful after freezes.
Flower: August–October; clusters of small white flowers.
Fruit: hard, red drupes.
Soil: adaptable; well draining.
Exposure: full sun, partial shade.
Temperature Tolerance: heat tolerant, cold hardy to 10°F.
Water: drought tolerant, 12 inches/year minimum.
Propagation: fresh scarified seeds.
Profile: If you have a sunny site and need a moderate-sized evergreen, evergreen sumac could be the plant for you. It needs little pruning to grow into a beautiful, rounded specimen plant. You can use it in a screen or background planting, as a border hedge, or trimmed into a small tree. However you use it, you, the birds, bees, and butterflies will enjoy the late-summer flowers and ornate red fruit. The deep green, glossy leaves provide year-round foliage color and contrast well with Texas ranger, sand sagebrush, brittlebush, and barberries. For seasonal color, mix it with dogweed, damianita, or chuparosa. If you live in Phoenix, this sumac will appreciate a little extra summer water.

Rhus virens foliage and flowers

Rhus virens fall color

Ribes aureum
Golden currant

Native Distribution: grasslands, mountain scrublands, forests; 3,500–8,000 feet; California to Texas, north to Montana, Canada.
Landscape Zone: 2–7.
Size: 3–6 feet tall.
Leaves: deciduous, three lobed, red fall color.
Flower: March–June; clusters of 2-inch golden flowers.
Fruit: 1/4-inch berries maturing reddish black by late summer.
Soil: adaptable; well draining.
Exposure: full sun, partial shade.
Temperature Tolerance: cold hardy to −30°F.
Water: moderately drought tolerant, 16 inches/year minimum.
Propagation: stratified seeds, layering, dormant hardwood cuttings.
Profile: When golden clusters of trumpet-shaped, spicy-scented flowers turn this plant into a mound of color in the spring, you'll know how golden currant got its name. The dense covering of small, maple-like leaves, absence of prickles or spines, colorful summer fruit, and brilliant autumn shades of burgundy, red, and yellow make this a premier plant for your pool, patio, or landscape planting. Since it spreads by rhizomes, it is well-suited for mass plantings. You can prune it lightly to make it more dense, or shear it to fit confined areas. Numerous cultivars and varieties exist, so choose one adapted to your region. The variety *Ribes aureum* var. *aureum* is adapted to rocky, sandy soils and grows well with Apache plume, mountain mahogany, Fremont barberry, and starleaf Mexican orange. At lower elevations, golden current needs regular, deep watering in the summer. Wildlife devour the sweet fruit, which makes a fine jelly.

Ribes aureum fruit

Ribes aureum

Rosa woodsii
Wood's rose

Rosa woodsii flowers

Native Distribution: foothills, streamsides, Ponderosa and Aspen woodlands; 3,500–10,000 feet; Arizona to Texas, north into Canada.
Landscape Zone: 3–7.
Size: 3–6 feet tall and wide.
Leaves: deciduous.
Flower: June–August; 1–4 inches in diameter, 5 pink petals, lasts one day.
Fruit: fall; deep red rose hips.
Soil: adaptable; well draining.
Exposure: full sun, partial shade.
Temperature Tolerance: high to medium heat tolerance, cold hardy to −20°F.
Water: drought tolerant.
Propagation: Fall-sown seeds, cold stratify for two months.
Profile: When pruned into a rounded bush and covered with pink flowers with showy yellow stamens, Wood's rose adds class to any garden setting. You can also let this aggressive, thicket-forming, rhizomatous bush sprawl for a wildscape look. The fragrant flowers and deep green leaves accent pools and patios, landscape islands, and foundation plantings. As a mid-garden show plant, it will stand out against a background of fernbush, juniper, silktassel, and New Mexican privet. For a dramatic contrast, mix it with gray-foliated buffaloberry, chamisa, or winterfat; or, team it up with the white-flowering cliff fendler-bush, Apache plume, or manzanita. In the spring, new canes emerge red and are lined with prickles. Flowers develop on old wood.

Rosa woodsii

Salvia greggii
Autumn sage or cherry sage

Salvia greggii

Native Distribution: rocky soils, sunny slopes; 2,000–8,000 feet; Texas, Mexico.

Landscape Zone: 2–4.

Size: 1–3 feet.

Leaves: semi-evergreen.

Flower: spring–winter; clusters of 1-inch, red, purple, pink, or white flowers.

Soil: adaptable; well draining.

Exposure: full sun, partial shade.

Temperature Tolerance: limbs cold hardy to 15°F, root hardy to 0°F.

Water: drought tolerant.

Propagation: spring-planted seeds, softwood and semi-hardwood tip cuttings.

Profile: Once again, I am including a Chihuahuan Desert native from Texas because of its widespread use in Southwest landscapes. Autumn sage is popular as far north as Prescott and Albuquerque, but to survive the torrid summer heat of Phoenix, it needs regular water and shade from the afternoon sun. Rosy-red, tube-shaped blooms cover this flamboyant plant from June through November. The brilliant 1-inch flowers bloom profusely after rains or when water is available. The flowers provide a striking contrast against the bright green, aromatic leaves. You can use this densely foliated, low-growing shrub as a natural border hedge to add color to walks, drives, and walls. When planted in mass, autumn sage spreads a spectacular blanket of color across your yard. As a xeriscape garden accent, it makes a colorful companion for joint fir, red yucca, nolina, and agaves. Keep this *Salvia* densely foliated by trimming before spring growth, with severe pruning every few years. The plants lose their leaves in freezing weather,

Salvia greggii flowers

and at higher elevations they grow as an annual. You can choose varieties with red, pink, purple, and white blossoms. Hybrids with other *Salvia* species are often called *Salvia greggii* "types." Hummingbirds love the flowers.

Senna wislizeni (Cassia wislizeni)
Shrubby senna

Native Distribution: dry hills, rocky soils; 3,000–5,000 feet; Arizona to west Texas, Mexico.
Landscape Zone: 1–2.
Size: 4–6 feet.
Leaves: deciduous, compound, 1/2–1 1/2 inches long with 1/4-inch leaflets.
Flower: May–September; 4-inch clusters of yellow, pea-like blooms.
Fruit: 3- to 6-inch-long bean pods.
Soil: adaptable; limestone, igneous, well draining.
Exposure: full sun, partial shade.
Temperature Tolerance: heat tolerant, cold hardy to 0–10°F.
Water: drought tolerant, 12 inches/year.

Propagation: fresh seed, semi-hardwood cuttings.
Profile: The masses of showy, bright yellow flowers and contrasting dark green leaves, as well as the long blooming season, make shrubby senna a colorful choice for hot, arid landscapes. You know it's hardy because it's native to the hottest, driest regions of the Chihuahuan Desert. Its rigid, spreading limbs, dense branching, and moderate size make it a good background shrub, although it loses it leaves in the winter—not ideal for a specimen plant. Group it with a mixed planting of compatible species, such as sumacs, red yucca, barberries, acacias, and mimosas. To develop a compact shape, shrubby senna will require a winter trim before it leafs out in the spring. Reportedly, allowing the soil to completely dry between deep watering will stimulate profuse blooming.

Senna wislizeni flowers

Shepherdia argentea
Silver buffaloberry

Shepherdia argentea

Native Distribution: moist soil along water, Chaparral and Pinyon-Juniper woodlands; 3,000–7,500 feet; New Mexico to California, north to Canada.
Landscape Zone: 3–7.
Size: 6–10 feet tall.
Leaves: deciduous, 1–2 inches long, silver.
Fruit: summer; 1/4 inch, edible, red to yellow drupes on females.
Soil: adaptable; well draining.
Exposure: full sun, partial shade.
Temperature Tolerance: cold hardy.

Shepherdia argentea

Water: drought tolerant, 12 inches/year minimum.
Propagation: fresh or stratified seeds.
Profile: The ornate, 2-inch silver leaves give this shrub both its name and its landscape value. Silver buffaloberry makes a beautiful background plant, and since it forms thickets in the wild, it is great for mass plantings and erosion control. You can plant silver buffaloberries close together and trim them into a hedge, or put them in mixed plantings to contrast with the green foliage of pinyons, mountain mahogany, manzanita, and shrubby cinquefoil. You'll need both male and female plants to get the colorful summer fruit. Wildlife enjoy the berries, which make a tart jelly. You can use *Shepherdia argentea* as a native substitute for the all-too-common Russian olive (*Elaeagnus angustifolia*). The roundleaf buffaloberry, *S. rotundifolia*, is a compact, 3-foot shrub that occurs at 5,000 to 8,000 feet and has excellent potential for higher elevation landscapes.

Simmondsia chinensis
Jojoba

Native Distribution: washes, rocky slopes, chaparral and foothills; 1,500–5,000 feet; southwestern Arizona to California, Mexico.
Landscape Zone: 1.
Size: 3–6 feet tall, 10 feet wide.
Leaves: evergreen, 1 1/2 inches long, grayish green.
Fruit: summer; 1-inch, acorn-like nuts on females.
Soil: sandy, rocky, well draining.
Exposure: full sun.
Temperature Tolerance: heat tolerant, twig damage at 20°F.
Water: drought tolerant, 10 inches/year minimum.
Propagation: spring-planted seeds.
Profile: Dense, grayish-green, leathery leaves cover this rounded shrub all the way to the ground, making it ideal for a hedge or screen. Space jojoba plants 2 feet apart for a clipped hedge that resembles boxwood, or 4 feet apart for a background or screen planting. With a symmetrical shape and ornate paired leaves, jojoba provides year-round foliage as a specimen or a component of a mixed planting. Combine with damanita, dogweed, desert marigold, and blackfoot daisy for foreground color and with palo verde, huisache, ironwood, and tree yuccas for background structure. You'll need both male and female plants to produce the fruit, which have become commercially important because of the fruit's high oil content. Jojoba grows slowly, but requires no maintenance or extra water. Frost kills the seedlings of this low-desert plant. The cultivar 'Vista' is a smaller, compact version.

Above: *Simmondsia chinensis*

Below: *Simmondsia chinensis* hedge

Sophora secundiflora
Texas mountain laurel or mescal bean

Native Distribution: limestone hills; to 5,000 feet; New Mexico to central and south Texas, Mexico.
Landscape Zone: 1–2.
Size: shrubby to 15 feet.
Leaves: evergreen.
Flower: March–April; cascades of fragrant purple flowers.
Fruit: woody pods with poisonous red seeds.
Soil: adaptable; alkaline, well draining.
Exposure: full sun, partial shade.
Temperature Tolerance: heat tolerant, cold hardy to 10°F.
Water: drought tolerant, 14 inches/year minimum.
Propagation: scarified seeds.
Profile: Many landscapers consider Texas mountain laurel one of the ten best ornamental shrubs in the Sun Belt. In March and April, showers of vibrant purple flowers cover the plant and perfume the air with the scent of grape Kool-Aid. Its compact, upright shape—and the striking contrast between the deep purple flowers and shiny green leaves—make this shrub eye-catching as either a specimen plant or a component of a mixed planting. It colorfully accents a patio or pool decor, whether in a small landscape garden or a large planter. You can prune (but not shear) it into an informal hedge. Since it's an understory tree in nature, it will grow in filtered shade, though not as fast. Extra water speeds its growth, while cool summers impede it. A late spring freeze will nip the flowers. Even small plants bloom, and with time, Texas mountain laurel develops into an ornate small tree. The red seeds, known as mescal beans, are deadly, but fortunately, the hard seed coat usually prevents children from chewing them.

Sophora secundiflora

Tecoma stans

Yellow trumpet flower or yellow bells

Native Distribution: rocky slopes, desert washes, scrubland, chaparral, 2,000–5,500 feet; southern Arizona to Texas; Mexico through South America.

Landscape Zone: 1–2.

Size: 6–15 feet.

Leaves: frost deciduous, bright green, 6 inches long, narrow.

Flower: May–October; clusters of 4-inch, yellow flowers.

Fruit: 6-inch-long capsules.

Soil: limestone, loam, sand, well draining.

Exposure: full sun.

Temperature Tolerance: heat tolerant, limb damage at 28°F, freezes to ground at 20°F.

Water: drought tolerant, 12 inches/year minimum.

Propagation: fresh seeds, semi-hardwood cuttings.

Profile: True to its common names, this shrub has gorgeous trumpet- or bell-shaped flowers, making it one of the most beautiful landscaping plants in the Southwest. Dense clusters of lemon-yellow flowers cover the ends of the branches. With profuse blooms and a long flowering period, *Tecoma stans* makes a multiseason accent for entry gardens, courtyards, pools, and patios. It brightens corner plantings, enlivens walls and fences, and adds foliage and flower interest to landscape islands. Use this versatile shrub as a colorful mass, screen, or background plant, or if you want the formal look, shear it into a hedge. It complements evergreens such as jojoba, hopbush, Texas mountain laurel, and evergreen sumac. Trumpet flower freezes to the ground in mild winters, but recovers rapidly to form a 4- to 5-foot-tall shrub. Specimens tend to become upright as they grow larger. Remove dried seedpods and prune dead branches before spring growth begins. A number of hybrids and cultivars exist that vary in flower color, size, and frost hardiness. 'Orange Jubilee' has orange flowers and produces very few seed-pods. 'Gold Star' is a dwarf clone that grows 4 feet tall and 3 to 4 feet wide. Hummingbirds love trumpet flowers.

Tecoma stans

Tecoma stans flowers

Vauquelinia californica
Arizona rosewood

Native Distribution: desert canyons, chaparral, and mountains; 2,500–5,000 feet; Arizona, New Mexico, Mexico.
Landscape Zone: 2–6.
Size: 6–20 feet.
Leaves: evergreen, 2 inches long, narrow.
Flower: May–June; 3-inch clusters of white flowers.
Soil: adaptable; well draining.
Exposure: full sun, partial shade.
Temperature Tolerance: heat tolerant, cold hardy to 15°F.
Water: drought tolerant, 12 inches/year minimum.
Propagation: fresh seeds, softwood and semi-hardwood cuttings.
Profile: Arizona rosewood, a member of the rose family, has an erect profile, dense evergreen foliage, and long, narrow, sharply toothed, dark green leaves that cover the plant to the ground. Planted alone, it makes a large specimen shrub suitable for corner or background plantings. It's large enough to provide a visual screen when planted in

Vauquelinia californica flowers

mass. You can trim Arizona rosewood into a shaped shrub or small tree, but it loses its character. The slender, serrated leaves and abundant flower clusters give an ornamental accent to entry walks, patios, and poolside gardens. In companion plantings, the lustrous green color and narrow width of the leaves naturally complement desert willow and yellow trumpet flower. It's compatible in appearance and growth habitat with chokecherry, barberries, and fragrant

Vauquelinia californica

ash. Like many species adapted to drought and poor soil, Arizona rosewood grows slowly, but it speeds up once its root system becomes established if given extra water. A similar Texas species, Chisos rosewood (*Vauquelinia corymbosa*) is often available.

Viguiera stenoloba
Skeleton-leaf goldeneye

Native Distribution: sandy soils, rocky hills; 2,000–6,000 feet; southern New Mexico to Texas, Mexico.
Landscape Zone: 1–3.
Size: 2–4 feet.
Leaves: persistent to evergreen, 1–2 1/2 inch long, threadlike.
Flower: June–October; 1 to 2 inches, yellow, daisy-like.
Soil: adaptable; well draining.
Exposure: full sun, partial shade.
Temperature Tolerance: extremely heat tolerant, cold hardy to 10°F.
Water: drought tolerant, 12 inches/year minimum.
Propagation: fresh seeds, softwood tip cuttings.
Profile: Golden flowers blanket this low-growing, rounded sub-shrub in the summer and even more profusely in the fall. The mass of lemon-yellow blooms on 8-inch stems provides a pleasing contrast with the bright green, thread-like foliage. This bushy, long-flowering plant makes a colorful addition to informal perennial gardens and slope plantings for much of the year. You can use it as a border plant or a foreground accent in landscape islands. It is compatible in size with the gray-foliated brittlebush, chamisa, and mariola, and with the green-leafed star-leaf Mexican orange, joint fir, and small yuccas and agaves. To keep it compact and neat in appearance, remove the barren flower stalks after flowering and trim it back. Don't despair if it freezes to the ground—it's root hardy. Two

Viguiera stenoloba

similar goldeneyes, *Viguiera parishii* and *V. dentata*, have the same growth habit but larger leaves.

Yucca baccata

Native Distribution: throughout the Southwest.

Landscape Zone: 1–7, depending on species.

Size: 1–3 feet tall.

Leaves: evergreen, sword-like.

Flower: spring–summer; large clusters of white flowers on tall stalks.

Fruit: leathery capsules, 1–4 inches long.

Trunkless *Yucca* Species

Soil: variable, well draining.

Exposure: full sun.

Temperature Tolerance: cold hardy.

Water: drought tolerant.

Propagation: fresh seeds.

Profile: Small, shrubby yuccas give your landscape a distinctive Southwestern flavor. Their height adapts them to foregrounds and limited areas, such as patio and pool gardens or corner plantings. The blade-like leaves add variety to cactus or xeriscape gardens. Small yuccas make ideal accent plants, and when they send up their stalks of flowers, they become the center of attention. Like their larger counterparts, these yuccas have needle-tipped leaves, so don't plant them near play or walk areas. All the trunkless yuccas in the Southwest have great landscape merit and make great companion plants for agaves, chollas, and prickly pears.

Be sure to choose a species adapted to your elevation and landscape zone. Narrowleaf yucca (*Yucca angustissima*), with 1/2-inch-wide leaves, grows in north- and central-western New Mexico and bordering Arizona at elevations of 2,700 to 7,500 feet. Banana yucca (*Y. baccata*) has heavy, stiff, 3-foot-long leaves and is abundant in deserts and mountains. It grows at 3,000 to 8,000 feet and is cold hardy to −20°F. Navajo yucca, *Y. baileyi* var. *navajoa* (*Y. navajoa*) forms dense clumps with leaves 1/4 inch wide and 9 inches long; it grows at 4,500- to 7,500-foot elevations. Small soapweed yucca, *Y. glauca* (*Y. angustifolia*), has leaves 1/2 inch wide to 3 feet long. It grows in grassy plains from central New Mexico and Arizona into Wyoming at 5,000 to 7,000 feet and survives to −35°F. The creamy flowers cover the 4-foot stalks.

Tree *Yucca* Species

Yucca elata

Native Distribution: throughout the Southwest, Mexico.

Landscape Zone: 1–6, depending on species.

Size: 3–20 feet tall.

Leaves: evergreen, sword-like.

Flower: spring–summer; large clusters of white flowers on tall stalks.

Fruit: leathery capsules 1–4 inches long.

Soil: variable, well draining.

Exposure: full sun.

Temperature Tolerance: cold hardy.

Water: drought tolerant.

Propagation: fresh seeds.

Profile: With their large multiple branches and tall flower stalks, tree yuccas gracefully dominate almost any

landscape design. If you plant one in your xeriscape garden, make it the center of interest. Several planted together create a dramatic setting. Because of their stiff, needle-tipped leaves, tree yuccas should not be planted near walks and play areas. They grow slowly and may take decades to develop their characteristic trunk. Large specimens are dug from the wild, which unfortunately has decimated some native populations. All have the same general habitat requirements and landscape applications.

Two tree yuccas stand out as premier landscape specimens suitable for home and commercial designs. Soaptree yucca, *Yucca elata*, reaches 8 to 12 feet tall and has picturesque, symmetrical rosettes of narrow leaves that crown the trunks and branches. It grows at elevations of 1,500 to 6,000 feet. The popular blue yucca, *Y. rigida*, is a native of northern Mexico at 3,000 to 5,500 feet. It has a single trunk crowned with a compact rosette of stiff, 3-foot-long, bluish leaves. It's

Yucca rigida

cold hardy to 5°F. For a less refined look, plant mountain or Schott's yucca (*Y. schottii*), which grows 6 to 20 feet tall, usually without branching, and is cold hardy to −10°F. It grows naturally at elevations of 4,000 to 7,000 feet. Mohave yucca, *Y. schidigera*, reaches 9 to 15 feet in height with multiple arms and grows from deserts to the edge of the Pinyon-Juniper woodlands at 2,000 to 5,000 feet. The large-scale Joshua tree, *Y. brevifolia*, grows 30 feet tall and 3 feet in diameter with multiple branches. Naturally occurring at elevations of 2,000 to 3,500 feet, it is suitable primarily for parks and campus landscaping.

Wildflowers

Abronia fragrans

Abronia fragrans
Sweet sand verbena

Native Distribution: sandy soils, roadsides, plains, hills; Arizona to Texas, north to Canada.
Landscape Zone: 1–6.
Size: 1–2 feet.
Perennial.
Flower: spring through late summer; 3-inch round clusters, white, aromatic.
Soil: sand, well draining.
Exposure: full sun.
Temperature Tolerance: cold tolerant.
Water: drought tolerant.
Planting: fall-sown seeds; in spring, scarify seed with sandpaper or soak in water 6–8 hours.

Profile: Give *Abronia fragrans* plenty of room to sprawl, and it will cover a sandy area with dense, snowballs of white flowers. You can plant it in mass for a showy spring groundcover, or in the foreground of a perennial garden. The abundant flowers bloom on short stalks and fill your garden with the scent of vanilla. For an interesting effect, consider a mixed planting with sand verbena, *Abronia villosa*, a Southwest annual with large, fragrant clusters of purple to rose-pink flowers.

Achillea millefolium var. *occidentalis*

Achillea millefolium var. occidentalis
Western yarrow or milfoil

Flower: April–July; round clusters of white or yellow flowers.
Soil: adaptable.
Exposure: full sun, partial shade.
Water: moderately drought tolerant.
Planting: fall-sown seeds.
Profile: The yarrow's rosette of delicate, fernlike leaves looks like lace spread on the ground. In moist soil, the plant spreads by underground rhizomes and can form an attractive groundcover. From spring through the summer, a cluster of snowy flowers atop a slender stalk crowns the basal rosette. Crush a leaf, and you will smell the pungent volatile oils that have made yarrow an historically important medicinal plant. You can add color to your perennial garden by choosing the yellow-flowered 'Moonshine' cultivar, or a rose-colored cultivar. Yarrows planted in full sun may need extra water.

Native Distribution: widespread across United States.
Landscape Zone: 1–7.
Size: 12–18 inches.
Perennial.

Achillea millefolium flowers

Aquilegia chrysantha
Golden columbine

Aquilegia chrysantha

Native Distribution: moist soils in canyons and mountains above 3,000 feet; Arizona, New Mexico, Texas, Colorado, Utah.
Landscape Zone: 3–7.
Size: 1–3 feet.
Perennial.
Flower: April–September; yellow, 3–5 inches long with spur.
Soil: loam, well draining.
Exposure: shade, partial shade.
Water: requires moisture.
Planting: fresh seeds in fall, stratified seeds in spring.
Profile: Protect this delicate plant from full sun or arid locations, and you'll marvel at the abundant golden flowers and fine-textured foliage. The flowers waving in the breeze seem to float on a cloud of light green leaves. In rich, well-draining soil, columbines reach 3 feet high and wide, with scores of blooms. Columbines make a colorful perennial border or provide a splash of color for an entryway. They're most dramatic when cascading over an accent boulder, wall, or fountain, similar to its natural habitat of porous boulders and seeping cliffs.

The Southwest is blessed with yellow-, red-, and blue-and-white-flowered species of columbines. All make colorful specimen plants or accents. At low elevations and hot climates, be sure they get enough water in the summer or they will go dormant—or worse, die. However, high humidity and waterlogged roots are just as deadly. Nurseries carry the Southwest native red columbine, *Aquilegia triternata*, and the blue-and-white Rocky Mountain columbine, *A. caerulea*.

Asclepias tuberosa
Butterfly weed

Asclepias tuberosa

Asclepias tuberosa flowers

Native Distribution: prairies, open woods, mountains; 4,000–8,000 feet; California to Texas, through the Midwest and eastern half of the United States, Canada.
Landscape Zone: 1–7.
Size: 1–3 feet.
Perennial.
Flower: April–September; clusters of orange-and-red flowers.
Soil: adaptable; well draining.
Exposure: full sun, partial shade.
Water: drought tolerant.
Planting: fall-sown seeds.
Profile: The brilliant clusters of multicolored flowers crowning the stout, waving stalks make butterfly weed an impressive background accent in your perennial garden. Or you can mass plant them in a corner plot or against a wall. I planted mine just outside my window so I could see the monarchs and other butterflies that flock to the vivid blooms all summer. Mine bloomed the first year from seed, but others report that the plants spend several years developing their taproot before flowering. The deep taproot allows the plant to survive drought conditions, but it needs regular water to maintain flowers. Unlike other milkweeds, butterfly weed has clear sap.

Baileya multiradiata
Desert marigold

Native Distribution: sandy and gravelly desert soils; below 6,000 feet; California to Texas, Mexico.
Landscape Zone: 1–6.
Size: 1 1/2 feet.
Annual or short-lived perennial.
Flower: anytime; 1 to 2 inches diameter, yellow, daisy-like.
Soil: adaptable; well draining.
Exposure: full sun, radiated heat.
Temperature Tolerance: damaged below 32°F.
Water: drought tolerant.
Planting: fall-sown seeds.
Profile: This wildflower of the low deserts rivals the most pampered garden variety for beauty and showmanship. Its mound of lemon-yellow flowers grow on 1- to 2-foot stems above the grayish green, woolly foliage, presenting a striking color combination, especially in a cactus garden or mixed planting. It loves radiated heat and is perfect for an accent by a boulder, masonry wall, or

Baileya multiradiata

rock garden. The fall-sown seeds form a small basal rosette of leaves, with the bright bouquets of flowers appearing about three months after planting and continuing until frost. For profuse blooming, water weekly if rains fail. The flowers reseed themselves readily, allowing for year-round flowers in mild winters. The only maintenance required is to remove the spent flower heads.

Callirhoe involucrata
Winecup

Native Distribution: sandy, gravelly soils; throughout Arizona, New Mexico, and Texas, north to North Dakota.
Landscape Zone: 1–6.
Perennial.
Size: 1 foot tall, 3-foot sprawling stems.
Leaves: divided into 5–7 finger-like lobes.
Flower: February–July; 2 inches wide, purple-to-red.
Soil: adaptable; well draining.
Exposure: full sun, partial shade.
Water: drought tolerant.
Planting: scarified, fall-sown seeds, rake into soil.
Profile: With water, this proficient bloomer will decorate your yard with bouquets of gorgeous flowers until the heat of summer burns it back. The dense array of sprawling stems makes a colorful groundcover or mass planting. For colorscapes, mix winecups with

yellow-blooming evening primroses, desert marigolds, and Mexican gold poppies and with blue-flowered flax, prairie gentian, and verbenas. An accent patch will beautify a landscape island of shrubs, and it adds brilliant colors to a perennial border. Let the trailing stems spill over a wall for a dramatic effect. Wherever you plant a winecup, give it plenty of elbow room to spread. It overwinters as a small rosette of leaves.

Above: *Callirhoe involucrata*
Left: *Callirhoe involucrata* flowers

Calochortus kennedyi
Desert mariposa lily
Calochortus nuttallii
Sego lily

Native Distribution: *Calochortus kennedyi*: deserts and grasslands; below 5,000 feet; Arizona, California, Utah, Nevada. *Calochortus nuttallii*: sagebrush valleys, open slopes, pine forests; 4,500–8,000 feet; Arizona, New Mexico north to Canada.
Landscape Zone: *C. nuttallii*: 2–7; *C. kennedyi*: 1–4.
Size: 8–18 inches.
Perennial, bulb.
Flower: 3 petals, 2–3 inches wide; *C. nuttallii*: May–July, white or yellow; *C. kennedyi*: March–May, red, lavender, or orange with purple/black center.
Soil: adaptable, well draining.

Exposure: full sun.
Water: drought tolerant.
Planting: fall-sown seeds; may take two years to bloom.
Profile: With such spectacular flowers, it's no wonder that Utah chose the sego lily as its state flower. Numerous species of sego lilies grow throughout the Southwest, but *Calochortus kennedyi* and *C. nuttallii* are the most common. Both species are threatened or endangered in much of their range, so don't transplant one from the wild. The delicate blooms seem to burst from parched soils like jewels scattered across the countryside. Desert mariposa lily can cover the desert floor in April with rich orange-red blooms. Be sure your flower bed has perfect drainage, and then wait to be delighted when these treasures burst from the ground. Use the plants to soften cacti and boulder accents or at the base of a palo verde as a highlight. For a gorgeous mid-spring display of sunrise colors, group them with Mexican gold poppy, paintbrush, and desert marigold. The golden mariposa lily, *C. aureus* (*C. nuttallii* var. *aureus*), has brilliant golden-yellow flowers. The walnut-sized bulbs of mariposa lilies are readily available commercially.

Calochortus nuttallii

Calochortus nuttallii

Castilleja species
Indian paintbrush

Native Distribution: sandy, loam soils, desert grasslands to alpine meadows; more than two dozen species in Arizona and New Mexico.
Landscape Zone: 1–7.
Size: 6- to 12-inch-tall clumps.
Annual.
Flower: March–September; spikes of showy red bracts enclosing small flowers.
Soil: adaptable; well draining.
Exposure: full sun.
Water: drought tolerant.
Planting: fall-sown seeds, rake into loose topsoil; wet winter increases germination.
Profile: Your colorscaped garden will get rave reviews with a mixed planting of paintbrushes, lupines, and penstemons, each complementing the vertical profiles and intensifying the vivid colors of the other. Indian paintbrush's upright bouquets of blooming spikes make a colorful foreground for corner and courtyard gardens or a border accent. Mass plant for eye-catching drama and to provide forage for hummingbirds. Two dozen species, including yellow and purple variations, grow across the Southwest, ranging from low and high deserts to mountain meadows. Obtain seeds of species that are adapted to your habitat and climate. Another consideration: Most paintbrushes are partially parasitic on grass roots, which makes them difficult to establish from seed and almost impossible to transplant from the wild. Ask your nursery for seeds of non-parasitic species, such as owl's clover paintbrush, *Castilleja exserta*. Otherwise, purchase a seed pack that contains grama grass as a host.

Above: *Castilleja exserta*

Left: *Castilleja scabrida*

127

Cleome serrulata
Rocky mountain beeplant

Native Distribution: roadsides, open range, foothills, disturbed soils; 4,500–7,000 feet; Arizona, New Mexico, widespread west of Mississippi River.
Landscape Zone: 1–7.
Size: 2–5 feet.
Annual.
Flower: June–September; clusters of pink to purple flowers with feathery, 2- to 3-inch-long stamens.
Soil: adaptable; well draining.
Exposure: full sun.
Water: drought tolerant.
Planting: spring- or fall-sown seeds, self-sows readily; copious seeds in 2- to 3-inch-long pods.
Profile: Plant one of these aggressive annuals, and next year you'll have dozens. Sow the seeds, or transplant the seedlings, in the background of your garden, along a fence, or as a border to a drive, and you will enjoy dazzling pink clouds of flowers until first frost. The spectacular airy flowers

bloom upward along the stalks for a long season of color. Numerous pencil-thin pods form below, each with scores of tiny seeds, so gather and save for next year's planting. In my yard, rain washed some seeds down the drive, and the hardy plants sprouted in cracks of the street pavement. No wonder they blanket abandoned fields and thrive in vacant lots. Doves relish the seeds, and butterflies the flowers. A yellow-flowering species, yellow beeplant (*Cleome lutea*) is also available.

Above: *Cleome serrulata*

Left: *Cleome lutea*

Coreopsis tinctoria
Golden wave or plains coreopsis

Native Distribution: moist soils and roadsides; throughout the United States, Canada.
Landscape Zone: 1–7.
Size: 1–2 feet.
Annual.
Flower: February–December; 1-inch, yellow heads with reddish-brown center.
Soil: adaptable; well draining.
Exposure: full sun.
Water: drought tolerant.
Planting: early-spring-sown seeds; in areas with mild winters, late-summer- and fall-sown seeds for winter and spring flowers. Reseeds itself readily.
Profile: Mass plant this bright flower in a naturalized area and, as the name implies, you'll have waves of golden blooms dancing in the spring breezes. It flowers periodically after its spring burst of color, depending on the rains. Golden wave coreopsis competes well

Coreopsis tinctoria flowers

with grasses and reseeds itself, making it a popular component of meadow mixes, along with paintbrush, Indian blanket, lemon mint, black-eyed Susan, and Mexican hat. It thrives in hot, dry areas and spots with reflected heat from drives and walls, but it might need supplemental water to sustain a long blooming season. Several varieties are available, including a dwarf, a red-and-yellow, and a double-flowered selection. If you want a long-lived perennial, plant the all-yellow lanceleaf coreopsis, *Coreopsis lanceolata*.

Coreopsis lanceolata

Datura wrightii (Datura meteloides)
Sacred datura or jimsonweed

Native Distribution: loose sand, bottomlands; 1,000–7,000 feet; common from the western United States to Maine.
Landscape Zone: 1–6.
Size: 2–4 feet.
Perennial.
Flower: May–November; 6–8 inches long, white, funnel shaped.
Soil: adaptable; deep, well drained.
Exposure: full sun, partial shade.
Water: drought tolerant.
Planting: spring- or fall-sown seeds.
Profile: A dozen delicate white flowers may cover this large mounding, spreading plant in the morning, before the midday sun causes them to fold.

The snow-white flowers contrast vividly against the dark green foliage. As with many fragrant white-flowered plants, datura blooms open at night and are pollinated by moths. Plant this vigorous grower where it has plenty of room to expand, because each year it gets bigger and bushier. With its long blooming season, you'll see flowers accompanied by the unusual fruit—a 1- to 2-inch spine-covered capsule. The non-native annual *Datura stramonium* is prized for its purple flowers. All parts of the *Datura* plant are poisonous. Because of the plant's hallucinogenic properties, shamans have long considered the plant sacred.

Datura wrightii

Delphinium parishii
Desert larkspur

Native Distribution: desert hills, mesas, washes; below 5,000 feet; Arizona, Nevada, Utah, California.
Landscape Zone: 1–6.
Size: 1–4 feet.
Perennial.
Flower: February–May; spikes of pale blue, 1-inch flowers with spurs.
Soil: adaptable; well draining.
Exposure: full sun, partial shade.
Water: drought tolerant.
Planting: fall- or spring-sown seeds.
Profile: Larkspurs are old-time garden favorites. I can remember them in my grandmother's yard, waving in the breeze with hollyhocks. They're still a favorite, and our native species is just as attractive as the domestic garden

varieties. The spurred flowers crowd the erect stalk of each plant. Since each plant has only one flowering stem, you'll need to plant them about 6 inches apart to get a thick display. Sow the seeds and thin after germination. You can plant an accent patch or use them along a border. Larkspurs go dormant in the summer, so for all-season color, plant them with summer and fall bloomers, such as mealyblue sage, blazing star, prairie gentian, and Indian blanket. You'll find these perky flowers in most meadow mixes. More than a dozen species and subspecies of *Delphinium* grow across the Southwest, so finding seeds for your garden shouldn't be a problem.

Delphinium parishii

Dodecatheon pulchellum

Dodecatheon pulchellum
Shooting star

Native Distribution: moist meadows, seep springs, stream sides; 6,500–9,500 feet; New Mexico to California, north into Canada.
Landscape Zone: 6–7.
Size: 1–2 feet.
Perennial herb.
Flower: June–August; red to blue, 3/4 inch long, 4–5 lobed petals swept back to show yellow center.
Soil: moist, rich, well draining.
Exposure: cool semi-shade.
Water: regular watering required.
Planting: fall-sown seeds; in spring, cold stratify for 30 days, or root division.
Profile: If you live in Flagstaff, Sedona, Taos, or Santa Fe and you have an alpine garden, you will want this dramatic little flower for sure. When the rocket-shaped flowers start blooming atop one-foot stalks, you'll drop to your knees for a closer look. Spread the seeds freely and a squadron of red flowers will dazzle your summer garden. Mix with crimson and golden monkey flowers, spiderworts, and violets for a delightful colorscape. Though they require a humid microhabitat, shooting stars grow easily in cool, moist, humus-rich soil. Nurseries sell seeds and pots of several cultivars and similar species.

Engelmannia peristenia (Engelmannia pinnatifida)
Cutleaf daisy

Engelmannia peristenia

Native Distribution: rocky, sandy soils; New Mexico to Texas, north to Kansas and Colorado, Mexico.
Landscape Zone: 1–6.
Size: 1–3 feet.
Perennial.
Flower: spring, decreasing through fall; 1-inch yellow heads.
Soil: adaptable; well draining.
Exposure: full sun, partial shade.
Water: drought tolerant.
Planting: fall-sown seeds, transplanted winter rosette.
Profile: This is no timid plant, so give it room to show off in your garden. Cutleaf daisy bursts into bloom in early spring and continues all summer. Its deep taproot makes it drought tolerant, but a little extra water will keep it blooming longer. The dense rosette of deeply lobed leaves has an ornate appeal, and the flowers form a mound of bright yellow blooms on 1- to 2-foot stalks. Use cutleaf daisies as accent plants or borders, massed in the outskirts of your garden, or as part of a naturalized lawn. The flowers curl under during the heat of the day.

Eriogonum fasciculatum
Flat-top buckwheat or California buckwheat

Eriogonum fasciculatum

Native Distribution: desert flats, slopes, washes; 1,000–4,500 feet; Arizona, California, Nevada, Utah.
Landscape Zone: 1–6.
Size: shrubby, 1–2 feet tall, to 4 feet wide.
Perennial evergreen.
Flower: March–November; white to pink, 1/8 inch wide, in dense terminal clusters.
Soil: adaptable; well draining.
Exposure: full sun.
Temperature Tolerance: heat tolerant, hardy to 15°F.

Water: drought tolerant.
Planting: seeds or cuttings.
Profile: Buckwheats are great additions for your butterfly garden, and they are attractive long-bloomers for xeriscape beds. Flat heads of dense white flowers cover the shrub-like mounds from early spring through fall; in Phoenix, a summertime drink encourages prolonged blooming. The tiny, dark green leaves have a woolly covering underneath, which adds year-round visual interest to the plant. To maintain its ornamental appearance, *Eriogonum fasciculatum* should be cut back in mid-winter to encourage new, dense growth. With its mounding shape and 6-inch-long flower stalks, flat-top buckwheat makes a good companion plant for the more vertical mealycup blue sage, paintbrushes, Coulter's lupine, and desert marigold. Four varieties of *E. fasciculatum* grow across the West. The Mojave buckwheat, var. *foliolosum*, reportedly is more drought tolerant and a better bloomer than the straight species.

Eriogonum umbellatum
Sulphur flower buckwheat

Eriogonum umbellatum

Native Distribution: mesas, mountain hillsides; 5,000–9,000 feet; New Mexico to California, north to Washington.
Landscape Zone: 5–7.
Size: mounding, 1–2 feet tall and wide.

Perennial evergreen.
Flower: April–September; yellow, 1/8 inch wide, in dense terminal clusters on 4- to 6-inch-long stalks.
Soil: adaptable; well draining.
Exposure: full sun.
Temperature Tolerance: cold hardy.
Water: drought tolerant.
Planting: seeds or cuttings.
Profile: This mile-high member of the wide-ranging buckwheat genus dazzles any garden with its display of buttery blossoms. Umbrella-like clusters of yellow flowers protrude above the green vegetation on short stalks. The flowers tend to turn rusty as they age, bringing a variety of hues to a mixed planting. Sulphur flower looks great on the border of a raised bed or as a color accent to chamisa, Apache plume, winterfat, or buffaloberry. It is perfectly adapted for a high-altitude xeriscape garden and adds a soft touch to yucca, agave, and beargrass. Its long blooming period makes it a good component of a colorscape design.

Eschscholzia californica subsp. mexicana (Eschscholzia mexicana)
Mexican gold poppy

Eschscholzia californica subsp.
Mexicana flowers

Native Distribution: desert plains, foothills, mesas; below 5,000 feet; California to Texas, north to Utah, Mexico.
Landscape Zone: 1–6.
Size: 6–18 inches tall.
Annual.
Flower: February–May; 2–3 inches diameter, golden yellow.
Soil: adaptable; well draining.
Exposure: full sun.
Water: drought tolerant, 6–8 inches/year minimum.
Planting: fall- or winter-sown seeds.
Profile: This spectacular flower blankets the Southwestern deserts with gold when winter rains have been sufficient. If you have a bright, sunny garden spot, you'll want to find a place for these gorgeous poppies in your yard. The large clumps of green foliage and vibrant flowers add an eye-catching accent to any landscape garden. They are most beautiful when planted in mass, but you can use this popular annual as a bedding plant or in mixtures. The delicate texture of the lacy foliage provides a pleasing complement to the brilliantly colored petals. Occasionally, pink or white mutants will spring up. Mexican gold poppies reseed well, but for heavy cover, you may need to sow additional seeds until a good seed bank is established in the soil. For colorscaping, plant summer-blooming species such as prairie gentian, penstemons, blue flax, and desert marigold.

Eschscholzia californica subsp. mexicana

Eustoma exaltatum subsp. *russellianum*
(*Eustoma grandiflorum*)
Prairie gentian or tulip gentian

Native Distribution: along rivers and streams, meadows below 5,000 feet; California to Florida, Texas north into Canada, Mexico.
Landscape Zone: 2–6.
Size: 1–2 feet.
Annual or short-lived perennial.
Flower: June–September; blue, 2–3 inches diameter.
Soil: adaptable; moist, poor or well draining.
Exposure: full sun, partial shade.
Water: moderately drought tolerant.
Planting: fall-sown seeds on top of soil.

Profile: Many botanists still classify this spectacular flower by the species name *grandiflorum*. Pay special attention to any plant called *grandiflorum*: it means large flowers. With their gorgeous tulip-shaped blossoms, prairie gentian will be the hit of your wildflower garden from summer until frost. Use them as a colorful border, as an accent group, in pots, or as long-lasting cut flowers. It's easier to buy rosettes in the spring than to try growing the tiny seeds. Prairie gentian has long been cultivated, and you can choose among pink, white, rose, lilac, and double-flowered varieties. Its summer flowers add handsomely to a colorscaped garden.

Eustoma exaltatum subsp. *russellianum*

Gaillardia pulchella
Indian blanket or firewheel

Above: *Gaillardia pulchella* flowers
Left: *Gaillardia pulchella*

Native Distribution: roadsides, fields, sandy soils, Pinyon-Juniper and Ponderosa woodlands; 3,000–6,000 feet; widespread California to Florida, north to Canada, Mexico.
Landscape Zone: 1–6.
Size: 1–2 feet.
Annual.
Flower: May–July; yellow-and-red rays with 3 lobes, 1–2 inches across.
Soil: adaptable; well draining.
Exposure: full sun.
Water: drought tolerant.
Planting: fall- or spring-sown seeds.

Profile: Indian blanket has the reputation of being one of the easiest wildflowers to establish. Just rake the seeds into loose topsoil, then let them reseed before mowing or clearing your garden in the fall. In nature's succession of color, Indian blanket will cover your naturalized yard or decorate your garden after the March-April bloomers have faded. You can plant it as a clumping border or as a component of a mixed planting. Red, white, and yellow color selections are available. Cut the blooms for showy arrangements

and to extend the flowering period. If you want a perennial, use *Gaillardia aristata*, a Southwest native that is similar in appearance and habitat requirements. It has a dwarf cultivar that grows to 10 inches high and comes in various color selections. The hybrid blanket flower, *Gaillardia* × *grandiflora* (*aristata* × *pulchella*), is also a perennial, and it has cultivars with 4-inch-wide flowers as well as a dwarf variety. It is suitable for xeriscaping. *Gaillardia* species are included in most wildflower seed mixes.

Glandularia bipinnatifida (Verbena bipinnatifida)

Prairie verbena or Dakota vervain

Native Distribution: roadsides, fields, conifer forests; 2,000–10,000 feet; California to Georgia, north to South Dakota, Mexico.
Landscape Zone: 1–7.
Size: 6–12 inches tall, 1–3 feet wide.
Short-lived perennial.
Flower: March–October; round clusters of 1/4-inch purple flowers.
Soil: adaptable; well draining.
Exposure: full sun.
Water: drought tolerant.
Planting: fresh seeds, basal stem cuttings.
Profile: Maybe you've seen the low-growing, round clusters of verbena growing in the wild and thought it would make an ideal landscape plant.

Glandularia bipinnatifida

You're right. With abundant brilliant flowers and fine-textured leaves, this plant fits a multitude of landscape niches. You can use it as an attractive border for walks and patios, as a foreground plant in your perennial bed, or as a patch of color in your rock garden. For a long-blooming groundcover, plant prairie verbenas 2 feet apart. The reclining stems root in loose soil to form mat-like colonies that stabilize slopes and bare spots; the plant reseeds itself readily. The flower color may vary from rose to lavender, purple, and maroon. For a striking color combination, plant them with dogweed, Indian blanket, or Mexican gold poppy. Nurseries also carry red- and purple-flowering hybrids. Also see the description for Goodding's verbena, *Glandularia gooddingii*, in the section on groundcovers.

Helianthus maximiliani

Maximilian sunflower

Native Distribution: moist prairies and ditches; New Mexico to Florida, central states to Canada.
Landscape Zone: 1–6.
Size: 4–8 feet.
Perennial.
Flower: August–October; yellow, 3 inches diameter.
Soil: adaptable; moist, well draining.
Exposure: full sun.
Water: drought tolerant.
Planting: fall- or spring-sown seeds; root and plant division.
Profile: If you have a place in your yard for a dense mass of head-high flower stalks covered with a profusion of brilliant yellow blooms, this vigorous plant is made to order. Plant Maximilian sunflower to highlight a

Helianthus maximiliani

wall or fence, to provide a background in your garden, or to accent a corner. In marginal conditions, such as shallow and dry soil, these sunflowers may reach only 3 to 4 feet, but they will bloom just as profusely. They spread by rhizomes, and in deep, moist soil they can take over 4 to 8 square feet of space. As with all perennials, dividing the plant every few years increases vigor and blooming. You will need to remove the dead stalks in the winter. Various cultivars are adapted for range planting to provide cover and forage for livestock, birds, deer, and other wildlife. Cultivars of the common sunflower (*Helianthus annuus*), a popular annual that is easily grown from seed, have giant flowers with yellow to red petals. Use is similarly as a background accent.

Ipomoea leptophylla
Bush morning glory

Native Distribution: sandy plains, hills; New Mexico to central Texas, north to Montana.
Landscape Zone: 2–6.
Size: 2–3 feet tall, 3–5 feet wide.
Perennial.
Flower: May–July; 3 inches diameter, 4 inches long, lavender.
Soil: sand, sandy loam, well draining.
Exposure: full sun.
Water: drought tolerant, 10 inches/year minimum.
Planting: fresh or packaged seeds in spring.
Profile: If you like the showy flowers of morning glory vines, this plant will really capture your attention. Spectacular magenta trumpets cover the dense, rounded bush with a coat of color that will enliven your yard. The flowers open in the morning and close by noon. Plant bush morning glory in mass for a colorful groundcover and soil binder in a sandy location, or to complement a planting of mixed shrubs and perennials. You may need to give it an extra drink to ensure profuse summer blooming. This cold- and drought-tolerant plant grows from a deep taproot that gets deeper and bigger every year. Once established, it's difficult to move, so be sure to plant it in an appropriate location. In nature's scheme of succession, it dies back in late summer, making it a good colorscaping companion to fall bloomers such as blazing star, goldeneye, paperflower, and golden crownbeard, which have similar habitat requirements.

Ipomoea leptophylla

Ipomopsis aggregata (Gilia aggregata)
Skyrocket or scarlet gilia

Native Distribution: plateaus, mountain slopes, coniferous forests; 5,000–9,000 feet; California to central Texas, north to Canada, Mexico.
Landscape Zone: 3–7.
Size: 2–4 feet tall.
Biennial.
Flower: May–September; red, 1 inch long.
Soil: adaptable; well draining.
Exposure: full sun.
Water: needs extra water in dry areas.
Planting: fall- or spring-sown seed.
Profile: You'll have to be patient to enjoy the scarlet, tube-shaped flowers of skyrocket, but it's worth the wait. If planted from seed, all you'll see the first year is a rosette of leaves. The second spring, the rosette sends up a single flower stalk covered with delicate red "rockets" with five spreading petals. If a nursery carries the rosettes, you can enjoy the bright flowers the first summer. For flowers every year, plant two years in a row, and let the flowers reseed. For a dramatic effect, plant them in mass for a colorful array waving in the breeze, or mix them in an accent patch with different colors of penstemons and cardinal flowers. As a bonus, you'll have hummingbirds whizzing in and out all day long. In hot exposures, skyrocket needs extra water. The similar Arizona skyrocket, *Ipomopsis arizonica*, is better adapted for desert areas.

Ipomopsis aggregata flowers

135

Liatris species

Native Distribution: mesas, foothills, canyons, prairies; Arizona to Louisiana, north to Canada.
Landscape Zone: 1–6.
Size: 1–3 feet.
Perennial.

Flower: August–October; spikes of small purple flowers.
Soil: well draining.
Exposure: full sun.
Water: drought tolerant, 12 inches/year minimum.
Planting: corm division, fall-sown seeds.

Liatris punctata
Blazing star

Profile: You'll need two ingredients to enjoy this striking wildflower: a sunny location and well-draining soil. I planted mine in too much shade, and the stalks bloomed lying on the ground instead of erect as they normally grow. The cluster of upright stems looks like a mass of purple bottlebrushes and provides beautiful fall color for your garden. Use blazing star to make a perennial border, to accent a pool or patio decor, or to add color to a landscape island. Several species of *Liatris* grow across the Southwest, so select one native to your area. Blazing stars are a common ingredient in meadow mixes and provide a colorful contrast against the brown of dormant fall grass in naturalized areas. Seedlings may sometimes take several years to produce blooms.

Linanthus nuttallii
(Linanthastrum nuttallii, Gilia nuttallii)
Nuttall gilia

Linanthus nuttallii

Native Distribution: rocky crevices and slopes, pine forests; 5,500–8,000 feet; New Mexico to California, north into Canada.
Landscape Zone: 3–7.
Size: 6–12 inches tall.
Perennial.
Flower: July–November; 1 inch, white.
Soil: adaptable; well draining.
Exposure: full sun, partial shade.
Water: drought tolerant.
Planting: fall-sown seeds.
Profile: You may have to gather your own seeds for this beauty, but if you do, it will make a perfect addition to your landscape design. The low, compact shape, dense green foliage, and profusion of dainty, white phlox-like flowers make *Linanthus nuttallii* a beautiful foreground or accent plant. You can mass plant it as a groundcover, use it to border walks, patios, or xeriscape gardens, or plant it in rock crevices. It develops a deep, woody taproot. I haven't found out much about propagating this desirable plant, so you're on your own here.

Linum lewisii
Blue flax

Native Distribution: roadsides, prairies, mesas, mountains; 3,500–9,000 feet; widespread in most states west of the Mississippi River, north to Alaska, Mexico.
Landscape Zone: 1–7.
Size: 1–2 feet.
Short-lived perennial.
Flower: April–September; blue, 1–2 inches diameter.
Soil: adaptable; well draining.
Exposure: full sun, partial shade.
Water: drought tolerant.
Planting: fall-sown seeds.
Profile: A profusion of sky-blue flowers covers the slender stems of this airy, erect plant. Each wand-like stem branches near the top and displays a bouquet of blooms and buds. The dainty blossoms fade and drop by afternoon, but new ones replace them the next morning. The petals can vary from light to dark blue to almost white; darker lines (guiding insects to the nectar) lead to the contrasting yellow centers. Flax lives for one or two years and reseeds itself readily. You can expect to see it in most seed mixtures

Above: *Linum lewisii*

Right: *Linum lewisii* flowers

you buy. Flax lives for one or two years and reseeds itself readily. Most seed mixtures contain blue flax. Trim it back and give it extra water in the summer to encourage fall blooming. In addition to this and other blue-flowered species, numerous yellow species of flax grow throughout the Southwest.

Lobelia cardinalis
Cardinal flower

Native Distribution: moist meadows, stream sides; 3,000–7,500 feet; throughout West and most of the United States, Canada, Mexico.
Landscape Zone: 2–7.
Size: 2–5 feet.
Perennial.
Flower: May–October; spikes of 2-inch red flowers.
Soil: moist, poor to well draining.
Exposure: partial shade, morning sun.
Water: requires regular moisture.
Planting: fall-sown seeds, cuttings, layering, division.
Profile: This tall plant with crimson flowers thrives in moist, rich soil and partly sunny locations, such as pond

sides. However, it does surprisingly well in a shady garden setting if kept moist during the blooming season. The tall, leafy stems and brilliant scarlet flowers make for an eye-catching accent plant with a long bloom period. If you bend down a stem and cover it with soil, it will root at the leaf nodes. Transplant the new plant in the spring. The moisture-loving monkey flowers, columbines, and shooting stars make ideal companion plants. Plant cardinal flowers and you'll get hummingbirds as a bonus.

Lobelia cardinalis

Lupinus argenteus
Silver lupine
Lupinus sparsiflorus
Coulter's lupine

Native Distribution: widespread in western United States. *Lupinus argenteus*: clearings, slopes, open woodlands, conifer forests; 7,000–10,000 feet. *Lupinus sparsiflorus*: sandy, rocky desert soils; below 3,000 feet.
Landscape Zone: *L. argenteus*: 4–7; *L. sparsiflorus*: 1–3.

Size: 1–2 feet.
L. argenteus: **perennial**; *L. sparsiflorus*: **annual**
Flower: spikes of blue flowers; *L. argenteus*, June–October; *L. sparsiflorus*, January–May.
Soil: rocky, sandy, well draining.
Exposure: full sun.

Water: drought tolerant.
Planting: fall-sown seeds; scarify or soak seed in water for 6–8 hours to improve germination.
Profile: In the spring, lupines blanket roadsides, desert flats, mountain slopes, and meadows across the Southwest. The erect spikes of fragrant, pea-like flowers thrive in sunny, well-draining locations and make dramatic naturalized mass plantings or accent patches in your yard or garden. More than two dozen species, both annuals and perennials, grow in the Southwest, from the parched deserts to mountain meadows. I have included a representative species from each extreme. Check the habitat requirements of any seeds you buy to make sure that they match your conditions. All lupines have a tough seed coat adapted to harsh and unpredictable growing conditions, which allows the seeds to germinate periodically over a several-year period. Soak the desert species and scarify the mountain species to ensure that some germinate immediately. Dusting the wet seeds with the bacterial inoculant Rhizobium may produce hardier plants. Plant in the fall, 1/4 to 1/2 inch deep, in lightly tilled soil. Twelve seeds per square foot will give a dense display. The seeds overwinter as a small rosette, so water them if fall rains fail. In the spring, don't mow until the seeds have matured and dispersed, and you'll have a colorful show every spring.

Above: *Lupinus sparsiflorus* flowers

Left: Lupines at Angel Peak, New Mexico

Melampodium leucanthum
Blackfoot daisy

Native Distribution: dry, rocky slopes, grasslands, woodlands; 2,000–5,000 feet; Arizona to Texas, north to Colorado, Kansas, Mexico.
Landscape Zone: 1–5.
Size: 1–2 feet tall, spreading mounds.
Perennial.
Flower: March–December; 1 1/2 inches diameter, white with yellow centers.
Soil: adaptable; well draining.
Exposure: full sun.
Water: drought tolerant.
Planting: fall-sown seeds, self-seeding.
Profile: Heat can't kill them, nor will poor, rocky soil thwart their energetic blooming. Sound perfect for your xeriscape garden? It is, and more.

Blackfoot daisy forms a dense, rounded, evergreen mound up to 2 feet wide. White flowers with buttery-yellow centers cover the plant for months on end. It's great for borders, mass plantings, and colorful accents for cacti gardens. Use blackfoot daisies as companion plants for damianita, dogweed, flat-top buckwheat, and desert or plains zinnia. Their round shape complements taller bloomers such as desert marigold, mealycup blue sage, penstemons, and blazing star. In midsummer in Phoenix, a weekly watering will sustain blooming. To encourage dense spring foliage, trim back to 5 inches before spring blooming, especially if severe winters damage the stems.

Melampodium leucanthum

Mimulus cardinalis
Crimson monkey flower
Mimulus guttatus
Golden monkey flower

Native Distribution: along flowing water, seeping springs; below 8,500 feet; New Mexico to California, north to Canada.
Landscape Zone: 1–7
Size: 6–18 inches tall, spreading clumps.
Perennial.
Flower: March–October; tubular, 2 inches long, 1 inch wide. *Mimulus cardinalis*, red; *M. guttatus*, yellow.
Soil: adaptable; moist.
Exposure: afternoon shade.
Water: requires regular moisture.
Planting: seeds or potted nursery stock.
Profile: If you have a corner in your garden that is protected from afternoon sun and reflected heat, you may be a candidate for a monkey flower. These summer-blooming, water- and humidity-loving natives produce a mass of tubular flowers with lobed

Mimulus cardinalis

Mimulus guttatus

petals. The brilliant scarlet or gold flowers stand out in sharp contrast to the large, dark green leaves. Plant a monkey flower, and every hummingbird on the block will thank you. Given the proper microhabitat, monkey

flowers grow well from the low desert to mountain forests; just don't let them dry out. They make good neighbors for other humid-loving flowers, such as columbine, skyrocket, and cardinal flower.

Mirabilis multiflora
Giant four-o'clock

Mirabilis multiflora flowers

Native Distribution: sandy, rocky plains, hills, mesas, grasslands; 2,500–7,000 feet; Arizona to Texas, Colorado, Nevada, Mexico.
Landscape Zone: 1–6.
Size: 2 feet tall, 4 feet wide.
Perennial.

Flower: April–September; purplish red trumpets, 2 inches long, 1 inch across.
Soil: adaptable; well draining.
Exposure: sun.
Water: drought tolerant.
Planting: fall-sown seeds; in spring, scarify the seeds and stratify one month; soft cuttings.
Profile: The mass of vivid, tubular flowers nestled against the bright green, heart-shaped leaves of *Mirabilis multiflora* creates a spectacular accent in your yard. With dense foliage and a rounded profile, this robust plant presents a commanding appearance when used as a mounding groundcover or border plant. An extensive tubular root system helps the plant stabilize slopes and prevent erosion, but it also enables it to crowd out less vigorously growing plants. So give it plenty of room. Each cluster of the majestic flowers has three to six blooms, which close in the afternoon—hence the common name. The plant dies back in freezing winters. Hummingbirds and hawk moths sip from the flowers and birds feed on the seeds.

Mirabilis multiflora

Monarda citriodora
Lemon beebalm

Monarda citriodora

Native Distribution: sandy and rocky hills, prairies, roadsides; 4,000–8,500 feet; Arizona east to South Carolina, north to Nebraska, Mexico.
Landscape Zone: 1–6.
Size: 1–2 feet tall.
Annual or biennial.
Flower: May–August; 3/4-inch, pink-to-purple flowers on 6-inch spikes.
Soil: adaptable; alkaline, well draining.
Exposure: full sun, afternoon shade.
Water: moderately drought tolerant.
Planting: fall- or spring-sown seeds.
Profile: This picturesque plant is outstanding in its field, or any field for that matter. It forms dense colonies in prairies, pastures, and naturalized areas. It flowers after the early spring bloomers and lasts until midsummer. It will bloom with Indian blanket, cutleaf daisy, and prairie gentian. The showy spikes of flowers make good borders, background plantings, or cut flowers, and the leaves and flowers make a strong herbal tea. Supplemental water in the spring and summer will ensure flowering if rains fail. Delay mowing to give this annual a chance to reseed itself, and you'll have a colorful display every year. Five species of beebalm, all suitable for landscaping, grow across Arizona and New Mexico. Beebalms are excellent for hummingbird and butterfly gardens.

Nama hispidum
Rough nama or sand bell

Native Distribution: sunny, sandy soil on roadsides, desert hills, washes; below 7,000 feet; California to Texas, Oklahoma to Nevada, Mexico.
Landscape Zone: 1–6.
Size: 4–20 inches tall, upright to sprawling.
Annual.
Leaves: 1/2 to 1 1/4 inches long, narrow, covered in rough hairs.
Flower: March–November; pink to purple, bell shaped, yellow centered, 5/16 to 5/8 inch diameter
Soil: sandy, gravelly, well draining.
Exposure: full sun.
Temperature Tolerance: extremely heat tolerant.
Water: drought tolerant.
Propagation: spring sown seeds, readily reseeds itself.
Profile: This sprawling flower will bring you to your knees—to get a closer look at the array of purple flowers set in a thick mat of gray leaves. The densely blooming clumps of flowers brighten bare patches in cactus or xeriscape gardens throughout the summer, especially if given an extra drink now and then. The stems sometimes grow as tall as 4 to 20 inches, but usually they are prostrate. Sow the seeds in the spring and enjoy the pink-to-purple blooms throughout the summer. Though an annual, Rough nama reseeds itself for next year's display. The mounds of narrow gray-green leaves and dime-sized flowers complement hedgehog and barrel cacti and clumping wildflowers such as blackfoot daisy, desert zinnia, limoncillo, and paperflower. Ten species of *Nama* grow in the Southwest. Purplemat, *Nama demissum*, adds color to the low Sonoran and Mojave deserts.

Nama hispidum

Oenothera caespitosa
Tufted evening primrose

Native Distribution: rocky slopes, hillsides, Ponderosa forests; 3,000–7,000 feet; California to Texas, north to Canada.
Landscape Zone: 1–7.
Size: 6–12 inches tall, 1–2 feet wide.
Perennial.
Flower: April–September; white, 3–4 inches across.
Soil: adaptable, rocky, well draining.
Exposure: full sun.
Water: drought tolerant.
Planting: fall-sown seeds.
Profile: The tissue-like, snow-white flowers and slender dark green leaves of tufted evening primrose create a cheerful color combination for your landscape. This low-sprawling plant makes a delightful border flower for

Oenothera caespitosa

Calylophus lavandulifolius

entry or patio gardens or a colorful accent for rock gardens. The stems may spread out over 2 feet, so give it enough room to show off. The blooms open in the evening and close during the heat of the next day. Nurseries carry seeds for the numerous species of evening primrose that grow throughout the Southwest. You can choose among yellow or white flowers, tall or prostrate growth habits, and annuals or perennials. The yellow, crinkled flowers of the perennial sundrops, *Calylophus lavandulifolius*, add an interesting texture to a colorscape design. For a vertical accent, *Oenothera hookerii* bears bright yellow flowers profusely on 2- to 6-foot stalks.

Oenothera speciosa
Pink ladies or Mexican evening primrose

Oenothera speciosa flowers

Native Distribution: dry slopes, roadsides, forest openings; below 4,000 feet; California, east to Pennsylvania and south into Mexico.
Landscape Zone: 1–7.
Size: 1 foot.
Perennial.

Flower: March–July, 2 inches diameter, pink.
Soil: adaptable; well draining.
Exposure: full sun.
Water: drought tolerant.
Planting: fall-sown seeds.
Profile: Plant pink ladies and watch rippling waves of rosy pink brighten your garden. This sprawling plant forms colonies so dense that the vivid flowers obscure the ground. It blooms heaviest in the spring and on through the summer until heat and drought burn it back. Give it extra water, and it's almost evergreen. Use as a bedding plant or groundcover or to add color to a naturalized area. For a beautiful color combination, plant with winecups. Since pink ladies spreads vigorously by rhizomes, be careful about planting it in a flower bed with rich garden soil, or it may take over. Pink ladies die back to the roots in the winter. Above 6,000 feet or at 0°F temperatures, it grows as an annual.

Oenothera speciosa

Pectis angustifolia
Limoncillo or lemon scent

Native Distribution: dry, sandy, hills, mesas, desert washes; below 7,000 feet; Arizona to Texas, north to Wyoming, Mexico.

Landscape Zone: 1–6.
Size: 6 inches tall.
Annual.
Flower: summer–fall; 1/2 inch diameter, yellow.
Soil: adaptable; well draining.
Exposure: full sun, partial shade.

Water: drought tolerant.
Planting: fall- or spring-sown seeds.
Profile: With this little herbaceous wildflower, what you see is only half of what you get. Pinch the leaves and smell the lemon scent, and you won't know whether to plant limoncillo in your herb garden or use it as a landscape plant. Do both. The delicate leaves and abundant yellow flowers form a thick mat of contrasting colors that will accent your rock garden or flower bed. And after a hard day's work in the yard, you can use a twig of leaves to brew a refreshing lemon-flavored tea, iced or hot. The leaves also make a good seasoning for soups, stews, and fish. About a dozen other species with similar characteristics are available in nurseries across the Southwest.

Pectis angustifolia

Penstemon species
Beard tongues

Native Distribution: varies with species, from low deserts to mountain meadows.
Landscape Zone: 1–6.
Size: 1–6 feet.
Perennial.
Flower: spring–summer.
Soil: adaptable; well draining.
Exposure: full sun, partial shade.
Water: drought tolerant.
Planting: fall-sown seeds, potted nursery stock.
Profile: With their stately spikes of tubular flowers, penstemons are truly aristocrats of the garden, and we have scores of species in the Southwest to choose from. The three dozen species of penstemons in New Mexico and Arizona grow from the low deserts to alpine meadows, and from shaded canyons to sandy, arid hillsides—so you can select species suited for your growing conditions no matter where you live. Some grow 6 feet tall, others just 1 foot, and they come in a rainbow of reds, pinks, oranges, blues, purples, and whites. Use shorter species as border plants and the taller ones as desert garden accents against a tall cacti or boulder. Mass plant them for a stunning effect, especially if you like hummingbirds. To ensure next year's bloom, remove the spent flower stalks. Penstemons have an attractive basal rosette of leaves year round. Protect penstemons from rabbits and deer, who enjoy nibbling the plants.

Listed here are just a few of the various species and colors available from seed or in pots. Cultivars adapted to lower elevations also are available. When buying a penstemon, be sure to look at the scientific name, since common names vary widely.

Above: *Penstemon barbatus*
Left: White and blue penstemons
Photos continued on next page

Clockwise, from above:
Penstemon pseudospectabilis
Penstemon ambiguus
Blue penstemons
Penstemon jamesii

Red-to-Pink Penstemons

Penstemon barbatus, beardlip or scarlet penstemon: pine-oak woodlands 4,000–10,000 feet, throughout the Southwest. Landscape zones 1–7. Perennial, 2–4 feet tall, blooms June–October.

Penstemon eatoni, Eaton's penstemon or firecracker penstemon: desert shrub to pinyon-juniper woodlands, 2,000–7,500 feet, throughout the Southwest. Landscape zones 1–7. Perennial, 2 feet tall, blooms February–June.

Penstemon parryi, Parry's penstemon: roadsides, canyons, mesas, 1,500–5,000 feet, Arizona. Landscape zones 1–4. Perennial, 2–4 feet tall, blooms March–April.

Penstemon pinifolius, pineleaf penstemon: deserts to mountains, below 7,000 feet, Arizona, New Mexico. Landscape zones 2–7. Perennial, blooms spring–summer.

Penstemon pseudospectabilis, desert penstemon: desert shrub to Pinyon-Juniper woodlands, 2,000–7,000 feet, Arizona, New Mexico. Landscape zones 1–6. Perennial, 2–4 feet tall, blooms April–July.

Blue-to-Pink Penstemons

Penstemon angustifolius, pagoda penstemon: sandy mesas, dunes, grasslands, 5,000–6,500 feet, New Mexico, Arizona. Landscape zones 3–7. Perennial, 1–2 feet tall, blooms May–June.

Penstemon clutei (*Penstemon pseudospectabilis* subsp. *clute*), Sunset Crater penstemon: volcanic cinder soil, 6,500–8,500 feet, Sunset Crater National Monument, Arizona. Landscape zones 4–7. Perennial, 2–3 feet tall, blooms April–August.

Penstemon jamesii, James penstemon: sandy mesas, Pine-Juniper woodlands, 4,000–7,000 feet, New Mexico. Landscape zones 4–7. Perennial, 1 foot tall, blooms June–July.

Penstemon neomexicanus, New Mexico penstemon: ponderosa pine to spruce forests, 6,000–9,000 feet, southern New Mexico. Landscape zones 3–7. Perennial, 2 feet tall, blooms July–August.

Penstemon strictus, Rocky Mountain penstemon: mountain slopes, mesas, seeded on roadsides, 6,000–11,000 feet, northern Arizona. Landscape zones 3–7. Perennial, 1–3 feet tall, blooms June–July.

Penstemon virgatus, upright blue beardtongue: dry grasslands to conifer forests, 6,000–11,000 feet, New Mexico. Landscape zones 3–7. Perennial, 2–3 feet tall, blooms June–September.

White-to-Pink-to-Yellow Penstemons

Penstemon ambiguus, bush penstemon: sandy soils, mesas, woodlands, 4,500–6,500 feet, Arizona, New Mexico. Landscape zones 2–6. Perennial, 3-foot-wide rounded bush, blooms May–October.

Penstemon palmeri, Palmer's penstemon: sagebrush grasslands to Pinyon-Juniper woodlands, 3,500–6,500 feet, Arizona, New Mexico. Landscape zones 3–6. Perennial, 3–5 feet tall, blooms May–September.

Phlox nana

Phlox nana
Santa Fe phlox

Temperature Tolerance: cold hardy to 0–10°F.
Water: drought tolerant.
Planting: fall-sown seeds, spring-planted seedlings.
Profile: This common flower of the Pinyon-Juniper hills around Santa Fe will grace your garden with mounds of dainty pink flowers through the spring and, with ample moisture, into the summer. Its deep taproot ensures that it will survive harsh winters, as well as browsing by deer or rabbits. To increase your garden's palette of colors, use Santa Fe phlox as a companion plant with Rocky Mountain zinnia, woolly paperflower, blackfoot daisy, sulphur flower, and dogweed. *Sunset* Magazine rates Santa Fe phlox on its top-10 list of perennials for spectacular summer gardens in the mountain West.

Native Distribution: mesas, Pinyon-Juniper woodlands; 5,000–8,000 feet; Arizona, New Mexico.
Landscape Zone: 4–7.
Size: 1 foot tall and wide.

Perennial.
Flower: spring, summer; 1 inch diameter, rosy pink.
Soil: adaptable; well draining.
Exposure: full sun, partial shade.

Psilostrophe tagetina
Woolly paperflower

Psilostrophe tagetina

Native Distribution: desert plains, mesas; to 7,000 feet; Arizona to Texas, Utah to Kansas, Mexico.
Landscape Zone: 1–6.
Size: 1–2 feet tall, 3 feet wide.
Short-lived perennial.
Flower: April–October; 1 inch diameter, yellow.
Soil: adaptable; well draining.
Exposure: full sun.
Water: drought tolerant.
Planting: spring- or fall-sown seeds.
Profile: This densely branching perennial forms a rounded mass of bright, butter-colored flowers so thick that you won't be able to see the grayish green foliage. The mounding shape of woolly paperflower makes it an attractive border or accent plant, and it matches well with desert zinnia, blackfoot daisy, desert marigold, and evening primroses. When the vibrant flowers fade with age and become papery, you can use them in dried-flower arrangements. Three species of *Psilostrophe* grow throughout the Southwest, all with similar habitat requirements and landscape applications.

Ratibida columnifera (Ratibida columnaris)
Mexican hat

Native Distribution: roadsides, grass-lands, mesas, mountain openings; California east to North Carolina, north to Canada, Mexico.
Landscape Zone: 1–7.
Size: 1–3 feet.
Perennial.
Flower: June–October; 2 inches diameter, red-to-yellow or blotched petals, tall central cone.
Soil: adaptable; well draining.
Exposure: full sun, partial shade.
Water: drought tolerant.
Planting: fall- or spring-sown seeds.
Profile: In any one field of wildflowers (or seed pack), you'll find Mexican hats with red-to-maroon petals, yellow petals, and solid and mixed colors of every hue. Maybe it's nature's way of showing us how beautiful a diversity of colors can be. If you can spread seed, you can grow this robust flower in your yard. It's one of the most common ingredients in wildflower mixes for the Southwest. A stand of these tall flowers swaying in the breeze adds not only color, but also a dynamic dimension to naturalized areas, borders, background beds, and accent patches. Extra water in the summer helps extend the bloom into the fall. The unusual flowers, with their drooping, multicolored petals and protruding cones, make an attractive addition to cut-flower arrangements.

Ratibida columnifera

Rudbeckia hirta
Black-eyed Susan

Native Distribution: roadsides, prairies; widespread throughout the United States except Arizona and Nevada, Canada, Mexico.
Landscape Zone: 1–7.
Size: 1–3 feet.
Short-lived perennial.
Flower: May–October; 2–3 inches diameter, yellow with black-brown center.
Soil: adaptable; well draining.
Exposure: full sun, partial shade.
Water: drought tolerant.
Planting: fall- or spring-sown seeds.
Profile: A rounded clump of these bright lemon-yellow flowers with contrasting centers adds color to your flower bed or naturalized area all summer. This long-blooming species begins flowering after early-spring bloomers fade and continues until the fall species begin their show. Give black-eyed Susan extra water to keep it dense and lush and covered with a profusion of gold and brown. Though living only one or two years, this hardy flower readily reseeds itself to ensure an annual bloom. Let the seed heads fully mature and disperse before mowing, and don't remove the shredded mulch. 'Goldenglow', a cultivar of the Arizona species *Rudbeckia laciniata*, has double rays and a yellow center.

Rudbeckia hirta

Salvia farinacea
Mealycup blue sage

Native Distribution: prairies, canyons, woodlands; New Mexico to Florida.
Landscape Zone: 1–6.
Size: 2–3 feet tall, to 3 feet wide. Perennial.
Flower: April–September; bluish, 1/2 inch long.
Soil: adaptable; well draining.
Exposure: full sun, partial shade.
Water: drought tolerant.
Planting: seeds, cuttings.
Profile: This fast-growing plant forms a rounded mound of grayish green foliage with numerous spikes of crowded, tiny, tube-shaped flowers. The purple to light-blue flowers whorl around 1- to 2-foot-tall leafless stems and provide color for your garden through the summer and into fall. They have a tendency to get leggy, so trim back the flowering stalks during the summer to maintain a thick fall bloom. The plant reseeds easily, so you'll have either a garden full of mealycup blue sage or plenty of starts for your friends. You can mass plant them for a background plant or border. Prolonged freezing kills them, so don't plant them in the mountain climates. Several varieties, including one with white flowers, are available.

Salvia farinacea flowers
Salvia farinacea

Solidago species
Goldenrod

Native Distribution: throughout the United States.
Landscape Zone: 1–7.
Size: 1–6 feet.
Perennial.
Flower: summer–fall; spikes of small yellow flowers.
Soil: adaptable; poor to well draining.
Exposure: full sun, partial shade.
Water: some species drought tolerant.
Planting: fresh seeds, root division when dormant.
Profile: From deserts to mountains and marshes to prairies, you'll find numerous species of goldenrod throughout the Southwest. The large flowering spike, crowning a waving stalk, makes it among the most conspicuous of fall wildflowers. Because of the diversity in size and aggressiveness within the genus, choose your species and planting location carefully. *Solidago altissima* and *S. canadensis* grow head high, *S. missouriensis* reaches 3 feet, and *S. decumbens* peaks at 10 inches. The taller species make a colorful complement for meadows and naturalized areas, but they tend to overtake garden settings, spreading by rhizomes. Don't plant them in rich soil where you have to worry about control. Mass plant goldenrods to get extended color, since each plant has a short blooming period. Contrary to popular belief, these plants seldom cause hay fever; wind-pollinated ragweed, which blooms concurrently, is the major culprit.

Solidago altissima flowers with monarch butterfly

Sphaeralcea ambigua
Desert globemallow

Native Distribution: sandy, rocky soils, deserts, hills; below 3,500 feet; California to Texas and north throughout the West, Mexico.
Landscape Zone: 1–6.
Size: 1–6 feet tall.
Perennial.
Flower: throughout year; 1 1/2 inches diameter, red to pink to lavender.
Soil: adaptable; well draining.
Exposure: full sun.
Water: drought tolerant.
Planting: fall-sown seeds.
Profile: If you like hollyhocks, you'll want these miniature versions for your xeriscape garden. The cup-like flowers bloom all along the upper portion of the stalk in shades of orange, pink, peach, red, and lavender. Vigorous growers, they send up numerous stems from a single root. Plant these graceful perennials as a silhouette along a wall or fence line. The airy, spreading profile also complements agaves, beargrass, ocotillo, and yuccas as an accent in a cactus garden. The

Sphaeralcea ambigua

Sphaeralcea ambigua flowers

long blooming season fills a colorscape design and accents the sunset hues of desert marigold, Mexican gold poppy, and goldenrod. In the fall, cut the plant back to 6 inches in order to produce thick, new growth. Several clones are available that offer large, pink flowers and red flowers. Most

seed packs contain a variety of colors. If you can't find globemallows at a nursery, don't despair. Pick a few seed heads, and you'll have your own specimens in a few months. About 18 species grow in New Mexico and Arizona, from low deserts to 7,000-foot mountain slopes.

Thymophylla pentachaeta (Dyssodia pentachaeta)
Dogweed

Native Distribution: dry, rocky soils, slopes; 2,500–4,500 feet; California to Texas, Mexico.
Landscape Zone: 1–3.
Size: 4–10 inches tall, 1 foot diameter.
Short-lived perennial.
Flower: March–September; 1/2 inch diameter, yellow.
Soil: adaptable; well draining.
Exposure: full sun.
Water: drought tolerant.
Planting: fall-sown seeds.
Profile: What a delightful little plant dogweed is. Numerous dime-sized flowers on 1- to 4-inch stems cover mounds of dark green, fine-textured

Thymophylla pentachaeta

leaves. The petite clumps, which may range from the size of a dinner plate to 3 feet in diameter, make perfect border or accent plants for your cactus or patio garden—or plant one in a rocky crevice. As a groundcover, dogweed makes a colorful bouquet with blackfoot daisy, desert zinnia, and

damianita. You can count on a dogweed's delicate beauty year after year, because it reseeds itself readily. Six species and numerous subspecies of *Thymophylla* grow across the Southwest, all dainty and strongly scented. But don't be choosy—any one will look good in your yard.

Tradescantia occidentalis
Spiderwort

Tradescantia occidentalis

Native Distribution: sandy soils, slopes, mesas, mountain meadows; 2,500–7,000 feet; Arizona to Louisiana, north into Canada.

Landscape Zone: 1–7.
Size: 1–2 feet tall.
Perennial.
Flower: April–September; clusters of blue-to-rose, 1-inch flowers.
Soil: adaptable; well draining.
Exposure: full shade, partial shade.
Water: drought tolerant.
Planting: spring-sown seeds, root division.
Profile: Spiderwort is one of the most picturesque flowers I know. The three symmetrical, royal blue petals with contrasting golden anthers glisten in the mottled sunlight of their shady habitat. Each cluster of flowers nestles above nodding, unopened buds atop a slender stalk. The three-petaled blossoms fade in one day, but are replaced by one of the waiting buds. Spiderworts are ideal for shady borders, as groundcovers under trees, or in a foundation garden. The tidy clumps and arching blade-like leaves make an eye-catching addition to your perennial flower bed. They add color to a mixed planting with ferns, shooting star, columbine, and skyrocket. Six species of *Tradescantia* grow in Arizona and New Mexico.

Verbesina encelioides
Golden crownbeard or cow pen daisy

Native Distribution: sandy, disturbed soils, roadsides; below 7,000 feet; California to North Carolina and into Canada, Mexico.
Landscape Zone: 1–7.
Size: 2–3 feet tall.

Verbesina encelioides flowers

Verbesina encelioides

Annual.
Flower: March–December; 2 inches across, yellow.
Soil: adaptable; well draining.
Exposure: full sun.
Water: drought tolerant.
Planting: fall- or spring-sown seeds.
Profile: This rapidly growing annual will begin adding color to your landscape early in the spring, but it really puts on its show in the fall. Masses of lemon-yellow flowers with yellow centers cover the tall, spreading plant. Use golden crownbeard as a background or as a border along a wall or fence. It's too rangy looking for a formal garden, so keep it in the outskirts. It normally colonizes waste places, so you can use it as a tall component for a naturalized planting. It readily reseeds itself. Mix with comparably sized shrubby species, such as goldeneye, brittlebush, sand sagebrush, and chamisa, depending on the elevation of your site. The perennial dwarf crownbeard, *Verbesina nana*, grows to about 6 inches tall, with showy 1 1/2-inch flowers, and would make an excellent groundcover, accent, or foreground plant in landscape zone 2.

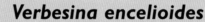

Viguiera dentata
Goldeneye

Native Distribution: dry hills, canyons, mesas; 3,000–7,000 feet; Arizona through central Texas.
Landscape Zone: 1–3.
Size: 3–6 feet.
Perennial.
Flower: June–November; 1 inch diameter, yellow.
Soil: adaptable; well draining.
Exposure: full sun, partial shade.
Water: drought tolerant.
Planting: fall- or spring-sown seeds.
Profile: If you want a waist- to head-high mass of color to border a fence, to provide a background in your perennial garden, or to cover a naturalized area, plant goldeneye. This vigorous grower needs elbow room or it will run over its neighbors—but allow it to spread, and it's spectacular. Goldeneye is large enough to make a colorful addition to a cactus garden with large-scale specimens of yucca, sotol, and prickly pear. It adds fall color to a landscape island of Texas ranger, brittlebush, chamisa, and palo verde. Parish's goldeneye, *Viguiera parishii*, is a spring-blooming shrub that grows to 4 feet, and it has similar landscape applications.

Viguiera dentata flowers

Viguiera dentata

Viola affinis

Viola affinis (Viola missouriensis)
Sand violet

Native Distribution: mountain stream banks and woodlands; Arizona, Texas, widespread east of the Rockies, Canada.
Landscape Zone: 3, 4, 6, 7.
Size: 3–6 inches tall.
Perennial.
Flower: February–May; 1 inch across, light blue-to-white.
Soil: adaptable; well draining.
Exposure: sun, light shade.
Water: moderately drought tolerant.
Planting: root division, fall-sown seeds.

Profile: Do you have a spot in your yard or garden that gets mottled shade and regular moisture? If you can simulate a woodland habitat, plant a dainty sand violet. The dense rosette of basal leaves with their exquisite little flowers make delightful accent plants for a shady patio garden, a filler between rocks, or a small-scale groundcover under a tree or shrub. They go dormant and disappear in the summer, but come back in the cool of the year. Numerous species of violets are available in the nursery trade, so don't deplete our wild populations.

Zinnia acerosa

Zinnia grandiflora

Zinnia acerosa
Desert zinnia
Zinnia grandiflora
Rocky Mountain or plains zinnia

Native Distribution: *Zinnia acerosa*: desert hills, mesas; 2,000–5,000 feet; Arizona to Texas, Utah. *Zinnia grandiflora*: mesas, Pinyon-Juniper woodlands; 2,000–6,000 feet; Arizona to Texas, Colorado, Kansas.
Landscape Zone: 1–6.
Size: 4–8 inches tall, 8–15 inches wide.
Perennial.
Flower: 1–2 inches diameter. *Zinnia acerosa*: March–October; white. *Zinnia grandiflora*: May–October; yellow.
Soil: adaptable; well draining.
Exposure: full sun.
Water: drought tolerant.
Planting: spring-sown seeds, plant division.

Profile: If you've ever seen mounding zinnias, you'll agree that they belong in a garden. Compact in size, covered with lemon-yellow or snow-white flowers, and long blooming, they provide everything you could ask for in a perennial. Mix or match them as bedding or border plants, or for a touch of color in a xeriscape or cactus garden. Set the plants about 8 inches apart for complete cover as a border, groundcover, or to stabilize a slope. These zinnias grow rapidly from seed, and their most profuse flowering is in the fall, which makes them an ideal colorscape companion for early blooming plants. The rounded mounds complement blackfoot daisy, dogweed, nama, and limoncillo, and they make an attractive accent paired with vertical elements such as yucca, sotol, chollas, and the green trunks of palo verde. After blooming, the petals dry to a straw color, revealing the light green leaves that densely cover the plant. In Santa Fe and Flagstaff, take a hint from the plant's common name and use Rocky Mountain zinnia. In Albuquerque and Phoenix, go for desert zinnia.

Vines

Campsis radicans
Trumpet creeper

Native Distribution: forests and edges of woods; eastern half of Texas to Florida, north to Canada.
Landscape Zone: 1–7.
Growth Habit: climbing to 40 feet; holdfasts, tendrils.
Woody perennial.

Leaves: deciduous.
Flower: May–October; 3 inches, trumpet shaped, orange.
Fruit: 6-inch cylindrical capsules.
Soil: adaptable; well draining.
Exposure: full sun, partial shade.
Temperature Tolerance: cold hardy.

Water: moderately drought tolerant.
Propagation: seeds, root suckers.
Profile: Trumpet creeper is not native to Arizona and New Mexico, and including this eastern vine here may violate the "Native Plant Code"—but it is so versatile and widely used in Southwestern landscaping that I believe it is worth mentioning. Trumpet creeper does everything vines are supposed to, and even better than you might wish for in your yard. It grows fast; climbs high on every conceivable object; develops a dense cover of heavy, stout stems and foliage; and spreads by root suckers. But you have to agree with the hummingbirds that its profuse clusters of flaming orange-red flowers are attractive. If you have a back fence or neglected area that needs some enhancement, plant this robust and hardy vine, but keep it off buildings. It suffers limb damage in hard winters and appreciates extra summer water west of its native range. Several horticultural varieties are available, some smaller and some with different shades of flowers. The variety 'Flava' has yellow flowers, and 'Madam Galen' has salmon-pink flowers.

Campsis radicans

Campsis radicans **flowers**

Clematis ligusticifolia
Western virgin's bower

Native Distribution: moist soils, roadsides, thickets, woods; 3,000–8,500 feet; New Mexico to California, north to Canada.
Landscape Zone: 2–7.
Growth Habit: climbing to 20 feet; twining leaf stalks.
Herbaceous perennial.
Flower: May–September; clusters of 1/2-inch, white flowers; feathery seed heads on female plants.
Soil: adaptable; well draining.
Exposure: full sun, partial shade.
Temperature Tolerance: cold hardy, freezes back.
Water: drought tolerant, 7 inches/year minimum.
Propagation: fresh seeds, semi-soft-wood cuttings.
Profile: This vigorously growing vine will quickly cover a lattice to shade your porch or patio, or it will sprawl across an open slope. Plant it on a fence or trellis to shade your windows or air conditioning unit in the summer. The dense flower clusters attract an abundance of bees and other insects, and the female plants have showy, feathery seed heads. Though western virgin's bower dies back in the winter, it is hard to eradicate once established. The vine prefers moist soil, but a deep tap root allows it to survive drought conditions. One wild specimen at the Grand Canyon covered 30 square feet with luxuriant foliage even after six months with no rain. Old man's beard, *Clematis drummondii*, is similar and also has the feathery seeds, but it has nondescript flowers and is nearly impossible to eliminate.

Clematis ligusticifolia flowers

Ibervillea lindheimeri
Globeberry or balsam gourd
Ibervillea tenuisecta
Slim-lobe globeberry

Native Distribution: rocky hills, dry woods, thickets; southern New Mexico and southeastern Arizona, east through coastal Texas, Oklahoma, Mexico.
Landscape Zone: 2–4.
Growth Habit: low climbing; tendrils.
Herbaceous perennial.
Flower: April–September; 1/2 inch, yellow.
Fruit: showy, bright orange to red, 1- to 2-inch globes.
Soil: adaptable; well draining.
Exposure: partial shade, full sun.
Temperature Tolerance: freezes back in winter.
Water: drought tolerant.
Propagation: fresh seeds.
Profile: You will hardly give these delicate low climbers a second glance until they begin to fruit. Then, brilliant reddish-orange balls dangle from the slender stems like Christmas ornaments. The picturesque tiny gourds colorfully accent a wire fence, patio lattice, or lamppost. The dark green, lobed leaves are scattered along the branching stems, giving the vines a dainty appearance. You don't have to worry about them getting out of hand, because the vines die to the ground in the winter. The thin-skinned, fleshy fruit is not edible.

Ibervillea lindheimeri fruit

Lonicera arizonica
Arizona honeysuckle

Native Distribution: mountains, open coniferous forests; 6,000–9,000 feet; Arizona, New Mexico.
Landscape Zone: 4–7.
Growth Habit: trailing woody vine to 3 feet.
Woody perennial.
Leaves: evergreen.
Flower: summer; clusters of 1- to 2-inch-long, trumpet-shaped, red flowers.
Fruit: fall; red berries, 2/5 inch diameter.
Soil: adaptable; well draining.
Exposure: partial shade, full sun.
Temperature Tolerance: cold hardy to −10°F.
Water: moderately drought tolerant.
Propagation: fresh seeds, softwood or semi-hardwood cuttings.
Profile: Unlike its Japanese relative *Lonicera japonica*, this native honeysuckle is well mannered and never trespasses. Give it some type of support, and it will form a dense, low-climbing shrubby plant. Clusters of flamboyant scarlet flowers contrast with the round evergreen leaves throughout most of the year, making this an eye-catching addition to your yard. You can plant it along a fence at about 4- to 6-foot intervals for a visual barrier, or let it sprawl over an open area as a groundcover. In central Texas, I used the look-alike *L. sempervirens* to surround a utility pole, and in two years it was a rounded mass about 5 feet high. The shrubby western honeysuckle, *L. albiflora*, has white flowers and grows at lower elevations in Arizona and New Mexico and is suitable for planting in landscape zones 2–4.

Lonicera sempervirens flowers

Maurandya antirrhiniflora
Snapdragon vine

Native Distribution: sandy soils, Pinyon-Juniper woodlands; 1,500–6,000 feet; New Mexico to California, Texas, Mexico.
Landscape Zone: 2–7.
Growth Habit: low climbing; twining.
Herbaceous perennial.
Leaves: evergreen unless frozen.
Flower: February–October; 1 inch, purple-to-pink.
Soil: adaptable; well draining.
Exposure: partial shade, full sun.
Temperature Tolerance: freezes back in winter.
Water: drought tolerant.
Propagation: seeds.

Profile: This prostrate to low-climbing vine has a jumble of slender, tangled stems, small leaves, and a few flowers blooming all the time—nothing glamorous, but definitely interesting, especially the unusual flowers. Each petite bloom has two brightly colored "lips" and a creamy yellow "throat." To best show off the subtle beauty of this vine, let it dangle over a rock wall, out of a crevice, or on a slope beneath a shrub. It reseeds itself readily, even in cold climates where it grows as an annual. Another western vine, balloonbush, *Epixiphium wislizeni* (*Maurandya wislizeni*), has very similar flowers.

Maurandya antirrhiniflora

Parthenocissus quinquefolia (Parthenocissus inserta)
Thicket creeper or woodbine

Native Distribution: moist canyons, bottomlands, roadsides; 3,000–7,000 feet; Arizona, New Mexico, east to the Atlantic Coast, Canada.
Landscape Zone: 1–7.
Growth Habit: high climbing; tendrils.
Woody perennial.
Leaves: deciduous, brilliant red-and-orange fall color.
Fruit: fall; blue berries, poisonous.

Soil: adaptable; well draining.
Exposure: full sun to full shade.
Temperature Tolerance: cold hardy.
Water: moderately drought tolerant.
Propagation: fresh seeds, cuttings.
Profile: Plant a robust creeper vine where it can climb unchallenged. It has dense foliage with five leaflets and will rapidly cover masonry, a fence, or a trellis with a luxuriant growth. The thick layer of leaves provides an insulating dead-air space against a building and, in the fall, paints it with brilliant shades of red, orange, and burgundy. You also can use these vigorous growers as groundcovers, if you keep them trimmed off trees and shrubs. Don't let the vine become established on wooden structures that need periodic painting.

Parthenocissus quinquefolia

Parthenocissus quinquefolia

Groundcovers

Acacia angustissima
Fern acacia

Native Distribution: grasslands, chaparral, mesas, oak woodlands; widespread in the Southwest, Texas, Mexico.
Landscape Zone: 1–7.
Size: 1–3 feet tall.
Leaves: deciduous.
Flower: summer–fall; 1/2 inch, white, round heads.
Fruit: 2- to 3-inch pods.
Soil: adaptable; well draining.
Exposure: full sun, partial shade.
Temperature Tolerance: cold hardy.
Water: drought tolerant.
Propagation: scarified seeds, softwood cuttings.

Profile: This thornless acacia has fine-textured, fern-like leaves and a low growth pattern, and it spreads by rhizomes—three ideal characteristics for a groundcover. It's also mowable and has dainty little flowers well into the fall. It grows equally well on rocky, sunny slopes or in mottled shade under an open shrub or tree. Fern acacia forms thick colonies along roadsides in the Southwest, so it should survive well in most yards. Still, an occasional watering will keep it lush. This widespread species has six varieties, so be sure to get one that is indigenous to your area.

Acacia angustissima

Allionia incarnata
Trailing four-o'clock

Native Distribution: sandy hills, flats, mesas; below 6,000 feet; California to Texas, Nevada to Oklahoma.
Landscape Zone: 1–6.
Size: stems to 10 feet long, trailing.
Herbaceous perennial.
Leaves: deciduous, oval, 1–2 inches long.
Flower: March–October; pink, 1 inch wide.
Soil: adaptable; well draining.
Exposure: full sun.
Temperature Tolerance: cold hardy.
Water: moderately drought tolerant.
Propagation: seeds.

Profile: Whether considered a groundcover, vine, or wildflower, this delightful little plant will beautify a bare spot for much of the year. It doesn't climb, but it sprawls across rocks, between shrubs, and around posts and poles. Its trailing branches form a mat of fuzzy, gray-green leaves accented with an abundance of dainty, rose-magenta flowers. Plant the seeds in cracks between boulders for a dramatic cascading effect. The foliage dies back in the winter but sprouts vigorously from a woody base.

Allionia incarnata

Artemisia ludoviciana
White sagebrush

Artemisia ludoviciana

Native Distribution: to 8,500 feet; throughout the United States, north into Canada.
Landscape Zone: 1–6.
Size: 1–3 feet tall.
Leaves: evergreen.
Flower: summer–fall; insignificant, releases allergenic pollen.
Soil: adaptable; well draining.
Exposure: full sun, partial shade.
Temperature Tolerance: heat tolerant, cold hardy to 0°F.
Water: drought tolerant.
Propagation: root division.
Profile: The silver evergreen foliage, low stance, and colony-forming habit make white sagebrush an ideal groundcover. In addition, it thrives from scorching desert to mountain forest environments, and it is deer and rabbit resistant. Plant white sagebrush as a border along a hot wall, walk, curb, or foundation and enjoy the highly aromatic scent. You can use it to surround a tree or upright shrub, or as an accent patch in a rock garden, but be careful about planting it in rich garden soil, since it might get out of hand. Mowing or cutting it back in the summer keeps it thick and densely foliated. Several compact cultivars are available with slightly different leaf structures and sizes. This is a wind-pollinated plant, so beware if you suffer from hay fever.

Dalea greggii
Gregg dalea

Native Distribution: hillsides, slopes, limestone mountains; 2,000–4,500; New Mexico and southeast Arizona, Texas, Mexico.
Landscape Zone: 1–6.
Size: 4–9 inches tall, 3 feet across.
Leaves: deciduous.
Flower: spring–fall; clusters of tiny purple flowers.
Soil: sand, loam, limestone, well draining.
Exposure: full sun.
Temperature Tolerance: heat tolerant, freezes to ground.
Water: drought tolerant, 12 inches/year minimum.
Propagation: fresh seeds, semi-hardwood cuttings.
Profile: You'll find this low-branching shrub with trailing limbs a perfect groundcover for dry, sunny exposures. The branches root at the nodes to form densely foliated clumps up to 3 feet in diameter. Plant them 1 1/2 to 2 feet apart for complete cover. This versatile

dalea fills border planters and beds and trails over walls. From spring through fall, clusters of purple pea-like flowers with yellow throats accent the woolly, grayish green foliage. The 1/4-inch flowers have the distinct keel common in members of the legume family. The grayish leaves and delicate flowers provide dramatic contrast

when combined with lustrous green plants, such as damianita, starleaf Mexican orange, and salvias. You'll have to prune it back if it freezes in hard winters, but it recovers rapidly in the spring. Occasional deep watering speeds growth. Just be sure the soil drains fast enough to keep the roots from getting waterlogged.

Dalea greggii

Top: *Dalea greggii* flowers

Glandularia gooddingii (Verbena gooddingii)
Goodding's verbena or desert verbena

Native Distribution: roadsides, desert hills, mesas; below 6,000 feet; widespread from Texas to California, north to Colorado, Nevada.
Landscape Zone: 1–6.
Size: 12–18 inches tall, spreads 2–3 feet or more.

Herbaceous perennial, lives 2 or 3 years.
Leaves: deciduous, bright green, pubescent, deeply cut, 1.5 inches long, 1 inch wide.
Flower: spring–fall; clusters of 1/2-inch-wide, purple flowers in round heads.

Soil: adaptable; well draining.
Exposure: full sun.
Temperature Tolerance: heat tolerant, freezes to ground in winter.
Water: drought tolerant, 12 inches/year minimum.
Propagation: fresh seeds, self-sows readily.
Profile: With ornately lobed leaves and flamboyant heads of blue-to-purple flowers, this verbena proves itself from early spring through fall. Mass planted as a seasonal groundcover, desert verbena paints your landscape in clouds of blue for much of the spring and summer, especially if given an extra drink in the heat of summer. As an accent, it draws attention to leafless plants such as ocotillo, yuccas, prickly pears, or against the smooth green bark of palo verde trees. Its color and size complement damianita, desert marigold, blackfoot daisy, and desert zinnia. Butterflies flock to the blooms. Remove the spent flower heads and cut back in the winter. This species is more upright than the introduced groundcover moss verbena, *Glandularia pulchella*. Also see the description for prairie verbena, *G. bipinnatifida*, in the Wildflowers section.

Glandularia gooddingii

Juniperus communis
Common juniper

Native Distribution: sunny mountain slopes; to 13,000 feet; widespread in eastern and western North America.
Landscape Zone: 3–7
Size: 2–6 feet, prostrate, shrubby
Leaves: evergreen, needle-like, 3/5 inch long.
Fruit: August–October; 1/3 inch diameter, bluish, berry-like, persistent.
Soil: adaptable; well draining.
Exposure: sun, partial shade.
Temperature Tolerance: cold hardy, not heat tolerant.
Water: moderately drought tolerant.
Propagation: cleaned and stratified seeds planted in spring.
Profile: Got a vacant space you want covered with an impenetrable groundcover? Choose one of the dozens of varieties of the versatile *Juniperus communis* and forget about maintenance, other than an occasional trim. This prostrate to shrubby juniper gives total ground coverage and adds year-round texture to its patch of landscape. Available cultivars include dwarf, drooping, mat-forming, or shrubby forms. For colorscaping, you can choose from among shades of green, gray, or bluish foliage. Use it as a border plant along sidewalks and drives; to stabilize slopes; or as a background or low-growing accent. Small mammals and more than 30 species of birds and feast on the fruit.

Juniperus communis foliage and fruit

Juniperus communis

Mahonia repens
(Berberis repens)
Creeping barberry

Native Distribution: shaded mountain slopes; 4,500–10,000 feet; California to west Texas, north to Canada.
Landscape Zone: 4–7.
Size: 4–12 inches.
Leaves: evergreen, red in winter.
Flower: spring; clusters of small, yellow blooms.
Fruit: black berries.
Soil: adaptable; well draining.
Exposure: full to partial shade.
Temperature Tolerance: cold hardy but not heat tolerant.
Water: moderately drought tolerant.
Propagation: fresh, triple-stratified, or scarified seeds, semi-softwood cuttings, suckers.
Profile: With holly-like evergreen leaves, colorful flowers, ornate fruit,

Mahonia repens

and a naturally low growth habit, creeping barberry is almost the perfect groundcover. Almost, that is, because it just can't tolerate desert heat. It likes the cool summers of higher elevations. If you live in an arid climate, try mulching around this beautiful groundcover to keep the soil cool and moist, and plant it in the shade. These plants grow moderately slowly, but the stems root where they touch the ground, and new sprouts grow from underground rhizomes to form a dense mat. Plant them 10 to 12 inches apart for fast cover.

161

Muhlenbergia rigens
Deer grass

Native Distribution: chaparral grasslands, mountain slopes, pine forests; 2,500–7,000 feet; Texas to California.
Landscape Zone: 1–7.
Size: clumps to 4 feet tall and wide.
Leaves: slender, gray-green, turn brown in cold winters.
Fruit: fall; fluffy seed plumes on stalk ends.
Soil: adaptable; well draining.
Exposure: full sun, partial shade.

Temperature Tolerance: root hardy to 10°F.
Water: drought tolerant.
Propagation: clump division, seeds.
Profile: You'll love the picturesque effect of this tall bunch grass when used as a lone accent, in a landscape mix, or grouped as a groundcover for a slope planting. You can plant it to droop over a wall, or as a focal plant to balance a corner garden. It's a perfect match for rockwork and to soften rock gardens. The erect seed heads decorate the plant in the fall, and the gracefully arching, pale green leaf blades contribute color until the plant goes dormant in late winter. Even then its artistic shape and grayish brown hues continue to complement your yard. Cut the clumps back to the ground in the winter for rigorous spring growth.

Muhlenbergia rigens

Nassella tenuissima (Stipa tenuissima)
Threadgrass or Mexican feathergrass

Native Distribution: rocky slopes, dry open woods, dry prairies; New Mexico, Texas, Mexico.
Landscape Zone: 1–4.
Size: clumps to 18–24 inches tall and 18–24 inches wide; flowering stalks 6–12 inches long.
Leaves: 6–14 inches long, slender, gray-green, turn brown in summer.
Fruit: early fall; fluffy seed plumes on stalk ends.
Soil: adaptable; well draining.
Exposure: full sun, partial shade.
Temperature Tolerance: root hardy to 10°F.

Water: drought tolerant.
Propagation: seeds, self-seeding, plant divisions.
Profile: The fine-textured threadgrass grows in a dense fountain-like clump with slender, wiry, thread-like leaves and a feathery seed stalk. The airy leaves sway gracefully in breezes, and the seed stalks will glow brilliantly when backlit by the afternoon sun. The flower clusters develop in the spring and last well into the fall as they ripen to golden brown. The foliage stays green in winter, but goes dormant during the heat of the summer. As a groundcover, *Nassella tenuissima* stabilizes sunny slopes. Planted alone, the fluffy seed heads and leaves add a soft accent to a bare spot, corner, or fence. In a xeriscape planting, the plant's size, green color, and vertical profile complement ground-hugging groundcovers and mounding flowers, such as damianita and zinnias. The plant self-seeds, so be sure to remove the seed heads before they ripen if you want to contain it. The 'Pony Tails' cultivar produces particularly abundant and showy seed heads.

Nassella tenuissima

Phyla species
Frogfruit

Native Distribution: moist soils, throughout most of New Mexico and Arizona; California to Florida, north to Pennsylvania.
Landscape Zone: 1–7.
Size: 3–8 inches tall.
Leaves: evergreen.
Flower: May–October; clusters of tiny, white flowers on 4-inch stems.
Soil: adaptable; well to poor draining.
Exposure: full shade to full sun.
Temperature Tolerance: cold hardy.
Water: moderately drought tolerant.
Propagation: plant division.

Phyla incisa

Profile: Frogfruit may have an unglamorous name, but the plant forms an attractive mat-like groundcover. The sprawling stems root at the leaf nodes to form thick colonies. Tiny verbena-like flowers contribute a little, but not much, to the plant's appearance. You'll need to give it extra water to keep it lush, especially during the hottest parts of the year. It goes dormant in hard winters. Numerous species of frogfruit grow throughout the Southwest. *Phyla incisa* and *P. nodililora* are probably the most widespread, growing from Houston to Yuma.

Pteridium aquilinum
Bracken fern

Native Distribution: meadows, canyons, dry woodlands; throughout North America.
Landscape Zone: 2–6.
Size: 1–3 feet tall.
Leaves: deciduous.
Soil: deep, loose, well draining.
Exposure: full to partial shade.
Temperature Tolerance: root hardy, freezes to ground.
Water: moderately drought tolerant.
Propagation: dormant root division.
Profile: Nothing creates that idyllic forest atmosphere like a stand of bracken fern underneath a canopy of trees. If you don't have your own private woods, use ferns to surround a mature pine or other tree with a tall trunk and shade-producing crown. Avoid planting in shallow, rocky soil types. This fern needs loose, rich soil to allow its rhizomes to spread and develop a thick colony. Keep it moist until the rhizomes become established. The variety *pubescens* grows at high elevations in the western United States. Other native ferns are also available from nurseries. Species with broad, luxuriant foliage generally require moist soil, semi-shade, and moderately humid conditions.

Pteridium aquilinum

Sedum species
Stonecrop

Native Distribution: throughout the Southwest.
Landscape Zone: 1–7.
Size: 2–12 inches tall.
Leaves: evergreen.
Flower: spring–fall; pink, white, or yellow, tiny.
Soil: adaptable; well draining.
Exposure: full sun to full shade.
Temperature Tolerance: cold hardy.
Water: drought tolerant.
Propagation: cuttings.
Profile: These sprawling little succulents make the perfect accent for your rock garden. Sedums thrive in dry locations, complement small cacti, and spread to cover bare ground. You can root them in a porous rock for a picturesque interest, or let them dangle out of a rock crevice. They have delicate stems, which break easily if you're trying to remove weeds or leaves from your garden. But not to worry. Just stick the pieces in loose soil, and they're guaranteed to root. Some imported species become rather aggressive in a rich garden setting.

Sedum nuttallianum

Cacti

Carnegica gigantea
Saguaro

Native Distribution: rocky foothills, plains, and washes of the Sonoran Desert; 600–3,600 feet; southwestern Arizona desert, Mexico.
Landscape Zone: 1–2.
Size: 20–50 feet.
Flower: May–June; white, 3–4 inches long.

Fruit: red to purple, 2–4 inches long, edible.
Spines: white to gray, 3 inches long
Soil: rocky, well draining.
Exposure: full sun.
Water: 8 inches/year maximum.
Propagation: seeds.

Profile: The saguaro is probably the best-known cactus in the United States. It's illustrated in practically every elementary school science textbook. Though synonymous with the Southwest in the minds of many Americans, saguaros grow only in a limited portion of the Sonoran Desert. If you live in the desert, you can have one in your yard—but you'll have to grow it yourself from seed, unless you have a few thousand dollars to spend, with no guarantee of a successful transplant. Nurseries price them by the size and number of arms. A large specimen weighs tons and requires guy wires for support until the anchor roots become established. The plant will slowly die if the taproot is damaged, though it may take years before you know it. Rigid laws restrict the collecting of saguaros from the wild, but seedlings are readily available. Don't plant one in sandy soil, or it will eventually topple over. As with most cacti, water is a saguaro's worst enemy; avoid lawn or irrigated locations. Typically, saguaros reach 1 foot in 15 years, 10 feet in 40 years, and 20 feet in 100 years, at which point the first arm develops.

Carnegica gigantea

Carnegica gigantean flowers

Echinocereus fendleri
Strawberry cactus or hedgehog

Native Distribution: deserts; west Texas to Arizona, Colorado, Mexico.
Landscape Zone: 1–3.
Size: 10-inch stems forming a mound 2- to 3-feet in diameter.
Flower: spring; 3–4 inches, red.
Fruit: 1–2 inches long, red to purple, spiny, edible.
Spines: 5–12 radials to 1/2–1 inch long, 1–3 centrals to 3 inches long.
Soil: sandy, rocky, well draining.
Exposure: full sun.
Propagation: seeds.
Profile: You'll run for your camera when the flamboyant reddish flowers of this cactus begin blooming. The spectacular blossoms will be the focal point of your rock garden, especially if the plant forms a large mound. When the fruit matures, you'll know why these plants are called strawberry cacti—but you'll have to fight your way through the dense spines that protect the succulent fruit. When planting this cactus, make sure its roots will never become waterlogged, or it will rot. About seven species and numerous varieties of strawberry hedgehogs grow throughout the Southwest, all with gorgeous bright red flowers. *Echinocereus fendleri* is the one of the more western species, and it is well established in Arizona. If you can find the golden hedgehog, *E. nichollii*, from southern Arizona, you should add one to your garden as a contrast. It has blond, golden spines and pink flowers.

Top: *Echinocereus nichollii*

Right: *Echinocereus fendleri*

Echinocereus pectinatus
Rainbow cactus

Native Distribution: limestone hills and desert grasslands, 4,000–6,000 feet; southern Arizona, New Mexico, west Texas, Mexico.
Landscape Zone: 1–6.
Size: 4- to 12-inch-tall cylindrical stem.
Flower: spring–summer; 2–5 inches, red to lavender.
Fruit: greenish, 1–2 inches long.
Spines: 15–23 recurved radials to 1/2 inch long, 2–3 centrals 1/8 inch long.
Soil: sandy, rocky, well draining.
Exposure: full sun.

Echinocereus pectinatus

Propagation: seeds.
Profile: A dense, lace-like mat of spines covers the stems of the rainbow cactus, making it a fine-textured accent for your rock garden. The stems usually grow solitary, but they may form a loosely clumped cluster. The large, brilliantly colored flowers, which later develop into fruit, seem out of place on the spiny cylinder. The flamboyant flowers vary from magenta to lavender, giving this cactus its common name. Botanists sometimes lump this species with the yellow-flowered Texas rainbow hedgehog, *Echinocereus dasyacanthus*, or consider them varieties of a single species.

Echinocereus triglochidiatus
Claret cup cactus or hedgehog

Native Distribution: rocky hillsides and mountains; 4,000–9,000 feet; Arizona and New Mexico, central Texas, Colorado, Mexico.

Landscape Zone: 1–7.
Size: 1-foot stems forming a mound 1–4 feet in diameter.
Flower: spring–summer; 1–2 inches, scarlet.

Fruit: spiny, red.
Spines: 5–7 radials to 1 inch long, 1–4 centrals to 1 3/4 inches long.
Soil: sandy, igneous, rich in humus, well draining.
Exposure: full sun.
Water: drought tolerant.
Propagation: seeds.
Profile: This wide-ranging and highly variable species has confused botanists since it was first named in 1848. Experts can't decide whether it's one species with numerous varieties or multiple species. But gardeners will agree that the waxy, long-lasting flowers are spectacular. With age, claret cups form rounded mounds, a picturesque addition to your desert garden, especially when covered with the scarlet blooms. Since some varieties are adapted to desert chaparral while others thrive in montane forests, try to buy one propagated from a locally indigenous plant. They normally grow in humus-rich soil, so plant them in a well-draining soil mix with leaf mold.

Echinocereus triglochidiatus

Ferocactus wislizeni (Echinocactus wislizeni)
Barrel cactus

Ferocactus wislizeni

Native Distribution: sandy, rocky soils, deserts and grasslands; 1,000–4,500 feet; Arizona east into Texas, Mexico.

Landscape Zone: 1–6.

Size: unbranched cylindrical stems, 4–10 feet tall, 2 feet in diameter, usually 2–3 feet tall in landscape settings.

Flower: spring–summer; yellow to orange, 1–3 inches, round.

Fruit: yellow, 1–2 inches long.

Spines: 12–20 or more bristle-like radials to 1–2 inches long, 4 stout centrals to 3 inches long.

Soil: gravelly, sandy, well draining.

Exposure: full sun.

Propagation: seeds.

Profile: Barrel cactus provides a medium-height accent between the taller chollas and prickly pears and the smaller hedgehogs and pincushions. A half dozen or more of the red-to-tangerine-to-yellow flowers bloom at once in a circle around the tip of the stem. Yellow, barrel-shaped fruit follow the flowers. Heavy, sometimes hooked, spines cover the stem to protect the plant's succulent flesh from thirsty predators. The dense cover of spines gives the cactus a yellow or reddish color.

About six species of barrel cactus are native to the Southwest deserts. The popular golden barrel cactus, *Echinocactus grusonii*, is from Mexico (where it is endangered from over-collection) and is widely available in the nursery trade. The basketball-sized specimens make a dramatic statement when mass planted on a sunny slope or rock garden. It is frost hardy to 14°F for brief periods, but requires an average minimum temperature above 55°F to thrive.

Echinocactus grusonii

Mammillaria vivipara

Mammillaria vivipara
Pincushion cactus

Native Distribution: dry, rocky soils in grasslands, plains, mountains; northern New Mexico, Arizona, north to Canada.
Landscape Zone: 1–7.
Size: 1–3 inches in diameter.
Flower: spring–summer; pink to purple, 1–2 inches across, in circle around top.
Fruit: 1/2–3/4 inch, oval, fleshy, green.
Spines: 12–21 radials to 5/8 inch long, 1–8 centrals 1/2–3/4 inch long.
Soil: gravelly, sandy, limestone, well draining.
Exposure: full sun.
Propagation: seeds.
Profile: Mammillarias, many from Central and South America, are some of the most popular cacti available in the nursery trade. Numerous species grow throughout the western states, but *Mammillaria vivipara* is one of the few that can withstand freezing. It grows in the northern plains and mountains, where few other cacti survive. Flower color among *Mammillaria* species varies from creamy to purple. The blooms cluster around the apex of the round, unbranched stems to form a circle. As many as a dozen flowers will open at the same time. A layer of fruit often surrounds the new blooms, adding bright red to green colors to the arrangement. Some pincushion cacti are golf-ball-sized; others grow to almost a foot in diameter. The name *mammillaria* comes from the nipple-shaped tubercles that cover the stems. If you want a rock garden that represents native species, buy plants that are propagated from pincushion species indigenous to your area.

Opuntia basilaris
Beavertail prickly pear

Native Distribution: sandy desert soils, canyons, dry mountain slopes; to 200–4,000 feet and higher; Arizona, California, Nevada, Utah.

Landscape Zone: 1–6.

Size: low growing, spreading, 2–4 feet high, 6 feet diameter.

Flower: March–June; pink to magenta, 3 inches across.

Fruit: oval, 3 inches, purple.

Spines: absent, or few along top of pad.

Soil: sandy, well draining.

Exposure: full sun, cold hardy to 0°F.

Propagation: scarified seeds, stem division.

Profile: In contrast to the yellow color of most prickly pears, beavertail produces an abundance of brilliant red to pink flowers. As a bonus, the pads of *Opuntia basilaris* lack the vicious, long spines found on other *Opuntia* plants. But if you think the pads are naked and harmless, think again. Clusters of tiny brown barbs (glochids) grow in rows all over the stems and fruit of all prickly pears—so hands off. The thornless pads of beavertail provide a textural contrast to other spine-covered cacti, and the pastel flowers add zip to a xeriscape garden. Nurseries carry cultivars with blue-gray to green pads and pink to magenta flowers. Also sometimes available, the Texas-native blind prickly pear, *Opuntia rufida*, is another spineless species with yellow flowers. Caution: All prickly pears have the tiny, hair-like glochid thorns in clusters on the pads. The barbed glochids cause extreme discomfort and must be meticulously removed with tweezers.

Opuntia basilaris flowers

Below: *Opuntia basilaris*

Opuntia bigelovii
Teddy bear cholla

Native Distribution: deserts, south-facing hillsides; to 3,000 feet; Arizona, California, Nevada, Mexico.
Landscape Zone: 1–4
Size: shrubby, 5–8 feet tall.
Flower: February–May; greenish, 1 1/2 inches across at end of jointed stems.
Fruit: yellowish, 3/4-inch knobby ovals.
Spines: silver to golden, 1 inch long, covered with sheaths.

Soil: sandy, well draining.
Exposure: full sun.
Propagation: scarified seeds, stem division.
Profile: The dense covering of golden spines gives teddy bear cholla a fuzzy appearance—but look closer, and you'll find that the thorny stems resemble a porcupine more than a teddy bear. Unlike the vivid red-flowered chollas, this dramatic species blooms with waxy, pale-green, almost translucent flowers highlighted with a dense cluster of yellow stamens. Chollas make spectacular focal plants for cactus gardens, but be sure to plant them far away from possible human contact. The brittle, spiny joints seem to jump onto pant legs and shoes. This hitch-hiking design makes growing chollas a snap: Just plant one of the easily rooting joints in a sunny, well-draining spot, and soon you'll have your own teddy bear.

Opuntia bigelovii

Opuntia macrocentra (Opuntia violacea)
Violet prickly pear
Opuntia santa-rita (Opuntia violacea var. santa-rita)
Santa Rita prickly pear

Native Distribution: desert grass-lands; below 5,000 feet; west Texas through southern New Mexico and Arizona, Mexico.

Landscape Zone: 1–6.

Size: 3–7 feet tall.

Flower: April–August; 2–4 inches, yellow.

Fruit: summer–fall; 1–2 inches long, purple-to-red, edible.

Spines: reddish brown to black, 2–8 inches long.

Soil: sandy, gravelly, well draining.

Exposure: full sun.

Propagation: scarified seeds, stem division.

Profile: The red-tinged pads distinguish these two cacti from the many other species of prickly pears common throughout the Southwest. During the winter or extreme droughts, the 4- to 8-inch roundish pads turn a maroon red, providing a striking accent for your otherwise dormant cactus garden. In the spring, the cactus comes to life, with yellow, rose-like flowers lining the spiny pads. *Opuntia macrocentra* has 4- to 7-inch-long spines, while the popular Santa Rita species is often spineless. As with most prickly pears, the pads root easily and grow rapidly when placed in loose, well-draining soil.

Top: *Opuntia santa-rita*

Right: *Opuntia macrocentra*

Opuntia phaeacantha
New Mexico prickly pear

Native Distribution: desert flats, arid hills, grasslands; to 7,500 feet; Texas to California, Kansas to Nevada, South Dakota.
Landscape Zone: 1–6.
Size: 3–7 feet tall, 10–15 feet in diameter.
Flower: April–June; 3–4 inches, yellow to orange.
Fruit: summer, fall; 2–3 inches long, purple to red, edible.
Spines: white, to 3 inches long.

Soil: sandy, well draining.
Exposure: full sun.
Propagation: scarified seeds, stem division.
Profile: This large proportioned prickly pear will grow to fill the space of a large shrub, but with the multi-leveled texture of dozens of prickly stems and pads. Start by rooting a single pad, and enjoy the evolving shape of the plant for years. Maintaining the size to match the scale of your site is easy: Just snap off a stem and start another plant. The profusion of yellow flowers and red fruit along the edges of the pads make prickly pears the highlight of any landscape. Combine the New Mexico species with chollas and other prickly pears for a spectacular desert exhibition garden. The most widespread species in the Southwest is Englemann prickly pear, *Opuntia engelmannii*; it is usually available at nurseries.

Opuntia phaeacantha

Opuntia engelmannii

Opuntia versicolor
Staghorn cholla

Native Distribution: desert grasslands, plains; 1,000–4,000 feet; Texas, New Mexico, Arizona, Mexico.
Landscape Zone: 1–6.
Size: shrubby, 3–15 feet tall.
Flower: April–May; 2 inches wide, red, yellow, orange, or brown.
Fruit: yellow, 1–2 inches long.
Spines: brownish, 1 inch long, covered with sheaths.
Soil: sandy, gravelly, well draining.
Exposure: full sun.
Propagation: scarified seeds, stem division.
Profile: You probably won't ever find a large cholla like *Opuntia versicolor* in a nursery; they're just too thorny to handle. To grow one, simply stick a stem joint in the ground and stand back. The intricately branching stems look like braided ropes, with each section ready to break off and hang onto any unfortunate passerby; then, it roots where it drops. Showy red, burgundy, or yellow flowers crown the tips of the cane-like stems in spring. This cactus' size makes it a good focal plant for your rock garden and a favorite nesting site for cactus wrens. To bring extra color to your cactus bed, look for specimens of staghorn cholla that have reddish joints. Numerous other cholla species with similar landscape applications are available. The dangling fruit of chain-fruit cholla, *O. fuldida*, make a dramatic accent piece.

Opuntia versicolor flowers

Opuntia versicolor

Pachycereus schottii (Cereus schottii, Lophocereus schottii)
Senita cactus

Native Distribution: desert valleys, south-facing hillsides; 1,000–2,000 feet; southwest Arizona, Mexico.
Landscape Zone: 1–2.
Size: columnar to 20 feet, with multiple trunks.
Flower: April–September, at night; lavender, funnel-shaped, 1 1/2 inches across.
Fruit: 1 inch long, egg-shaped, spiny, red.
Spines: 8–10 per areole, gray, bristle-like, 3 inches long.

Soil: gravelly, well draining.
Exposure: full sun, growing tips cold hardy to 25°F.
Propagation: seeds, cuttings, division.
Profile: Though it grows primarily in Organ Pipe National Monument in southwestern Arizona and Mexico, senita is widespread in landscapes across the Southwest. The tall, slender stems of mature specimens often twist and bend like octopus arms waving in the sky. Mexicans named the plant senita, or "old one," because the older stems develop a hairy growth on the ends reminiscent of an old man's whiskers.

Totem pole cactus, *Pachycereus schottii* var. *monstrosus*, is wildly popular for cactus and patio gardens and container plantings. The spineless, tubercled stems create a spectacular highlight, whether a two-foot plant in a container or a multi-stemmed specimen in a yard. In nature, this unusual form occurs only in Baja California, so it is less frost tolerant than senita. It needs protection below 25°F.

Take careful consideration when planting senita, organ pipe, or saguaro cacti. They all require an exacting sun and heat profile and suffer if planted where cold air settles in the winter or shade or moisture persists. If you buy a sizeable specimen, be sure it is properly labeled as nursery grown or salvaged from nature with proper permits attached.

Pachycereus schottii var. *monstrosus*

Pachycereus schottii

Stenocereus thurberi (Cereus thurberi)
Organ pipe cactus

Native Distribution: desert valleys, south-facing hillsides; 1,000–3,500 feet; southwest Arizona, Mexico.
Landscape Zone: 1–2.
Size: columnar to 20 feet, with multiple trunks.
Flower: May–June, at night; lavender, funnel-shaped, 3 inches across.
Fruit: 3 inches diameter, red, spiny.
Spines: 11–19 per areole, brown to black, 1/2 inch long.
Soil: gravelly, well draining.
Exposure: full sun, cold hardy to 25°F.
Propagation: seeds, cuttings, division.
Profile: In the South, homeowners plant a live oak so their grandchildren can play under the majestic spreading limbs of a mature specimen. In Phoenix or Tucson, you have to think that far ahead if you plant an organ pipe or a saguaro. Organ pipe cacti grow readily from seeds, but you'll be collecting Social Security before one gets as tall as head high. If you take a stem cutting, allow the cut surface to callous over before planting to inhibit fungi from invading. Plant only in locations that are protected from frost and cold temperatures during the winter, or the growing tips might become damaged.

Stenocereus thurberi

Stenocereus thurberi, with *Encelia farinosa*

Appendix 1
Colorscaping with Flowering Trees, Shrubs, Vines, and Groundcovers

Note: Dates refer to the range of flowering or fruiting times for the species through a variety of conditions; bloom times for individual plants may vary.

Trees

Acacia farnesiana, huisache
  zones 1–2
  February–April
Acacia greggii, catclaw acacia
  zones 1–6
  April–October
Arbutus arizonica, Arizona madrone
  zones 2–7
  February–March
Cercis orbiculata, western redbud
  zones 1–6
  February–April
Chilopsis linearis, desert willow
  zones 1–3
  April–August
Ebenopsis ebano, Texas ebony
  zone 1
  May–August
Fraxinus cuspidata, fragrant ash
  zones 1–3
  April–May
Leucaena retusa, goldenball leadtree
  zones 1–3
  April–October
Olneya tesota, desert ironwood
  zones 1–3
  May–June
Parkinsonia florida, blue palo verde
  zones 1–3
  March–May

Parkinsonia microphylla, foothills palo verde
  zones 1–3
  April–May
Prosopis glandulosa, honey mesquite
  zones 1–3
  May–June
Prosopis velutina, velvet mesquite
  zones 1–3
  May–June
Prunus serotina, southwestern black cherry
  zones 3–7
  March–April
Prunus virginiana, western chokecherry
  zones 2–7
  April–July
Rhus lanceolata, prairie flameleaf sumac
  zones 1–5
  June–August
Robinia neomexicana, New Mexico locust
  zones 2–7
  April–August
Sambucus nigra subsp. *canadensis*, Mexican elder
  zones 1–3
  September–June
Sapindus saponaria, western soapberry
  zones 1–6
  May–August
Ungnadia speciosa, Mexican buckeye
  zones 1–6
  March–April

Shrubs

Acacia constricta, white-thorn acacia
    zones 1–3
    May–August

Agave species, century plant
    zones 1–6
    June–August

Aloysia gratissima, bee brush
    zones 1–3
    March–November

Amelanchier utahensis, serviceberry
    zones 2–6
    April–May

Amorpha fruticosa, false indigo
    zones 2–6
    May–June

Anisacanthus thurberi, desert honeysuckle
    zones 1–6
    June–October

Arctostaphylos patula, greenleaf Manzanita
    zones 3–7
    March–May

Baccharis sarothroides, desert broom
    zones 1–6
    August–September

Bouvardia ternifolia, scarlet bouvardia
    zones 1–6
    June–September

Buddleja marrubiifolia, woolly butterflybush
    zones 1–3
    April–September

Caesalpinia gilliesii, desert bird of paradise
    zones 1–2
    April–September

Calliandra conferta, fairy duster
    zones 1–3
    October–April

Ceanothus greggii, desert ceanothus
    zones 2–4
    March–June

Chamaebatiaria millefolium, fernbush
    zones 2–7
    July–November

Choisya dumosa, starleaf Mexican orange
    zones 2–7
    June–October

Chrysactinia mexicana, damianita
    zones 1–4
    April–September

Dalea formosa, feather dalea
    zones 1–4
    March–June

Dalea frutescens, black dalea
    zones 1–4
    July–October

Dasiphora floribunda, shrubby cinquefoil
    zones 3–7
    June–September

Dasylinon species, sotol
    zones 1–6
    May–July

Encelia farinose, brittlebush
    zones 1–2
    November–May, after rains

Ericameria laricifolia, larchleaf goldenweed
    zones 1–6
    August–December

Ericameria nauseosa, chamisa
    zones 3–7
    July–October

Fallugia paradoxa, Apache plume
    zones 3–7
    April–October

Fendlera rupicola, cliff fendlerbush
    zones 2–6
    March, June

Fouquieria splendens, ocotillo
    zones 1–2
    March–June

Hesperaloe parviflora, red yucca
    zones 1–6
    May–October

Justicia californica, chuparosa
    zones 1–2
    year-round, periodically

Justicia canadicans, jacobinia
    zones 1–2
    year-round, periodically

Larrea tridentata, creosote bush
    zones 1–3
    February–October

Leucophyllum frutescens, cenizo
  zones 1–2
  year-round, after rain
Mahonia fremontii, Fremont barberry
  zones 4–7
  March–April
Mahonia haematocarpa, red barberry
  zones 2–6
  February–April
Mahonia trifoliolata, agarita
  zone 2
  February–April
Mimosa biuncifera, catclaw mimosa
  zones 1–4
  May–September
Mimosa borealis, fragrant mimosa
  zones 1–4
  May–September
Mimosa dysocarpa, velvet pod mimosa
  zones 1–4
  May–September
Nolina species, beargrass
  zones 1–6
  March–July
Parthenium argentatum, guayule
  zones 1–6
  April–October
Parthenium incanum, mariola
  zones 1–6
  July–October
Psorothamnus scoparius, broom dalea
  zone 10
  August–September
Purshia stansburiana, Stansbury cliffrose
  zones 2–6
  April–July
Rhus glabra, smooth sumac
  zones 3–7
  June–August

Rhus ovata, sugar sumac
  zones 1–4
  March–May
Rhus trilobata, skunkbush
  zones 2–6
  March–June
Rhus virens, evergreen sumac
  zones 1–4
  August–October
Ribes aureum, golden currant
  zones 2–7
  March–June
Rosa woodsii, wood's rose
  zones 3–7
  June–August
Salvia greggii, autumn sage
  zones 2–4
  April–November
Senna wislizeni, shrubby senna
  zones 1–2
  May–September
Sophora secundiflora, Texas mountain laurel
  zones 1–2
  March–April
Tecoma stans, yellow trumpet flower
  zones 1–2
  May–October
Vauquelinia californica, Arizona rosewood
  zones 2–6
  May–June
Viguiera stenoloba, skeleton-leaf goldeneye
  zones 1–3
  June–October
Yucca species, yucca
  zones 1–7
  March–June

Vines and Groundcovers

Acacia angustissima, fern acacia
    zones 1–7
    summer–fall
Allionia incarnata, trailing four-o'clock
    zones 1–6
    March–October
Campsis radicans, trumpet creeper
    zones 1–7
    May–October
Clematis ligusticifolia, western virgin's bower
    zones 2–7
    May–September
Dalea greggii, Gregg dalea
    zones 1–6
    spring–fall

Glandularia gooddingii, Goodding's Verbena
    zones 1–6
    spring–fall
Ibervillea lindheimeri, globeberry
    zones 2–4
    April–September
Lantana urticoides, West Indian lantana
    zones 1–6
    spring–winter
Mahonia repens, creeping barberry
    zones 4–7
    spring
Maurandya antirrhiniflora, snapdragon vine
    zones 2–7
    February–October

Appendix 2
Plants with Evergreen, Semi-Evergreen, or Persistent Leaves

Trees

Arbutus arizonica, Arizona madrone
Cupressus arizonica, Arizona cypress
Ebenopsis ebano, Texas ebony
Juniperus deppeana, alligator juniper
Juniperus scopulorum, Rocky Mountain juniper
Picea pungens, Colorado blue spruce
Pinus cembroides, Mexican pinyon pine
Pinus edulis, New Mexico pinyon pine

Quercus arizonica, Arizona oak
Quercus emoryi, Emory oak
Quercus grisea, gray oak
Quercus oblongifolia, Mexican blue oak
Sambucus nigra subsp. *canadescens*, Mexican elder
Washingtonia filifera, California fan palm
Washingtonia robusta, Mexican fan palm

Groundcovers

Artemisia ludoviciana, white sagebrush
Juniperus communis, common juniper
Mahonia repens, creeping barberry
Phyla species, frogfruit
Sedum species, stonecrop

Shrubs

Agave species, century plant
Arctostaphylos patula, greenleaf manzanita
Artemisia filifolia, sand sagebrush
Artimesia tridentata, big sagebrush
Baccharis sarothroides, desert broom
Buddleja marrubiifolia, woolly butterflybush
Calliandra conferta, fairy duster
Ceanothus greggii, desert ceanothus
Celtis pallida, desert hackberry
Cercocarpus montanus, mountain mahogany
Chamaebatiaria millefolium, fernbush
Choisya dumosa, starleaf Mexican orange
Chrysactinia mexicana, damianita
Dasiphora floribunda, shrubby cinquefoil
Dasylirion species, sotol
Dodonaea viscosa, hopbush
Encelia farinosa, brittlebush
Ephedra species, joint fir
Ericameria laricifolia, larchleaf goldenweed
Ericameria nauseosa, chamisa
Fallugia paradoxa, Apache plume
Fraxinus greggii, Gregg ash

Garrya wrightii, Wright silktassel
Hesperaloe parviflora, red yucca
Krascheninnikovia lanata, winterfat
Larrea tridentata, creosote bush
Leucophyllum frutescens, Texas ranger
Lycium species, wolfberry
Mahonia fremontii, Fremont barberry
Mahonia haemetocarpa, red barberry
Mahonia trifoliolata, agarita
Nolina species, beargrass
Parthenium argentatum, guayule
Parthenium incanum, mariola
Purshia stansburiana, Stansbury cliffrose
Rhus ovata, sugar sumac
Rhus virens, evergreen sumac
Salvia greggii, autumn sage
Simmondsia chinensis, jojoba
Sophora secundiflora, Texas mountain laurel
Vauquelinia californica, Arizona rosewood
Viguiera stenoloba, skeleton-leaf goldeneye
Yucca species

Glossary of Terms

Biennial: a flower that takes two years to mature and bloom.

Bract: Usually small and leaf-like structures located below the petals of a flower. In some plants, the bracts are as colorful and showy as the petals.

Budding (propagation): A twig axis with a dormant bud is removed and inserted into an actively growing limb by making a T-shaped cut, peeling back the bark, and inserting the bud section into the incision.

Caliche: Rocky, limestone soil; covers much of Central, North, and West Texas.

Chlorosis: Iron deficiency usually caused by soil with a pH greater than 7.5. The high calcium content inhibits iron utilization by the plant. This abiotic disease causes yellow leaves, slow growth, and branch dieback.

Cold hardy: Able to survive hard winter freezes.

Corm: An underground structure similar to a bulb but without scales.

Cuttings, hardwood: Cuttings taken from the current season's growth of a plant, after the wood matures in the fall or dormant season. Take a section from just above a leaf node, about 12 to 16 inches long and up to 1/2 inch in diameter. Store the cuttings in moist sand until spring. To root, dust with a rooting powder and place in moist sand, vermiculite, or peat. Cover with polyethylene, which is permeable to oxygen but holds in water vapor.

Cuttings, semi-hardwood: Cuttings taken from a plant soon after seasonal growth stops but before the wood hardens, usually in the summer.

Cuttings, softwood: Cuttings taken from actively growing wood, usually in the spring.

Dieback: The gradual dying back of plant shoots, beginning from the growing tips.

Division (propagation): Separating a plant and its roots into two or more sections for replanting.

Drought tolerant: Requiring no supplemental water to survive extended periods of drought, but may need periodic deep watering to maintain maximum flowering, foliage, and growth.

Grafting (propagation): A delicate procedure whereby a twig is removed with a leaf and leaf bud and inserted into a growing limb.

Holdfast: A root-like structure that a vine uses to attach to a surface.

Layering (propagation): A growing limb is bent and covered with soil, leaving 6 to 12 inches of the end exposed. The buried portion will grow roots and can then be cut from the parent plant to grow on its own.

Microhabitat: A combination of physical and biological conditions that is different from the surrounding conditions. For example, a flower bed located at the southwest corner of a house receives more sun and reflected heat than those in a shady entryway.

Rosette: A small, stemless plant or flower with radial symmetry.

Scarifying seed: Mechanically pricking, filing, or wearing down tough seed coat so it will absorb water and germinate.

Shade, full: No direct sun; heavily filtered sun okay.

Shade, partial: Less than six hours of full or filtered sun per day.

Shrub: A woody plant that usually has multiple trunks or stems and a mature height of less than 15 feet.

Stolon: An underground stem that roots at nodes to form new plants.

Stratification: Placing seeds in moist sand or other medium, sealing in polyethylene bags, and storing in the refrigerator for a designated time, typically three months at 40ºF.

Sub-shrub: A multi-stemmed perennial larger than a wildflower but smaller than a shrub, usually 2 to 3 feet tall and wide.

Sun, full: At least six hours of direct or reflected sun per day.

Tree: A woody plant that usually has a single trunk and a mature height of more than 15 feet.

Tubercle: A knob-like protrusion on the surface of a plant. Found most notably on *Mammillaria* cactus plants.

Vegetative propagation: Seedless reproduction, such as bulbs, softwood cuttings, layering, and root suckers.

Xeriscape: A landscape utilizing plants that require little water or additional irrigation, even during droughts.

Useful Organizations and Demonstration Gardens

Arizona and New Mexico have a number of public gardens, arboretums, parks, native plant associations, and special-interest groups that offer information on landscaping and conserving native plants. Other sources for information include your county water district, agricultural extension services, and the agriculture departments at major universities; they offer printed material on landscaping with native plants.

ARIZONA

Demonstration Gardens, Programs, and Plant Sales

The Arboretum at Arizona State University
826 Apache Boulevard
P.O. Box 872512
Tempe, AZ 85287-2512
http://www.azarboretum.org
Arboretum guides are available at the ASU visitors information center.

Arizona-Sonora Desert Museum
2021 North Kinney Road
Tucson, AZ 85743
(520) 883-1380
info@desertmuseum.org
http://www.desertmuseum.org

Boyce Thompson Southwestern Arboretum
37615 U.S. Highway 60
Superior, AZ 85273
(602) 689-2723
http://cals.arizona.edu/BTA

Phoenix Desert Botanical Garden
1201 North Galvin Parkway
Phoenix, AZ 85008
(480) 941-1225
http://www.dbg.org
For more information on desert-related plants or problems, call the plant hotline, (480) 941-1225.

Tohono Chul Park
7366 North Paseo del Norte
Tucson, AZ 85704
(520) 742-6455
http://www.tohonochulpark.org

Tucson Botanical Gardens
2150 North Alvernon Way
Tucson, AZ 85712
(520) 326-9686
TBG@tucsonbotanical.org
http://tucsonbotanical.org

University of Arizona Campus Arboretum
P.O. Box 210036
Tucson, AZ 85721
http://arboretum.arizona.edu
Includes 83 trees on campus.

Flagstaff Arboretum
4001 South Woody Mountain Road
Flagstaff, AZ 86001-8775
(928) 774-1442
http://www.thearb.org
Provides list of drought-tolerant landscape plants.

Organizations and Agencies

Arizona Native Plant Society
Box 41206
Tucson, AZ 85717
http://aznps.org

Central Arizona Cactus and Succulent Society
info@centralarizonacactus.org
www.centralarizonacactus.org
Meets at the Phoenix Desert Botanical Garden on the
last Sunday of most months.

Tucson Cactus and Succulent Society
P.O. Box 64759
Tucson, AZ 85728-4759
TCSS@tucsoncactus.org
http://tucsoncactus.org

University of Arizona Cooperative Extension
Yavapai County
840 Rodeo Drive #C
Prescott, AZ 86305
(928) 445-6590
http://cals.arizona.edu/yavapai/anr/hort
Provides list of drought-tolerant landscape plants and
a weekly column, "Backyard Gardener."

University of Arizona Cooperative Extension
Pima County
4210 North Campbell Avenue
Tucson, AZ 85719-1109
(520) 626-5161
http://cals.arizona.edu/pima/gardening
Provides list of drought-tolerant landscape plants.

University of Arizona Cooperative Extension
Maricopa County
4341 East Broadway Road
Phoenix, AZ 85040-8807
(602) 470-8086
http://cals.arizona.edu/maricopa/garden
Provides list of drought-tolerant landscape plants.

NEW MEXICO

Demonstration Gardens, Programs, and Plant Sales

Albuquerque Garden Center
10120 Lomas Boulevard NE
Albuquerque, NM 87112
(505) 296-6020
gardencenter@intergate.com
http://www.abqgardencenter.com

Living Desert Zoo and Gardens State Park
P.O. Box 100
Carlsbad, NM 88221
(505) 887-5516
ken.britt@state.nm.us
http://www.emnrd.state.nm.us/emnrd/parks/
LivingDesert.htm

**Plants of the Southwest Nursery
    (Albuquerque location)**
6680 4th Street NW
Albuquerque, NM 87107
(505) 344-8830
plantsofthesw@juno.com
www.plantsofthesouthwest.com

Plants of the Southwest Nursery (Santa Fe location)
3095 Agua Fria Road
Santa Fe, NM 87507
(505) 438-8888
plantsofthesouthwest@hotmail.com
www.plantsofthesouthwest.com

Rio Grande Botanic Garden
2601 Central Avenue NW
Albuquerque, NM 87104
(505) 764-6200
http://www.cabq.gov/biopark/garden

Santa Fe Botanical Garden
Santa Fe Community College
Lower Level, Room 301
P.O. Box 23343
Santa Fe, NM 87502-3343
(505) 428-1684
bot_gardens@sfccnm.edu
http://www.santafebotanicalgarden.org
Manages two off-site preserves.

Santa Fe Greenhouses
2904 Rufina Street
Santa Fe, NM 87507-2929
(877) 811-2700
info@santafegreenhouses.com
http://www.santafegreenhouses.com

Organizations and Agencies

New Mexico Native Plant Society
P.O. Box 2364
Las Cruces, NM 88004
http://npsnm.unm.edu

NATIONAL

Lady Bird Johnson Wildflower Center
4801 La Crosse Avenue
Austin, TX 78739
(512) 292 4100
www.wildflower.org

The Lady Bird Johnson Wildflower Center is a nation-wide clearinghouse and information source for all aspects of native plants. The center offers information sheets on growing different species of plants, recommended species for each state, how-to plant guides, guidelines for collecting seeds, a data file of regional organizations offering information and activities about native plants, and lists of nurseries and seed sources for each state. Individual membership includes a quarterly magazine.

Bibliography

Arizona Native Plant Society. *Desert Shrubs*. Arizona Native Plant Society, 1989.

Arizona Native Plant Society. *Desert Trees*. Arizona Native Plant Society, 1988.

Arnberger, Leslie. *Flowers of the Southwest Mountains*. Globe, Ariz.: Southwest Parks and Monuments Association, 1974.

Benson, Lyman. *The Cacti of Arizona*. Tucson: The University of Arizona Press, 1969.

Benson, Lyman, and Robert Darrow. *Trees and Shrubs of the Southwest Deserts*. Tucson: The University of Arizona Press, 1981.

Bowers, Janice Emily. *100 Desert Wildflowers of the Southwest*. Globe, Ariz.: Southwest Parks and Monuments Association, 1989.

Bowers, Janice Emily. *100 Roadside Wildflowers of the Southwest*. Globe, Ariz.: Southwest Parks and Monuments Association, 1987.

Carter, Jack. *Trees and Shrubs of New Mexico*. Silver City, Nev.: Mimbres Press, 1998.

Carter, Jack, et al. *Common Southwestern Native Plants*. Silver City, Nev.: Mimbres Press, 2003.

Cooperative Extension Service. *Native Plants for New Mexico Landscapes*, Circular 513. Albuquerque: New Mexico State University, 1984.

Desert Botanical Garden Staff. *Desert Wildflowers*. Phoenix: Arizona Highways, 1988.

Dodge, Nat. *100 Roadside Wildflowers of the Southwest Uplands*. Globe, Ariz.: Southwest Parks and Monuments Association, 1967.

Dodge, Nat. *Flowers of the Southwest Deserts*. Globe, Ariz.: Southwest Parks and Monuments Association, 1976.

Duffield, Mary Rose, and Warren D. Jones. *Plants for Dry Climates*. Tucson: HP Books.

Elmore, Francis. *Shrubs and Trees of the Southwest Uplands*. Globe, Ariz.: Southwest Parks and Monuments Association, 1976.

Epple, Anne. *A Field Guide to the Plants of Arizona*. Guilford, Conn.: Falcon Press, 1955.

Fagan, Damian. *Canyon Country Wildflowers*. Helena, Mont.: Falcon Press, 1988.

Gentry, Howard Scott. *Agaves of Continental North America*. Tucson: The University of Arizona Press, 1982.

Grant, Karen, and Verne Grant. *Hummingbirds and Their Flowers*. New York: Columbia University Press, 1968.

Ivey, Robert. *Flowering Plants of New Mexico*. Albuquerque: R D Ivey, 2003.

Johnson, Eric, and David Harbison. *Landscaping to Save Water in the Desert*. Rancho Mirage, Calif.: E&P Products, 1985.

Julyan, Robert, Mary Stuever, eds. *Field Guide to the Sandia Mountains*. Albuquerque: University of New Mexico Press, 2005.

Kearney, Thomas, and Robert Peeples. *Arizona Flora*. Berkeley: The University of California, 1964.

Larson, Peggy, and Lane Larson. *The Deserts of the Southwest: A Sierra Club Naturalist's Guide*. 2nd ed. Berkeley: University of California Press, 2000.

Martin, William, and Charles Hutchins. *Fall Wildflowers of New Mexico*. Albuquerque: The University of New Mexico Press, 1988.

Martin, William, and Charles Hutchins. *Spring Wildflowers of New Mexico*. Albuquerque: The University of New Mexico Press, 1984.

Martin, William, and Charles Hutchins. *Summer Wildflowers of New Mexico*. Albuquerque: The University of New Mexico Press, 1986.

Martino, Steve, and Vernon Swaback. *Desert Excellence: A Guide to Natural Landscapes*. Phoenix: Bellamah Community Development, 1986.

Mielke, Judy. *Native Plants for Southwestern Landscapes*. Austin: The University of Texas Press, 1993.

Miller, George O. *A Field Guide to Wildlife of Texas and the Southwest*. Austin: Texas Monthly Press, 1988.

Miller, George O. *Landscaping with Native Plants of Texas*. St. Paul, Minn: Voyageur Press, 2006.

Miller, George O., and Delena Tull. *A Field Guide to Wildflowers, Trees, and Shrubs of Texas*. Lanham, Md.: Taylor Trade Publishing, 2003.

Moffat, Ann, and Mark Schiler. *Landscape Design That Saves Energy*. New York: William Morrow, 1981.

Natural Vegetation Committee, Arizona Chapter, Soil Conservation Society. *Landscaping with Native Arizona Plants*. Tucson: The University of Arizona Press, 1973.

Nelson, Ruth. *Plants of Zion National Park*. Springdale, Utah: Zion Natural History Association, 1976.

Nokes, Jill. *How to Grow Native Plants of Texas and the Southwest*. Austin: Texas Monthly Press, 1986.

Patraw, Pauline. *Flowers of the Southwest Mesas*. Globe, Ariz.: Southwest Parks and Monuments Association, 1977.

Phillips, Arthur, III. *Grand Canyon Wildflowers*. Grand Canyon, Ariz.: Grand Canyon Natural History Association, 1979.

Phillips, Judith. *Southwestern Landscaping with Native Plants*. Sante Fe: Museum of New Mexico Press, 1987.

Phillips, Steven J., ed. *A Natural History of the Sonoran Desert*. Tucson, Ariz: Arizona-Sonora Desert Museum, 1999.

Powell, Michael, and Shirley Powell. *Native Plants in Landscaping: Trees, Shrubs, Cacti, and Grasses of the Texas Desert and Mountains*. Marathon, Tex.: Iron Mountain Press, 2005.

Shuler, Carol. *Low-Water-Use Plants for California and the Southwest*. Cambridge, Mass: Fisher Books, 1993.

Sunset Book Editors. *Sunset Western Garden Book*. Menlo Park, Calif.: Lane Publishing Co., 1988.

Warnock, B. H. *Wildflowers of the Guadalupe Mountains and the Sand Dune Country, Texas*. Alpine, Tex.: Sul Ross University, 1974.

Wasowski, Sally, and Andy Wasowski. *Native Landscaping from El Paso to LA*. New York: McGraw Hill, 2000.

Weniger, Del. *Cacti of Texas and Neighboring States*. Austin: The University of Texas Press, 1985.

West, Steve. *Northern Chihuahuan Desert Wildflowers*. Helena, Mont.: Falcon Press, 2000.

Wooton, E. O., and Paul Standley. *Flora of New Mexico*. New York: Weldon & Wesley, Ltd., 1915.

Index